Robert E. Stevens
Bruce Wrenn
Philip K. Sherwood
Morris E. Ruddick

The Marketing Research Guide

Second Edition

Pre-publication
REVIEWS,
COMMENTARIES,
EVALUATIONS . . .

*"T*his clearly written research guide contains contemporary business examples from NASCAR to Hummer. Tables, graphs, and worksheets supplement the easy-to-read text, making it not only a hands-on publication that teaches concepts but also an instruction manual that propels one's thoughts into action. The research process is covered comprehensively, providing in-depth insight from the formulation of a plan through its implementation and assessment."

David Dyson, PhD
Professor of Management
and former Dean,
Oral Roberts University
School of Business

*"T*he development of a marketing plan has consistently been one of the most difficult tasks for both my marketing students and business clients. *The Marketing Research Guide* is a comprehensive handbook that provides a detailed format for developing a marketing plan that can be used by both students and professionals. The components of the guide are supported by sound theoretical frameworks, which makes the book appropriate for academic use. Moreover, the book provides examples and templates necessary for use by professionals. Its most significant attribute is the effective alignment of marketing research, marketing planning, and marketing strategy. It provides an excellent overview of the marketing research process and how this process impacts both marketing strategy and marketing planning."

James T. Simpson
Professor and Chair,
Department of Management
and Marketing, The University
of Alabama in Huntsville

The Marketing Research Guide

Second Edition

BEST BUSINESS BOOKS®
Robert E. Stevens, PhD
David L. Loudon, PhD
Editors in Chief

Doing Business in Mexico: A Practical Guide by Gus Gordon and Thurmon Williams

Employee Assistance Programs in Mananged Care by Norman Winegar

Marketing Your Business: A Guide to Developing a Strategic Marketing Plan by Ronald A. Nykiel

Customer Advisory Boards: A Strategic Tool for Customer Relationship Building by Tony Carter

Fundamentals of Business Marketing Research by David A. Reid and Richard E. Plank

Marketing Management: Text and Cases by David L. Loudon, Robert E. Stevens, and Bruce Wrenn

Selling in the New World of Business by Bob Kimball and Jerold "Buck" Hall

Many Thin Companies: The Change in Customer Dealings and Managers Since September 11, 2001 by Tony Carter

The Book on Management by Bob Kimball

The Concise Encyclopedia of Advertising by Kenneth E. Clow and Donald Baack

Application Service Providers in Business by Luisa Focacci, Robert J. Mockler, and Marc E. Gartenfeld

The Concise Handbook of Management: A Practitioner's Approach by Jonathan T. Scott

The Marketing Research Guide, Second Edition by Robert E. Stevens, Bruce Wrenn, Philip K. Sherwood, and Morris E. Ruddick

Marketing Planning Guide, Third Edition by Robert E. Stevens, David L. Loudon, Bruce Wrenn, and Phylis Mansfield

Concise Encyclopedia of Church and Religious Organization Marketing by Robert E. Stevens, David L. Loudon, Bruce Wrenn, and Henry Cole

The Economies of Competition: The Race to Monopoly by George G. Djolov

Market Opportunity Analysis: Text and Cases by Robert E. Stevens, Philip K. Sherwood, J. Paul Dunn, and David L. Loudon

Concise Encyclopedia of Real Estate Business Terms by Bill Roark and Ryan Roark

Concise Encyclopedia of Investing by Darren W. Oglesby

Marketing Research: Text and Cases, Second Edition by Bruce Wrenn, Robert Stevens, and David Loudon

The Marketing Research Guide

Second Edition

Robert E. Stevens
Bruce Wrenn
Philip K. Sherwood
Morris E. Ruddick

Best Business Books®
An Imprint of The Haworth Press, Inc.
New York • London • Oxford

For more information on this book or to order, visit
http://www.haworthpress.com/store/product.asp?sku=5156

or call 1-800-HAWORTH (800-429-6784) in the United States and Canada
or (607) 722-5857 outside the United States and Canada

or contact orders@HaworthPress.com

Published by

Best Business Books®, an imprint of The Haworth Press, Inc., 10 Alice Street, Binghamton, NY 13904-1580.

PUBLISHER'S NOTE
In some cases, names, selected data, and corporate identities have been disguised.

First edition published in 1997.

Cover design by Kerry E. Mack.

Library of Congress Cataloging-in-Publication Data

The marketing research guide / Robert E. Stevens . . . [et al.].—2nd ed.
    p. cm.
Includes bibliographical references and index.
    ISBN-13: 978-0-7890-2416-9 (hc. : alk. cover)
    ISBN-10: 0-7890-2416-0 (hc. : alk. cover)
    ISBN-13: 978-0-7890-2417-6 (pbk. : alk. cover)
    ISBN-10: 0-7890-2417-9 (pbk. : alk. cover)
    1. Marketing research. I. Stevens, Robert E., 1942-

HF5415.2.M35585 2005
658.8'3—dc22
                                                           2005003578

CONTENTS

ABOUT THE AUTHORS

Robert E. Stevens, PhD, is Professor of Marketing in the Department of Management and Marketing at the University of Louisiana at Monroe. During his distinguished career, Dr. Stevens has taught at the University of Arkansas, the University of Southern Mississippi, and Hong Kong Shue Yan College. His repertoire of courses has included marketing management, business research, and strategic management. The author or co-author of 22 books and over 150 other publications, he has published his research findings in a number of business journals and numerous professional conference proceedings. He is a past co-editor of the *Journal of Ministry Marketing & Management* and currently co-editor of Haworth's *Services Marketing Quarterly,* and serves on the editorial boards of four other professional journals. Dr. Stevens has acted as a marketing consultant to local, regional, and national organizations and is the owner of two small businesses.

Bruce Wrenn, PhD, is Professor of Marketing in the School of Business and Economics at Indiana University South Bend. The author of several books on marketing management, planning, research, and marketing for religious organizations, Dr. Wrenn has also written numerous articles on marketing strategy, research, and marketing techniques for not-for-profit and health care organizations. He spent several years with a major pharmaceutical company performing market analysis and planning and has served as a consultant to a number of industries, religious denominations, and organizations in the food, high tech, and health care industries.

Philip K. Sherwood, EdD, is Director of Research Services for Maritz Research. Dr. Sherwood has over twenty years of marketing research experience on both the supplier and client side. For fourteen of those years, he has been a research director at Research International and Maritz. For seven years he directed the primary and secondary research programs for the data storage division at 3M and Imation Corporations. He was involved in the design, execution, and analysis of custom primary research designed to improve market position in the billion-dollar data storage business. In addition to being an active participant in the marketing research world as a supplier and a client of marketing research, Dr. Sherwood has co-authored six books in the areas of market research, feasibility analysis, market opportunity analysis, and product development. Prior to his career in research, he was a business professor for seven years.

Morris E. Ruddick, MS, is President of the Ruddick International Group, a market research and planning consulting firm with headquarters in Denver, Colorado, and branches in Houston, Texas, and Washington, DC. His areas of expertise include corporate development and planning, marketing management, product development, and advertising and market research in the industrial, electronic media, consumer services, and not-for-profit sectors. Having held key roles in two major successful corporate turnarounds, Mr. Ruddick possesses sharp analytic skills for performing corporate image evaluations and for assessing the dynamics impacting demand, acceptance, and timing of emerging technologies and markets.

Preface

This book is designed primarily for two groups of readers. The first group is managers who must negotiate, evaluate, and use marketing research as a part of the decision-making process. The second group is those individuals involved in the research process who need to review marketing research procedures or find examples of specific techniques. This book could also serve as a basic text for an introductory course in marketing research, especially if a research project approach is used in the course.

Three primary considerations were used in preparing the book. The first was length. We wanted to keep the amount of reading material brief enough to be read and reviewed quickly. Therefore, we had to omit many topics and also provide only a limited discussion of others. However, the essential concepts and techniques are presented in a much more concise form.

The second consideration was to present material that was theoretically sound, but practical. We wanted the reader to be able to put the concepts presented to immediate use in decision making. A unique feature of this book is that forecasting, sampling, and analysis techniques are described without the use of mathematical formulas. The worksheets at the end of each chapter are provided to help you apply chapter concepts.

The final consideration was to provide a thorough set of appendixes to illustrate various aspects of a research project such as a research proposal, questionnaire, final report, etc. Thus, the reader can read about a research proposal and actually see what one looks like. This is useful in evaluating proposals done by others or in preparing your own.

The end result is a book that is both readable and helpful to those involved with research. We hope this book serves you as both a tutorial and an easily accessible reference for research projects.

Acknowledgments

Many individuals contributed to the development of this book. We owe special thanks to Vicki Mikulak, who typed the many drafts of the book; Rajni Nair, who helped with checking references, artwork, and proofreading early drafts; and the College of Business Administration at the University of Louisiana Monroe for encouragement to undertake the project.

Chapter 1

Introduction to Marketing Research

THE MARKETING DECISION ENVIRONMENT

Marketing decisions in contemporary organizations are some of the most important decisions made by managers. The decisions of what consumer segments to serve with what products/services, at what prices, through which channels, and with what type and amounts of promotion not only determine the marketing posture of a firm but also affect decisions in other areas as well. The decision to emphasize quality products, for example, places restraints on procurement, production personnel, quality control, etc.

Many companies are discovering that the decisions involved in creating and distributing goods and services to selected consumer segments have such long-run implications for the organization that they are now being viewed as strategic decisions necessitating input by top management. Some marketing decisions, such as those relating to strategy, may involve commitments and directions that continue to guide efforts as long as they prove successful. A belief that future success requires the organization to become "market driven" or "market sensitive" has increased the importance of the intelligence function within organizations as they seek to make the right responses to a marketplace. Marketing research is the specific marketing function relied upon to provide information for marketing decisions.

MARKETING RESEARCH

Research, in a business context, is defined as an organized, formal inquiry into an area to obtain information for use in decision making. When the adjective marketing is added to research, the context of the area of inquiry is defined. Marketing research, then, refers to procedures and techniques involved in the design, data collection, analysis, and presentation of information used in making marketing decisions. More succinctly, *marketing research produces the information managers need to make marketing decisions.*

Although many of the procedures used to conduct marketing research can also be used to conduct other types of research, marketing decisions require approaches that fit the decision-making environment to which they are being applied. Marketing research can make its greatest contribution to management when the researcher understands the environment, industry, company, management goals and styles, and decision processes that give rise to the need for information.

MARKETING RESEARCH AND DECISION MAKING

Although conducting the activities of marketing research requires using a variety of research techniques, the focus of the research should *not* be on the techniques. Marketing research should focus on *decisions to be made* rather than the collection techniques used to gather information to facilitate decision making. This focus is central to understanding the marketing research function in terms of what it should be and to the effective and efficient use of research as an aid to decision making. Any user or provider of marketing research who loses sight of this central focus is likely to end up in one of two awkward and costly positions: (1) failing to collect the information actually needed to make a decision, or (2) collecting information that is not needed in a given decision-making context. The result of the first is ineffectiveness—not reaching a desired objective, and the result of the second is inefficiency—failing to reach an objective in the least costly manner. The chances of either of these occurring are greatly reduced when the decision to be made is the focus of the research effort.

To maintain this focal point, an understanding of the purpose and role of marketing research in decision making is necessary. The basic purpose of marketing research is to *reduce uncertainty or error in decision making.* It is the uncertainty of the outcome surrounding a decision that makes decision making difficult. If the outcome of choosing one alternative over another is known, then choosing the right alternative would be simple, given the decision-making criteria. If it was certain that alternative A would result in $100,000 in profit and that alternative B would result in $50,000 in profit, and the decision criterion was to maximize profits, then the choice of alternative A would be obvious. However, business decisions must be made under conditions of uncertainty—it is unknown if alternative A will produce $50,000 more than B. In fact, either or both alternatives may result in losses. It is the ability to reduce uncertainty that gives information its value.

Analyzing what is involved in making a decision will help in understanding how information aids decision making. Decision making is defined as a choice among alternative courses of action. For purposes of analysis, a decision can be broken down into four distinct steps as shown in Figure 1.1. Using this approach, decision making is viewed as a four-step process: (1) recognize the existence of problems and opportunities, (2) define the problem or opportunity, (3) identify alternatives, and (4) select an alternative.

Recognize the Existence of Problems and Opportunities

A problem or opportunity is the focus of management efforts to maintain or restore performance. A problem is anything that stands in the way of achieving an objective, whereas an opportunity is a chance to improve an overall performance.

Managers need information to aid in recognizing problems and opportunities, because before a problem can be defined and alternatives developed, it must be recognized. An example of this type of information is attitudinal data that compares attitudes toward competing brands. Since attitudes usually are predictive of sales behavior, if attitudes toward a company's product were less favorable than before the attitudinal information would make the managers aware of the exis-

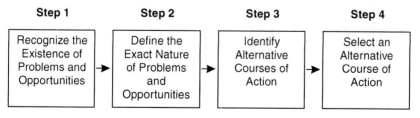

FIGURE 1.1. Steps in Decision Making

tence of a problem or potential problem. Opportunities.may depend upon the existence of pertinent information, such as knowing that distributors are displeased with a competitor's new policy of quantity discounts and as a result may be willing to place increased orders for your product.

Define the Problem or Opportunity

Once a problem or opportunity has been recognized, it must be defined. Until a clear definition of the problem is established, no alternative courses of action can be considered. In most cases a problem cannot be defined without some exploration. The symptoms of the problem are recognized first, and there may be several problems that produce the same set of symptoms. An analogy using the human body may help in understanding this point. A person experiencing a headache (symptom) could be suffering from a sinus infection, stress, the flu, or a host of other illnesses (potential problems). Treating the headache may provide temporary relief, but not dealing with the root problem will ensure its return, perhaps worsening physical conditions.

The same type of phenomenon occurs in marketing. A firm, experiencing a decline in sales (symptom), may find it to be the result of a decline in total industry sales, lower prices by competitors, low product quality, or myriad other potential problems. No alternative courses of action should be considered until the actual problem is defined. Thus, information aids the manager at this stage in the decision-making process by defining the problem.

In some cases an entire research project must be devoted to defining the problem or identifying an opportunity because of a lack of insight or prior knowledge of a particular area. This type of study is usually called an exploratory study and will be discussed more fully in Chapter 2.

Identify Alternatives

The third stage in the decision-making process involves identifying viable alternative courses of action. For some problems, developing alternatives is a natural outcome of defining the problem, especially if that particular problem or opportunity has occurred before. A manager's past knowledge and experiences are used to develop the alternatives in these situations. However, in other situations a real contribution of research is to inform the decision maker of the options available to him or her. A company considering introduction of a new product may use consumer information to determine the position of current offerings to evaluate different ways the new product could be positioned in the market. Information on the significant product attributes and how consumers position existing products on these attributes would be an evaluation of possible "openings" (options) available at a given time.

Select an Alternative

The final stage in the decision-making process is the choice among the alternative courses of action available to the decision maker. Information provided by research can aid a manager at this stage by estimating the effects of the various alternatives on the decision criteria. For example, a firm considering introduction of a new product may test market two versions of that product. The two versions of the product are two alternatives to be considered, and the sales and profits resulting from test marketing these two versions become the information needed to choose one alternative over another. Another example is the pretest of television commercials using different themes, characters, scripts, etc., to provide information on consumer reactions to alternative commercials. This information is helpful when selecting the best advertising approaches to use.

Information collected through research must be directly related to the decision to be made in order to accomplish its purpose of risk reduction. Thus, the focus of research should be the decision-making processes in general and, specifically, the decision to be made in a given situation, rather than the data or the techniques used to collect the data. A person involved in marketing research is in danger of viewing himself or herself as a research technician rather than as someone who provides information to help managers make decisions to solve problems and take advantage of opportunities. In fact, it is safe to say that the best researchers think as decision makers in search of information to make decisions rather than as researchers in search of answers to research questions.

STRATEGIC VERSUS TACTICAL INFORMATION NEEDS

Managers are called upon to make two broad categories of decisions—strategic and tactical. The strategic decisions are those that have long-run implications and effects. These decisions are critical to a firm's success and may not be altered if successful. Tactical decisions are short run in scope and effect and are usually altered on a regular basis. An example of these two types of decisions will help clarify the distinction and also clarify what many researchers and managers have failed to understand.

A company analyzing an industry for possible entry would be considering a strategic move—entering a new industry. This requires information on such topics as competitor strengths and weaknesses, market shares held by competitors, market growth potential, production, financial and marketing requirements for success in the industry, strategic tendencies of competitors, etc. This is strategic information. Once the decision to enter the industry has been made, information on current prices charged by specific competitors, current package designs and sizes, etc., is needed to make the tactical decisions for the short run—a year or less. This is tactical information.

Thus, *strategic decisions require strategic information, and tactical decisions require tactical information.* Failure to recognize the distinction between decision types and information types will result in information that deals with the right areas—prices for example—but with the wrong time frame. For tactical decisions, a manager needs to know competitive prices and their emphasis by both competitors and consumers. For strategic decisions, the manager is more interested in competitors' abilities and tendencies to use pricing as a retaliatory weapon.

The researcher and the manager must be certain the time frame for the decision is specified in advance to ensure that the right type of information is collected. This should be a joint effort by both information user and provider.

RESEARCH FOR STRATEGIC DECISIONS

The need for management to anticipate the future is becoming increasingly more important in the decision-making process. Future planning must consider the changing environment, the changing behavior of customers, the changing competitive forces, and the impact of these changes on current and future activities, but the key is understanding the impact that present decisions will have on future business environments. The truly successful business competitors of the future will be those who understand these dynamics and who can be the initiators and set the pace for market trends rather than reacting to the changes in the business environment.

Successful planning in today's highly competitive environment means that decision makers have been able to find the very narrow range of "doing the right things, the right way, at the right time." The school of hard knocks via trial and error demands a tuition rate unacceptably high in the twenty-first century. A shrinking margin of error requires decision makers to find ways to reduce the chances for making the wrong decisions. Marketing research can help avoid the high cost of errors in judgment by helping decision makers find that narrow range of correct decisions.

STEPS IN A MARKETING RESEARCH PROJECT

Ensuring that data collected in a research project is related to management's information needs and that it also fits management's time frame requires an approach to research that is centered on the management problem—the decision to be made. Such an approach, which is comprised of the planning phase and the execution phase, can be outlined as follows:

   I. Define the management problem
  II. Specify research objectives
 III. Develop research methodology
     A. Define information problem—specific needs
     B. Define population to be studied
     C. Develop sampling technique and determine sample size
     D. Determine how to measure variables or attributes
       to be studied
     E. Determine how to collect data
     F. Determine how to analyze data
 IV. Collect data

V. Analyze and interpret data
VI. Present findings
    A. Technical report
    B. Popular report

A venerable work adage states, "Plan your work; work your plan," and this is the approach that should be used in carrying out a research project. A research project does not begin with a questionnaire or a focus group interview or any other research technique, but with a carefully thought-out plan for the research that includes: (1) a statement of the management problem or opportunity, (2) a set of research objectives, and (3) a statement of the research methodology to be used in the project.

The Management Problem

The starting point in a research project should be an attempt by both the user and the provider of information to clearly define the problem. Mutual understanding and agreement are vitally necessary at this point in the research process. Failure by either party to understand or clearly define the major issue requiring information will surely lead to disappointment and wasted effort. Many information users, especially the uninitiated, have been "burned," never to be "burned" again, by someone who has collected some data, then collected his or her money and left with a lot of "useful" information. A health care administrator recently related such a story. He had heard a great deal about marketing and the need for having information on consumers, although he was unclear about both. He was approached by a marketing research firm that offered to supply a lot of "useful marketing information" for a reasonable fee. Several months after he had received the final report and the marketing research firm had received his check, he realized that he had no idea of how to use the information or if it was what he really needed.

This type of problem can be avoided, or at least minimized, through user-provider interaction, analysis, and discussion of the key management issues involved in a given situation. The information provider's task is to convert the manager's statement of symptoms to likely problems and decision issues and then finally to information issues. Two key questions that must always be dealt with at this stage are: (1) What information does the decision maker believe is needed to make a specific decision? and (2) How will the information be used to make the decision? Asking these questions will cause the information user to begin thinking in terms of the information needed to make the decision rather than the decision itself. Also, the user can move to a level of thinking specifically about how the information will be used.

An example of this interaction process will help clarify this point. An executive vice president for a franchise of a national motel-restaurant chain was evaluating his information needs with one of the authors about a major remodeling of one of the chain's restaurants. The author posed the question about how the information was going to be used in the decision-making process. The chain's vice president then realized that corporate policy would not permit deviating from the established interior designs currently used even if information were available that an alternate design would be more acceptable to consumers. He then concluded that he did not need the information! The information could have been easily obtained through a survey, but the bottom line would have been management's inability to act on it. The manager realized that he needed to work on a policy change at the corporate level, and if information was needed, it would be to evaluate that particular policy. Two types of questions that are often helpful in focusing the attention of the decision maker and the researcher on the information of real importance in arriving at a decision are "Why?" and "What if?" The "why" questions help to determine what is known from what is merely assumed to be true, the "what if" question helps to determine the value of the information in arriving at the decision. An example will illustrate the use of these questions:

DECISION MAKER: Our market share is slipping and we need to find what ad message will improve awareness of us and reverse that trend.

RESEARCHER: Why do you believe the drop is due to poor advertising?

DECISION MAKER: Because our share dropped soon after we changed our ad message.

RESEARCHER: So, one hypothesis is that poor advertising is responsible for the decline. Why else might we be losing share?

DECISION MAKER: Well, word has come back through the salesforce that dealers are pushing our competitor's product lately because of an award of a free Hawaiian vacation to their top dealer for the first quarter.

RESEARCHER: What if we did some research and discovered the sales decline was due primarily to competitive strategies? What would you do differently?

DECISION MAKER: Then we would change our promotional tactics with our dealers to beat the competition.

Here we see the "why" and "what if" questions being used to:

1. Distinguish between what is known (facts) from what is merely assumed to be true (hypothesis).
2. Determine the scope of the research.
3. Make certain that the research addresses subjects and provides information in a form that is useful to the decision maker in taking action. If the decision maker indicates that the answer to a "what if" question is that nothing will be done differently, then the researcher should be alert to the possibility that the research may be going down a fruitless path. If the decision maker receives information that does not translate into better decisions, then the researcher has failed in his or her job.

This step of clearly defining the real management issues must be foremost in the researcher's thinking. Information, regardless of quality or quantity, collected for the wrong problem or not relating to the right decision represents wasted resources and may even mislead management. The relationship of information needs to strategy decisions in marketing will be discussed in Chapter 2 to reinforce the concept of relating information to decisions made in marketing.

If the problem cannot be defined based on current information, an entire study may be necessary to complete this step. As previously mentioned, this is a project in itself and is called exploratory research. In such a situation, the problem in the exploratory study is to identify the variables in a given management situation and to develop a clear definition of the problem or opportunity facing the organization.

Research Objectives

Once the management problem has been identified it must be translated into a set of research objectives. The objectives represent a decomposition of the problem into a series of statements that constitute the end results sought by the research project. The objectives should be stated in such a way that their accomplishment will provide the information necessary to solve the problem as stated. The objectives serve to guide the research results by providing direction, scope of a given project, and serve as the basis for developing the methodology to be used in the project.

In the area of objectives, both the user and provider should interact to maximize the research results they are anticipating. The provider of the information usually assumes the role of interpreting needs and developing a list of objectives that serve as a basis of negotiation for final research objectives. Objectives should be stated in the form of questions so that the researcher can think in terms of finding ways to provide answers to those questions. The following illustration will help make this clear.

Management problem: A person who has a small company that installs in-wall wiring for home stereo systems wants to know if a market opportunity exists to work with builders of expensive "spec" homes to provide prewired installations for audio/video (A/V) systems.

Research Objectives:

1. What building contractors are building "spec" homes costing $400,000+?
2. What product and service features should be present to interest them in subcontracting for prewired A/V installations?
3. Would they want a variety of product/service packages at different price points?
4. What role does a home buyer play in making A/V installation decisions?
5. Should A/V equipment, satellite dishes, etc., be offered with the prewiring installation?
6. Who are the competitors and what do they offer?

Research Methodology

After the management problem has been defined and research objectives agreed upon by both user and provider, the next step in the research process is to develop a research methodology that will accomplish the objectives and provide the information needed to solve the management problem. Overall research designs will be dealt with at length in Chapter 2. The purpose here is to explain and identify the decisions that must be made in developing the methodology.

Defining Information Needs

The first step in developing the research methodology is to identify specifically the types of information needed to answer the research objectives/questions. Although this might appear to be an inherent part of the process of developing the objectives, it is usually wise to approach this in a more formal way by identifying specific information types. For example, a research objective could be stated as follows: What are the characteristics of heavy users, light users, and nonusers of our product? The word "characteristics" can take on a wide variety of definitions—socioeconomic, psychological, behavioral, and physical. What specific types of information are needed in this particular research project? Answering this question forces the researcher to consider research objectives, the management problem, and the decisions to be made based on the research.

Population or Universe

The next step in developing the research methodology is to define the population or universe of the study. The research universe includes all of the people, stores, or places that possess some characteristic management is interested in measuring. The universe must be defined for each research project and this defined universe becomes the group from which a sample is drawn. The list of all universe elements is sometimes referred to as the sampling frame.

It is extremely important that the sampling frame include *all* members of the population. Failure to meet this requirement can result in bias. If, for example, the researcher is trying to estimate the average income in a given area and intends to use the telephone book as the population listing or sampling frame, three problems would be encountered. First, not everyone has a land line telephone (i.e., replaced with cell phones). Second, there are usually 15 to 20 percent in an area with unlisted numbers, and third, new residents would not be listed. Thus, the difference between the sampling frame (telephone book) and area residents could be substantial and bias the results.

The population should be carefully identified and a sampling technique used that minimizes the chance of bias introduced through the sampling frame not containing all elements of the population. The techniques to successfully avoid such biases will be discussed in Chapter 8.

Sampling Technique and Sample Size

Two separate decisions are called for in this step. The first is how specific sample elements will be drawn from the population. There are two broad categories of sampling techniques: probability and nonprobability. The approach selected depends on the nature of the problem and the nature of the population under study. For probability sample designs the objective is to draw a sample that is both representative and useful. For nonprobability designs the objective is to select a useful sample even though it may not be representative of the population it comes from. These distinctions will be clarified later, but it is important to note that the sample design influences the applicability of various types of statistical analysis—some analysis types are directly dependent upon an assumption about how sample elements are drawn. Sampling issues are pertinent even when we are dealing with decision makers who say, "I can't afford the time or money to do a big survey. I just want to get a feel for the market opportunity and then I will take my chances." For example, if the installer of prewired A/V systems previously mentioned held such an attitude the researcher is still faced with the need to define the population of interest (building contractors of expensive homes), develop a sampling frame (list) of these people, and determine how many and who to talk with in order get answers to the research questions.

Sample size represents the other side of the decision to be made. Determining how many sample elements are needed to accomplish the research objectives requires both analysis and judgment. The techniques for determining sample size are discussed in Chapter 8 and Appendix D, including a whole series of other nonstatistical questions, such as costs, response rate, homogeneity of sample elements, etc., which must be considered to determine sample size. In some studies the cost may dictate a lower sample size than would be required given requirements about sampling reliability.

Measurement Decisions

The researcher must determine what is to be measured, in addition to answering this difficult question: "How will we measure what we need to measure?" For example, if attitudes are to be measured, which technique will be used? The method of equal-appearing intervals? The semantic differential? The Likert technique? In many cases no validated measuring techniques are available, so the researcher must rely on what has been used in past studies and on his or her own judgment to decide upon the appropriate technique.

It is extremely important that the researcher develop operational definitions of the concepts to be measured and that these are stated explicitly. Even seemingly simple concepts, such as awareness, can be defined in several ways, each having different meaning and relative importance. To know that 60 percent of the respondents said they had heard of Kleenex is not the same as 60 percent saying that Kleenex is what comes to mind when they think of facial tissues. Yet both of these approaches could be considered as measuring awareness.

Once the planning stages are complete the written results of the plan should be embodied in a document called a research proposal. A proposal should be prepared whether the project is done internally or by an outside research organization because it is the basis for allocating funds internally and for a contractual agreement when an outside firm is involved. When an outside firm is involved, staff normally prepare the proposal based on interaction with information users and those with authority to expend funds for outside research. (See Appendix A for two sample research proposals.)

Data Collection

The next decision area in a project concerns data-collection methods. The first choice is between observation and interrogation, and the second choice is the specific observation or interrogation technique to use. These decisions, in turn, depend on what information is needed, from which sample elements, in what time frame, and at what level of costs.

Depending on the nature of the project, data collection can be the single most costly or a relatively inexpensive element in a project. However, data collected are always an important determinant of research value because of the influence of the conditions surrounding data collection or the validity of the results obtained.

Using untrained interviewers to collect data, for example, can produce invalid and misleading data, thus causing management to make a wrong decision. Careful control of data collection is essential to effective research. Data-collection problems and techniques are examined in detail in Chapters 5 through 7.

Data Analysis

One final decision to be made regarding the research methodology concerns the methods used to analyze the data. The major criterion used in making this decision is the nature of the data to be analyzed. The purpose of the analysis is to obtain meaning from the raw data that have been collected.

For many researchers the area of data analysis can be the most troublesome. The basis for good techniques used in data analysis is discussed in Chapter 9. Although some data-analysis techniques do require an understanding of statistics, it is not true that all research results must be managed by statistical experts to be interpretable or useful. However, use of the *proper* data-analysis approach will mean the difference between not being able to discover the answers to research objectives, or worse, drawing erroneous conclusions, and capitalizing on all the careful work done to generate the data.

Identifying how the information will be analyzed before a data-collection instrument is developed is important because it is necessary to know how one plans to use the data in getting answers to research objectives before the question that generates the data can be asked. For example, if one needs to examine the differences in attitudes of people ages 13 to 16, 17 to 20, 21 to 24, and 25 to 28, one cannot ask about the respondent's age by using categories <18 yrs, 18 to 25, 25+. Less obvious and more sophisticated analytical reasons provide additional support for the need to determine data-analysis approaches before developing the data-collection instrument.

Collect, Analyze, Interpret, and Present Results

Once the previous steps have been completed and the planning stage of the research project has been carried out, the plan is now ready for execution. The execution stages involve developing the data-collection instrument, carrying out the plan for the research in terms of collecting the data from the population sampled in the ways specified, and analyzing the data using the analysis techniques already identified in the research plan. If the research plan or proposal has been well thought out and "debugged" early through revisions of objectives and research designs, then the implementation steps will flow much better.

Once the data are collected and analyzed the researcher must interpret the results of the findings in terms of the management problem for which the data were collected. This means determining what the results imply about the solution to the management problems and recommending a course of action to management. If the purpose of the research project was to determine the feasibility of introducing a new product and the results of the research project show that the product will produce an acceptable level of profits, then the research should recommend introduction of the product unless there are known internal or external barriers to entry that cannot be overcome. This means the researcher must move beyond the role of the scientist in objectively collecting and analyzing data. Now the role requires a management consultant in a science that states: Given these facts and this interpretation, I recommend this action. This does not, of course, mean that the action recommended will be followed by management. Since the researcher is usually in a staff capacity, only recommendations for action can be offered. Management can accept or reject the recommendations; this is management's prerogative. However, to be effective in getting results implemented, the researcher must assume this role of recommending action. Failure to do this is analogous to a dog chasing a car—the dog would not know what to do with the car once he or she caught it! The researcher should be involved in the problem definitions and objectives to be able to recommend courses of action based on interpretation of results.

To some this approach may seem to be overstepping the researcher's responsibilities to make recommendations. Yet most managers appreciate this approach since it at least represents a starting point in deciding what action should be taken given certain research results. Remember, information has not really served its basic purpose until it is used in decision making. Techniques aimed at increasing the impact of the written and/or oral report are discussed in Chapter 11.

APPLICATIONS OF MARKETING RESEARCH

A wide range of research applications provide the framework for the data analysis, resulting in the decision-making information to effectively keep in touch with the shifts, changes, and emerging trends reflective of market needs and preferences. A few examples of applications include:

Concept/Product Testing: A concept or product test consists of evaluating consumer response to a new product or concept. This is often a part of the test market in the development of a new product. It also helps determine how a product or service can best be positioned in a particular sector of the marketplace. For example, product testing would answer what the consumer's perception of new products or services to be offered might be. It can also examine how users perceive a product's value as well as its attributes and benefits or how perceived values and attributes relate to actual need and demand.

Tracking Study: A tracking study is an ongoing periodic survey of prerecruited consumers who rate their use of various products or services. Specific preferences are measured and compared to evaluate changes in perceptions, preferences, and actual usage over time.

Product/Brand Service Usage: Product or brand usage studies serve to determine current demand for the various brands of a product or service. This type of approach may also determine which brand name has primary awareness in the consumers' minds or which they prefer as well as how often and why it is used.

Advertising Penetration: Advertising penetration analyses evaluate the message that is actually being communicated to the target audience. This type of study serves to determine if the intended message is understood, how persuasive it is, or how well it motivates. These studies may also evaluate the effectiveness of individual media for a particular target market.

Image Evaluation: Image studies provide feedback relative to the image a company, product, or service has in the eyes of the consumers. Image studies may reveal attribute perceptions of a particular brand or determine its strengths and weaknesses.

Public Opinion Surveys: Public opinion studies are used to determine the key issues in the minds of the public or specific customers (or investors), relative to specific issues, individuals, or business sectors. They reveal whether opinion is positive or negative, determine the degree of importance of specific issues, or evaluate awareness levels of key issues.

Copy Testing: Copy testing allows for an evaluation of consumer response to ad copy being considered. It determines how well the intended message is actually being communicated. Copy tests ensure the wording used is consistent with the language of the target audience. Copy testing is used most effectively in the conceptual stages of copy development to allow for consumer feedback on concepts portrayed by various preliminary ad copy.

Test Marketing/Product Placements: Product placements are a bit more extensive than product tests. Product tests take place in a controlled setting, such as a shopping mall, in which consumers are recruited to test a product. In a product placement study, the product to be test marketed is placed in the home of the consumer for a specific period of time. After this period a personal or telephone interview is used to record the specific detailed responses of the user concerning the product. This type of study will determine how consumers respond to a product that often has no name or packaging appeals associated with it.

Taste Tests: Taste tests are conducted in a controlled environment in which consumers are recruited to taste a product and give their evaluations. Taste tests serve to determine the acceptance of a product without brand or packaging appeals relative to attributes of flavor, texture, aroma, and visual appeal. Taste tests may be conducted with variations of a single product or with samples of competitors' products tasted for comparison testing.

Market Segmentation: Market segmentation or market targeting studies determine how a market is segmented by product usage, demand, or customer profiles. These studies usually develop demographic, psychographic, product preference, and lifestyle profiles of key market segments.

Media Measurement: These studies determine what share of the market the medium being tested actually possesses and how a target market is identified demographically and psychographically. Media studies also evaluate preferences in programming as well as promotional appeals that are most effective in reaching and expanding a particular target audience.

Market Feasibility: A market feasibility study analyzes the market demand for a new product, brand, or service. This type of study usually evaluates potential market size, determines what kind of demand might be expected, what market dynamics are interacting, and what market segments might be most receptive to the introduction of a new product or brand. Feasibility studies may also determine market feedback relative to similar product or services, attributes sought, as well as pricing and packaging perspectives.

Location Studies: For local customer-intensive businesses, the location must be determined. Location studies serve to evaluate the size of the potential market surrounding a proposed location and whether local demand will support the facility.

Market Share/Market Size Studies: Market share/market size studies determine what products are being purchased at what volume and the actual size of sales being realized by each competitor. These studies also help to identify and determine the strength of new firms that have recently entered the market in a strong growth mode.

Competitive Analysis: A competitive analysis is often part of a market share/market size study. It consists of an evaluation of the strengths and weaknesses of competitors. It may also include pertinent data relative to locations, sales approaches, and the extent of their product lines and manufacturing capabilities.

Positioning Studies: Positioning studies evaluate how leading companies or brands are viewed in the minds of consumers concerning key product or image attributes. This type of study will evaluate perceived strengths and weaknesses of each as well as determine key attributes consumers associate with their idea of an "ideal" supplier of a particular product or service.

Customer Satisfaction Studies: Customer satisfaction studies evaluate the level of satisfaction existing customers have with the products or services of a company or organization. The basic philosophy is that it is cheaper to keep an existing customer than to try to attract a new one. Therefore, continuous analysis of existing customers provides input on how to change what is being done to increase or decrease dissatisfaction.

MARKETING INFORMATION SYSTEMS

Some organizations have moved beyond the stage of thinking of information needs in terms of projects and have focused attention on creating information systems that provide a continuous flow of information to users. Although such a focus may shift priorities in terms of the amounts spent on information for a database and that spent for specific projects, it should be pointed out that even if information is collected on a regular basis as a part of the information system, the principles of good marketing research set forth in this book are still applicable to these information systems. The fact that information is collected on a regular basis does not negate the need for relating it to the decisions to be made, for using correct sampling techniques, etc. The basic principles outlined are applicable to all information flows, some directly and others indirectly, but nonetheless applicable. Therefore, an understanding of these principles will help ensure better quality of information regardless of the nature of the system or procedures used to provide the information.

SUMMARY

This chapter has focused on the purpose, use, and overall approaches to gathering information for making marketing decisions. An understanding of the decision-making process and how information can aid a manager is the basis for planning and implementing research projects. Research projects, in turn, should be carried out in such a way that this focus of providing problem-solving information is central to the research process. This chapter outlined such an approach.

WORKSHEET

1. Can you define the exact nature of the problems and opportunities you face, or do you have only surface symptoms?

   _____

   _____

   _____

2. If you cannot define the problem, list the symptoms being experienced.

   a. _____

   b. _____

   c. _____

3. Are other organizations experiencing the same symptoms or are these symptoms unique to your organization?

   _____

   _____

   _____

4. Who could you contact at other organizations for insight into this problem? Think of suppliers, customers, and competitors who could provide insight into the problem.

   _____

   _____

   _____

5. If the problem or opportunity has been defined, what kind of information would help you solve the problem or take advantage of the opportunity?

_____

_____

_____

6. How would you use the resulting information to make the decisions necessary to resolve the problem or take advantage of an opportunity?

_____

_____

_____

7. Ask yourself "why" or "what if" questions in order to ensure that you are pursuing the proper focus and scope for the research.

_____

_____

_____

8. List the relevant research objectives, stated as questions the research will seek to answer.

a. _____

b. _____

c. _____

Now fill in these statements.

1. Person responsible for initiating the project: _____

2. Time frame for decision: _____

3. Person responsible for approval of the project: _____

4. Project completion: _____ Internal _____ External

    If external, potential providers:

    a. _____

    b. _____

    c. _____

5. Project budget: $_____

Chapter 2

Research Designs
for Management Decisions

THE DECISION-MAKING PERSPECTIVE
OF RESEARCH

Research has already been described as the process of systematically gathering and analyzing information. Strategy research is the integration of the tools and techniques of research, competitive analysis, and forecasting into the planning and decision process. Whereas the goal of strategy research is to provide decision-making information for management, the purpose of any research is to *reduce the error in decision making.*

Strategy research begins therefore within the context of the planning/decision process. Once research objectives are specified, the decision of what type of research design is to be developed and chosen must be made. The choice of design must reflect a keen understanding of the decision alternatives to be considered as well as the designs that will provide the best fit for the decision alternatives. Management, as well as the research director and research consultant, must be involved in the inception stages. Likewise, the research director and research consultant should be interacting with management decision makers in interpreting the subtleties of the results and their impact on the decision alternatives.

THE RESEARCH DESIGN DECISION PROCESS

The first step in the research process is reaching agreement on the purpose the particular research project is to serve, again, within the context of the planning/decision process. This usually consists of identifying the decision alternatives, the opportunities to be evaluated, or the market/environmental analysis that requires definition or clarification. Once this is established, the research purpose is then translated into specific research objectives. An estimation of the value of the information and the return on research is then made. The next step involves determining the research design that is the best fit for the information required. The research design will become the basis for the selection of the research methodology or methodologies, sampling procedures, as well as outlining the structure and sequencing of the overall research project. The final step in the research process is implementing the design. This begins with designing the data-gathering instrument (be it questionnaire or discussion guide); followed by the collection, manipulation, and analysis of the data; and is completed with the interpretation of the data as it relates to the specific decision alternatives.

TYPES OF RESEARCH DESIGNS

A research design is like a road map—you can see where you currently are, where you want to be at the completion of your journey, and can determine the best (most efficient and effective) route to take to get to your destination. As with such a journey, we may need to take unforeseen detours along the way, but by keeping our ultimate objective constantly in mind and using our map we can arrive at our destination. Our research purpose and objectives suggest which route (design) might be best to get us where we want to go, but there is more than one way to "get there from here." Choice of research design is not similar to solving a problem in algebra for which only one correct answer and an infinite number of wrong answers exist. It is closer to selecting a cheesecake recipe—some are better than others, but no one recipe is universally accepted "as best." Successfully completing a research project consists of making those choices that will fulfill the research purpose and obtain answers to the research objectives/questions in an efficient and effective manner.

Choice of design type is not determined by the nature of the strategic decision faced by the manager such that we would use research design A whenever we need to evaluate the extent of a new product opportunity, or design B when deciding on which of two advertising programs to run. If that approach would always work best for every decision maker, you would have bought a menu-driven software program to make research decisions instead of this book! Rather, choice of research design is influenced by a number of variables such as the decision maker's attitude toward risk, the types of decisions being faced, the size of the research budget, the decision-making time frame, the nature of the research objectives, and other subtle and not-so-subtle factors. Much of the choice, however, will depend upon the fundamental objective of doing the research.

- Conduct a general *exploration* of the issue, gain some broad insights into the phenomenon, and achieve a better "feel" for the subject under investigation (e.g., What do customers mean by "good value"?).
- *Describe* a population, event, or phenomenon in a precise manner where we can attach numbers to represent the extent to which something occurs or determine the degree two or more variables covary (e.g., the relationship between age and consumption rate).
- Attribute *cause* and effect relationships among two or more variables so that we can better understand and predict the outcome of one variable (e.g., sales) when varying another (e.g., advertising).

These three broadly different objectives give us the names of our three types of research designs: *exploratory, descriptive,* and *causal.*

Exploratory

Exploratory research is in some ways akin to detective work—there is a search for "clues" to reveal what happened or is currently taking place, a variety of sources might be used to provide insights and information, and the researcher/detective "follows where his or her nose leads" in the search for ideas, insights, and clarification. Researchers doing exploratory research must adopt a very flexible attitude toward collecting information in this type of research and be constantly asking themselves what lies beneath the surface of what they are learning and/or seeing. An insatiable curiosity is a valuable trait for exploratory researchers to bring to their search for this type of information.

Such curiosity will serve exploratory researchers well when, for example, they see the need to ask a follow-up question of a respondent who has mentioned some unanticipated answer to a researcher's query. The follow-up question is not listed on the researcher's interview guide, but the curious interviewer instinctively knows that the conversation should begin to deviate from the guide because the unexpected response may be revealing much more important issues surrounding the topic for investigation than were originally anticipated by the researcher. A willingness to follow one's instincts and detour into new territory is not only acceptable in exploratory research, it is commendable! Inspired insight, new ideas, clarifications, and revelatory observations are all the desired outcomes from exploratory research and decision makers should not judge the quality of the idea or insight based on its source.

A classic example of serendipitous exploratory research is the story of the advertising agency for Schlitz beer failing to come up with a new beer slogan after examining mounds of survey research done on beer drinkers, only to have one of the agency's staff overhear a patron at a bar exclaim, when the bartender reported that he could not fill the patron's order for Schlitz because he was temporarily out, "When you're out of Schlitz, you're out of beer." A new ad slogan was born! We do not want to give the impression that any approach is acceptable for doing exploratory research, or that all methods are of equal value in providing desired information, but it is true that exploratory research is characterized by a *flexibility* of method that is minimal with descriptive and causal designs.

Exploratory research is needed whenever the decision maker has the following objectives:

1. More precisely defining an ambiguous problem or opportunity (e.g., "Why have sales started to decline?").
2. Increasing his or her understanding of an issue (e.g., "What do consumers mean by saying they want a 'dry beer'?").
3. Developing hypotheses that could explain the occurrence of certain phenomena (e.g., "Different ethnic groups seek different levels of spice in our canned beans.").
4. Generating ideas (e.g., "What can be done to improve our relationships with independent distributors?").

5. Providing insights (e.g., "What government regulations are likely to be passed during the next year which will affect us?").
6. Establishing priorities for future research or determining the practicality of conducting some research (e.g., "Should we try to survey all our salespeople on this issue or just talk with the leading salesperson in each region?").
7. Identifying the variables and levels of variables for descriptive or causal research (e.g., "We will focus our attention on determining the level of consumer interest in these three product concepts because exploratory research shows no interest in the other two.").

The following are some of the common tools used to conduct exploratory research.

Secondary Information

More often than not the proper place to begin a research study is to investigate previous work related to the research issues under study. Exploratory research seeks to generate ideas, insights, and hypotheses, and reading what others have done and discovered about the topic in which you are interested can save valuable time and resources in the search for those ideas. For example, if your research objective consists of developing an instrument to measure customers' satisfaction with your product or service, a search of previously published studies measuring customer satisfaction could generate many ideas and insights useful in developing your own instrument. This may be done by using one or more of numerous books on the subject currently available, or by doing a computer search of a database similar to EBSCOHOST where key words such as "customer satisfaction" or "customer service" are used to reveal articles published on the subject during a specific time period (e.g., the previous three years). Chapter 5 discusses sources and uses of secondary data in more depth.

Personal Interviews

One of the best ways to obtain desired insights, hypotheses, clarifications, etc., is to talk with someone whose experience, expertise, or position gives him or her unique perspective on the subject of interest. In some cases such *key informants* are obvious, such as talking with secretaries about changes in your word processing software, but sometimes valuable insights come from not-so-obvious sources, such as talking with shoeshine people about executive footwear or golf caddies about golf equipment. The key to achieving your research objective of gaining insight, ideas, etc., through exploratory personal interviews is to be flexible and think about what you are hearing. Your objective in conducting the interview is not to get your seven questions asked and answered in the course of the conversation. The questions are the means to the objective of gaining insights; they are not the objective itself. My objective is to gain *insight* and I might be able to achieve that objective far better by asking questions related to what I am hearing than doggedly pursuing my original questions.

Researchers should never confuse the exploratory personal interview with one conducted in descriptive research. Descriptive research interviewing requires a consistency in the questions asked and the way the questions are asked that is not conducive to achieving exploratory objectives. With descriptive, we need to eliminate the variance of results due to differences in interviewing circumstances so that we can attribute the results to variances in respondent attitudes and behaviors, hence the need for consistent interviewing behavior. With exploratory, we are not trying to precisely measure some variable, we are trying to gain penetrating insights into some important issue. Hence, each of our exploratory interviews may take a different track as we seek to probe and query each key informant to gain full benefit of their unique experiences. In the same sense, descriptive research interviewing may require a probability sample of respondents so that we can compute sampling errors and be able to make statements such as, "We are 95 percent confident that somewhere between 77 percent to 81 percent of dealers prefer brand A over brand B." Never however, should exploratory research use a probability sample since our entire objective in talking with people is to select those who are in a position to shed an unusual amount of light on the topic of interest. They are chosen precisely because they are *un*usual (i.e., in the best position to shed some light on the subject), not because they hopefully represent the "usual." Another way of thinking about this is to answer the question "How many people do you need to talk with to get a good idea?" The answer of course is one person—the *right* person. We are not measuring behavior here, we are seeking inspiration, clarification, perspective, etc., so we must seek out those people who can do that for us. Chapter 5 discusses in more detail interviewing approaches that would be used in descriptive research.

Focus Groups

One of the most popular techniques for conducting exploratory research is the focus group, a small number of people (usually 8 to 12), convened to address topics introduced by a group moderator. The moderator works from a topic outline developed with input from moderator, researcher, and decision maker. Focus groups have proven to be of particular value in:

- Allowing marketing managers to see how their consumers act, think, and respond to the company's efforts.
- Generating hypotheses that can be tested by descriptive or causal research.
- Giving respondents impressions of new products.
- Suggesting the current temperament of a market.
- Making abstract data "real," such as seeing how a "strongly agree" response on a survey appears in the faces and demeanor of "real" people.

Focus groups are popular because they not only are an efficient, effective means of achieving these goals but also because decision makers can attend them, observing the responses of the participants "live." This observation can be a double-edged sword, for although it does make the abstract "real," it can deceive the novice into believing that the entire market is represented by the consumers in the focus group. Conducting more focus groups to see a larger number of respondents does not convert the exploratory findings into descriptive data. Focus groups are one of several means of achieving the objectives of exploratory research and should not be overused or believed to be generating results that were never the intent of this technique. Further discussion of focus groups is contained in Chapter 5.

Analysis of Selected Cases

Another means of achieving the objectives of exploratory research is to conduct in-depth analysis of selected cases of the subject under investigation. This approach is of particular value when a complex set of variables may be at work in generating observed results and intensive study is needed to unravel the complexities. For example, an in-depth study of a firm's top salespeople and comparison with the worst salespeople, might reveal characteristics common to stellar performers. Here again, the exploratory investigator is best served by an active curiosity and willingness to deviate from the initial plan when findings suggest new courses of inquiry might prove more productive. It is easy to see how the exploratory research objectives of generating insights and hypotheses would be well served by use of this technique.

Projective Techniques

Researchers might be exploring a topic where respondents are either unwilling or unable to directly answer questions about why they think or act as they do. Highly sensitive topics involving their private lives are obviously in this category, but more mundane behaviors may also hide deep psychological motivations. For example, in a case investigating why some women persisted in preferring a messy, expensive spray to kill roaches instead of using a more efficient trap that the women acknowledged to have more benefits than their sprays, researchers discovered that the women transferred hostilities for the men who had left them to the roaches and wanted to see the roaches squirm and die. The method used to uncover these hidden motives is one of the so-called *projective techniques,* named because respondents project their deep psychological motivations through a variety of communication and observable methods. These methods typically include:

1. *Word association.* Respondents are given a series of words and respond by saying the first word that comes to mind. The response, the frequency of the response, and time it takes to make the response are keys to understanding the underlying motives toward the subject. If no response is given, it is interpreted to

mean that emotional involvement is so high as to block the response.

2. *Sentence completion.* Similar to word association, sentence completion requires the respondent to enter words or phrases to complete a given sentence, such as "People who use the Discover credit card are _____." Responses are then analyzed for content.

3. *Storytelling.* Here respondents are given a cartoon, photograph, drawing, or are asked to draw a scene related to the subject under investigation and tell what is happening in the scene. In theory, the respondent will reveal inner thoughts by using the visual aid as a stimulus to elicit these deep motivations. Therefore, if the picture is of two people sitting and looking at a computer screen in an office, the story that is told about the people will reveal how the respondent feels about using computers in a work environment.

4. *Third-person technique/role-playing.* This technique is a reflection of what Oscar Wilde meant when he said, "A man is least himself when he talks in his own person; when he is given a mask he will tell the truth." Respondents are told to explain why a third person (a co-worker, neighbor, etc.) might act in a certain way. For example, a stimulus might appear as: *We are trying to better understand what features people might consider when buying a garden tractor. Please think about people you know and tell us what features would be important to them for such a product.* Role-playing requires the respondent to play the role of another party in a staged scenario, such as asking a retailer to play the role of a customer coming into a retail establishment.

As can be seen from the description of these techniques, one must be skilled not only in structuring these approaches, but also must be an experienced professional in interpreting the results. Also, their use is often bimodal—either an organization (e.g., an advertising agency or marketing consulting firm) uses them extensively or not at all. They have been shown to provide intriguing new insights into behavior, but are best left to experts to operate and interpret.

All of these exploratory techniques, when properly applied, can be successfully used to achieve the research objectives of generating ideas, hypotheses, clarifying concepts, etc. Quite often in a multistaged research project, one might start with exploratory research, then use the results to help structure a descriptive research questionnaire or a causal research experiment. Although that is frequently the case, exploratory results do not have value only as preliminary work before the "real" research takes place. Depending on the research purpose or attitude of the decision maker toward risk, exploratory research may be the only research that is done. For example, if in-depth interviews with twenty selected purchasing agents generate only ridicule of a new product idea, it is not necessary to conduct a structured survey of 500 to kill the idea. However, if you want to ultimately produce an ad which says your paintbrush is preferred two to one over a major competitor's by professional painters, exploratory research will not be sufficient to support your claims.

If a decision maker is a high risk taker, exploratory research may be all that is desired before a decision can be reached. If the stakes increase, however, that same decision maker may want to follow up the exploratory research with more structured and quantifiable descriptive or causal research. The point we are trying to make here is that well-conducted exploratory research can be extremely valuable in achieving the objectives endemic to that type of research, apart from its contribution to later phases of the research study. The fact that it does not generate precise quantifiable data is not a "weakness" of the approach. When properly conducted and interpreted it can serve as a powerful aid to decision making, depending upon the decisions being faced.

Descriptive Research

As the name implies, descriptive research seeks to *describe* something. More specifically, descriptive research is conducted when seeking to accomplish the following objectives:

1. To describe the characteristics of relevant groups such as the 20 percent of our customers who generate 80 percent of our business. Having a description of our "heavy users" can define a target for our future marketing efforts intended to find more prospects like our best customers.
2. To determine the extent to which two or more variables covary. For example, does consumption rate vary by age of consumer?

3. To estimate the proportion of a population who act or think a certain way. For example, how often do childless couples eat at restaurants in a typical month?
4. To make specific predictions. For example, we might want to forecast the number of wholesalers who will be converting to a new software inventory tracking system in the next year.

Descriptive research is highly structured and rigid in its approach to data collection compared to exploratory research's unstructured and flexible approach. As such, descriptive research presupposes much prior knowledge on the part of the researcher regarding *who* will be targeted as a respondent, *what* issues are of highest priority to be addressed in the study, *how* the questions are to be phrased to reflect the vocabulary and experience of the respondents, *when* to ask the questions, *where* we will find the respondents, and *why* we need these particular questions answered in order to make our decisions. Thus, exploratory research may often be needed to allow descriptive research requirements to be met.

Although exploratory research may generate a hypothesis (e.g., Hispanics offer a more attractive market for our product than do Asians.), it is descriptive research (or causal) that provides for a test of the hypothesis. Exploratory research may be needed to answer the who, what, when, where, why, and how of doing descriptive *research* (e.g., Who should be the respondents of the survey?), and descriptive research answers these same questions about the market (e.g., Who are the high consumers of our product?). Whereas exploratory research *suggests,* descriptive *quantifies.*

Descriptive research is more than an efficient means of collecting quantifiable facts. Facts can be a plentiful and useless commodity unless coupled with the "glue of explanation and understanding, the framework of theory, the tie-rod of conjecture."[1] We should determine how the information collected in a descriptive research study will be analyzed and used to test hypotheses, indicate the characteristics of a population, etc., before we ever design the data-collection instrument. For example, exploratory research conducted by a hospital may have generated the hypothesis that women of childbearing age with higher incomes and education demand a variety of birthing options, education classes, and father participation and presence in the delivery room, including during a cesarean section. Secondary data may reveal that the hospital is located in an area of high concentration of women of above-average income and education, and that pregnancy rates for the area are average. Descriptive research may seek to test the hypotheses that these women:

- Demand and expect their hospital to provide an obstetrics program with those characteristics.
- Are not presently satisfied with the options available from other hospitals.
- Are looking for and would be attracted to a hospital that did offer an obstetrics program which satisfied their wants and needs.

Here, the exploratory research generated, but could not test, the hypotheses, and the descriptive research generated facts in a form that provided the means of testing the hypotheses. It is important to note that researchers would have determined how the hypotheses would be tested before they designed questions in the questionnaire to generate the desired facts. That is, they would have set up *dummy tables* or chosen the *multivariate statistical techniques* to be used to test the hypotheses, then determined how data would be collected to allow for the use of these procedures for hypotheses testing. For example, one of the dummy tables can be seen in Figure 2.1.

By setting up this table before we even design the questionnaire or determine the number and type of respondents to survey, we have in effect helped specify the parameters for those parts of the research design. One hypothesis is that we should see the percentages on the top row of these tables get larger as we move to higher incomes (e.g., higher-income expectant mothers put more emphasis on such services in choosing a hospital than do lower-income expectant mothers). Other dummy tables would be developed to show how other hypotheses would be tested. This table was developed because researchers were intent on testing the hypotheses arising out of the exploratory research, and will be used once completed to influence decisions about service design, promotion, and other aspects of the marketing program. Design of such a table also permits researchers to develop a data-collection instrument such as a questionnaire that can provide the data in a form that permit the hypotheses to be tested. Although sounding somewhat convoluted, it is true that we determine how the data will be analyzed before we develop the questions that

Sibling Education Classes	Household Income Per Year			
	≤$25,000	$25,001-$40,000	$40,001-$55,000	>$55,000
High				
Medium				
Low				

Father in Delivery Room	Household Income Per Year			
	≤$25,000	$25,001-$40,000	$40,001-$55,000	>$55,000
High				
Medium				
Low				

Nurse Midwife	Household Income Per Year			
	≤$25,000	$25,001-$40,000	$40,001-$55,000	>$55,000
High				
Medium				
Low				

Physician Referral Service	Household Income Per Year			
	≤$25,000	$25,001-$40,000	$40,001-$55,000	>$55,000
High				
Medium				
Low				

Importance of Service or Program Feature in Determining Hospital Choice

FIGURE 2.1. Sample Tables or Hypotheses Testing

provided the data. The basic types of descriptive research studies used to provide such data are cross-sectional and longitudinal studies.

Cross-Sectional Designs

The best-known and most frequently used descriptive design, cross-sectional analysis involves a sampling of a population of interest at one point in time. This technique is sometimes referred to as a *sample survey,* because it often involves a probability sampling plan intended to choose respondents who will be representative of a certain population. As with all descriptive research, sample surveys are characterized by a high degree of *structure*—in both the data-collection instrument and in the data-collection process itself. The only way we can be sure we are measuring frequency or variation in the phenomenon under investigation is to build a high degree of structure into the instrument and process. That structure was not only *not* needed in exploratory research, it would have been a deterrent to achieving our objectives of insight, ideas, hypotheses, clarification, etc. Chapter 5 will discuss how to conduct sample surveys via questionnaires or observation in order to achieve the goals of a descriptive research study.

Cross-sectional surveys do not always involve selection of a one-time sample of respondents from the population. Several firms such as The Home Testing Institute, Market Facts, and National Family Opinion (NFO) operate *omnibus panels* that consist of hundreds of thousands of U.S. households that have been selected to proportionately represent the U.S. population along key dimensions such as age, income, sex, ethnic composition, and geographic dispersion. Members of such households are recruited to serve on the panel and agree to participate in answering questionnaires or trying products when requested to do so by the company maintaining the panel. Using such a panel allows an organization to select certain demographic characteristics for respondents (e.g., single males under thirty-five years of age) and send a questionnaire to them, knowing that the cost of finding and getting a response from a targeted number of this group (e.g., 1,000 completed questionnaires) is much less than trying to complete such a project in the general population where response rates may be as low as 1 or 2 percent. These panels are particularly cost-effective when research is being conducted on a topic where the incidence rate in the population is very low (e.g., vegens, people with four-car garages, people with cappuccino machines in their homes, etc.). In such cases it is possible to buy a few screening questions on the monthly questionnaire sent to, say, 50,000 panel members to identify those members who fit the desired profile, then send only those qualified panelists a longer questionnaire to obtain the detailed information being sought. Firms maintaining such omnibus panels turn over membership frequently to avoid participating households becoming "professional respondents," which would reduce the respondents' representativeness of the general population.

Some organizations recruit and maintain their own panels. For example, Parker Pen maintains a panel of people who use writing pens frequently. Such corporate panels are useful when the company wants to assess targeted consumers' attitudes on a scheduled basis, try out potential new products in an in-home setting before making a go, no-go decision, or seek information on awareness and knowledge of competitive promotions. These panels are used more than once over time, similar to the longitudinal panels discussed later, but since the subject of the research changes constantly it is best to think of these panels as company-run omnibus cross-sectional survey research panels.

Longitudinal Studies

Whereas cross-sectional studies are similar to taking snapshots of a target population at a point in time, longitudinal studies are similar to filming videotapes of the respondents. The primary objective of longitudinal research is to monitor behavior over time and thereby identify behavioral (or attitudinal) changes. Sometimes referred to as *true panels,* these longitudinal panels report the same information (e.g., grocery store purchases, or purchases and use of a particular product or service) at specific points in time. This information can be combined with other pertinent information to determine, for example, if brand switching occurred after exposure to a trial sample, coupon, or advertisement.

One of the best-known panels for consumer goods is Information Resource's BehaviorScan, which continuously tracks households in several markets by having panel members use a specially coded card that tracks optically scanned purchases by household members at selected grocery stores. BehaviorScan can be used for test marketing purposes by splitting the panel into two or more matched groups based on household demographics, and then sending different promotional appeals to the groups via direct mail, newspaper ads, or TV. Changes in purchasing patterns can be measured after the promotional appeal is made. A.C. Nielsen Company offers a similar service, in which households use handheld scanners in their homes to track purchases.

The ability to use longitudinal panels for tracking changes in purchase behavior and brand loyalty has advantages over the use of cross-sectional surveys. For example, consider Figure 2.2 and information taken from two cross-sectional sample surveys.

It appears that no brand switching occurred between the two surveys taken in time period 1 and 2. However, a longitudinal analysis might reveal a very different story as shown in Figure 2.3.

Figure 2.3 shows that in fact there was considerable brand-switching behavior, and that Brand C enjoyed the greatest brand loyalty, Brand A the least. Longitudinal panels also have an advantage over sample surveys in that panel members record purchases immediately and therefore generate accurate purchase data, whereas cross-sectional surveyors often must rely on respondents' memories for reporting purchases. However, cross-sectional studies may often be more representative of the target population, due to the difficulties of recruiting and maintaining a representative sample.

Causal Research

Although descriptive research is effective in identifying covariation between variables (e.g., blue packages outsell red ones, con-

	Number of Consumers	
	Period 1	Period 2
Brand A	100	100
Brand B	150	150
Brand C	250	250
	500	500

FIGURE 2.2. Two Cross-Sectional Sample Surveys

Brand Purchased in Period 1	Brand Purchased in Period 2			
	Brand A	Brand B	Brand C	Total
Brand A	50	20	30	100
Brand B	20	80	50	150
Brand C	30	50	170	250
Total	100	150	250	

FIGURE 2.3. Longitudinal Panel

sumption rate varies by education level), it cannot truly indicate causality (e.g., color causes sales, education causes consumption). Causal research procedures help determine if two or more variables are causally related. Although there might be a tendency to see many research objectives from a causal perspective ("We really want to know what causes consumers to act that way."), causality in the vernacular is different from how it is defined by scientists. Quite often decision makers do not need to test for a causal relationship in order to make good decisions. I might need to know only that blue packages outsell red ones or that consumption of my product increases with educational level in order to make appropriate marketing decisions. Testing for causality is a risky, expensive, time-consuming proposition and may not in the end permit better decisions than those made by simply acknowledging the covariation that descriptive research identified. However, in some cases a test of our hypothesis requires causal research (e.g., greater sales will result from having four shelf offerings of our product in stores under 60,000 square feet than having two facings in stores over 80,000 square feet). Descriptive research is characterized by its more *structured* approach as compared to exploratory. Causal research is also highly structured, but is characterized also by the use of *control* procedures used during the *experimental designs* associated with tests of causal relationships. Experimental design for causal research is discussed in Chapter 3.

Our interest in causal research is to determine the degree to which one variable is causally related to another (e.g., Does ad A cause people to remember its message better than ad B? or Does a 10 percent decrease in price cause an increase in profit compared to no price change?). Obviously, in all such cases we are concerned with truly determining the impact of our independent variable (ads A and B, or price in the previous examples) on our dependent variable (ad recall or profit in the examples), and not some extraneous variable that "leaks" into our test (e.g., a competitor's actions, an environmental event). Therefore, when we conduct a causal experiment we are concerned with three things:

- *Manipulation:* We manipulate the causal or independent variable such as ad message or price.
- *Measure:* We measure the effect or dependent variable such as ad recall or profit.
- *Control:* We control other variables that could have an impact on our dependent variable, such as making sure that our product with price P_1 in store S_1 is found on the same shelf level as that product with price P_2 in store S_2.

When we cannot exercise physical control (i.e., putting the products on the same level of store shelf) we can in effect still have control over the experiment by measuring the nonphysically controlled variable. For example, we cannot control our competitor's pricing in our test markets, but if we can measure the competitor's price, we can use our statistical analysis procedure to control for differences in competitive pricing by "making all else equal" and just measuring the effect of our price change on our sales. How this is done is beyond the scope of this discussion, but researchers should be aware that control can be exerted through both "physical" means as well as via measurement. The key in both cases is to anticipate what variables, other than the ones being manipulated, could have an effect on the dependent variable and then exercise control in some form over those variables.

Due to the complexity and importance of these designs we devote Chapter 3 to a discussion of experimentation and testing.

SUMMARY

Good strategy and good marketing decisions do not just "happen." They are grounded in accurate, timely, and useful market intelligence. Such information is obtained only through the careful translation of management problems into a research purpose, a research purpose into a set of research objectives, and those research objectives into a research design. Such a design is a road map that helps us arrive at our planned destination of having the information we need for decision making. The research design may involve one or more of the three categories of research: exploratory, descriptive, or causal. Our research objectives suggest that one or combinations of these types will be needed to obtain the desired information.

NOTE

1. Ferber, Robert, Donald F. Blankerty, and Sidney Hollander. 1964. *Marketing Research.* New York: The Ronald Press, p. 153.

WORKSHEET

1. Research Objectives/Questions (from #8, worksheet for Chapter 1)

   a. _____

   b. _____

   c. _____

2. What type(s) of research design do these objectives require?

Exploratory used to:	Descriptive used to:	Causal used to:
• More precisely define problems • Clarify concepts • Generate hypotheses • Generate ideas • Provide insights • Establish research priorities • Identify relevant variables	• Describe the characteristics of relevant groups • Determine extent to which two or more variables covary • Estimate proportion of population behaving in a certain way • Make specific predictions	• Determine a cause-effect relationship between two or more variables of interest

   Research Objectives   Research Objectives   Research Objectives

   _____   _____   _____

   _____   _____   _____

   _____   _____   _____

3. If an objective requires more than one type of design to be used to answer the research question, indicate the order of conducting the research:

                              Order of use (1=first, 2=second, 3=third)

   Research Objective   Exploratory   Descriptive   Causal

   _____

   _____

   _____

4. Exploratory Research Methods to be used:

Technique to be used (check as needed)

Research Objective	Secondary Research	Interviews	Focus Groups	Case Analysis	Projective Techniques

5. Secondary Research

Research Objective   Secondary Source

6. Personal Interviews

Research Objective   Interview Guide Questions

7. Focus Groups

Research Objective   Moderator Guide Questions

8. Analysis of Selected Cases

Research Objective   Case Selected for Investigation

_____

_____

_____

9. Projective Techniques

                                     Technique

Research Objective	Word Association	Sentence Completion	Story-telling	Third Person

_____

_____

_____

10. What descriptive research methods will be used?

                                     Technique

                              Cross-Sectional Research

Research Objective	Sample Survey	Omnibus Panel	Longitudinal Panel

_____

_____

_____

Note: Descriptive research interviewing techniques are discussed in Chapter 5; questionnaire design is discussed in Chapter 6.

11. Causal Research

	Variables to be:		
Research Objective	Manipulated	Measured	Controlled

Chapter 3

Experimentation

WHAT IS EXPERIMENTATION?

Experimental designs differ from other research designs in the degree of control exerted by the researcher over the conditions under which data are collected. When observational or survey designs are employed, the researcher measures the variables of interest but does not attempt to manipulate or control the variables. However, as mentioned in Chapter 2, in experimental (causal) designs, researchers measure, manipulate, and control different variables. For example, a retailer trying to isolate the influence of price changes on the sales volume of a product, must identify the nonprice variables such as location of the product in the store, time period of the day/week, promotion, etc., and control these variables because they also influence sales volume. Simply altering price and measuring sales is not an adequate design because of the impact of nonprice variables on sales.

Essentially, the key differences in experimentation and other designs are:

1. In an experiment, one or more of the independent variables are deliberately manipulated while others are controlled.
2. Combinations of conditions (particular values of the independent variables, e.g., different prices) are assigned to sample elements (e.g., different stores) on a random basis. This reduces the likelihood of preexisting conditions affecting the results.

So, if we were manipulating a grocery product's shelf facings and the size of store the product was sold in to determine the effect of these variables on sales, we would randomly assign the number of facings to stores of different sizes (e.g., store A of 10,000 square feet gets three facings, store B of 40,000 square feet gets one facing, store C of 20,000 square feet gets four facings, etc.).

Although all research is related to model building, the results of an experiment can become the basis of creating a model that provides an understanding of the relationship between some dependent variable (e.g., sales volume), and independent variables (e.g., price and promotion). If, for example, we could construct a valid model of the relationship between price levels and advertising levels, we could predict the extent of the impact of changes in the independent variables on dependent variables. We might be able to represent the relationship mathematically as follows:

$$Y_s = a + b_1X_2 + b_2X_2$$

where:
$$Y_s = \text{sales volume in units}$$
$$X_1 = \text{price level}$$
$$X_2 = \text{advertising level}$$
$$a = \text{constant}$$
$$b_1/b_2 = \text{coefficients}$$

Such a model would enable us to answer this type of question: "Given a change in X_1 (price) of a given amount, how much change would we expect in Y_s (sales volume) holding X_2 (advertising levels) constant?" Answers to these types of questions would be extremely valuable in studying price/volume relationships in attempts to increase profitability.

TERMINOLOGY

Several terms are used to describe the concepts involved in an experiment. Knowledge of these terms is essential to understanding experimental designs.

Experimental Treatment

Experimental treatment describes a specified combination of independent variables. For example, if an experiment was designed to measure the influence of three different levels of advertising on sales, then each level of advertising would be a different treatment. If the effects of the three levels of advertising were combined with two levels of price, then there would be six experimental treatments as shown in the following:

Price level one with

Advertising level one
Advertising level two
Advertising level three

Price level two with

Advertising level one
Advertising level two
Advertising level three

Since price level one with advertising level one represents a specified combination of independent variables, it is referred to as an experimental treatment. Each combination of price and advertising levels creates another experimental treatment. Therefore, this example consists of six different treatments.

Experimental Units

Experimental units are the geographic areas, stores, or people whose responses are measured in determining the effect of the different treatments. If the price and advertising levels described earlier are used in different geographical areas, then the areas represent experimental units. Each group of experimental units is a sample of all possible units and is used for comparing the impact of the treatments. Continuing the example, each of the six treatments may be assigned to forty different geographic locations for a total of 240 units. If we took a measure of sales before and after each treatment in each location we would have a total of 480 (i.e., 240 × 2) "observations."

Experimental Design

Experimental design is the specific process used to arrange independent variables into treatments and then assign treatments to units. Many designs are possible and great care should be exercised in choosing and/or modifying the design. Choosing the best design is the most important aspect of experimentation. Several designs will be discussed in a later section but it should be noted that researchers unfamiliar with experimentation should seek advice in setting up an experiment.

Control Group

In many experiments the use of a control group is a necessary element of the design. A control group is randomly selected just as other groups of units in the experiment are. However, the control group does not receive a treatment and thus serves as a benchmark for comparing the effects of treatments. If an experiment was used to determine the impact of two new levels of price on sales, prices held at the previous level in some areas would enable these areas to serve as controls in analyzing the results.

VALIDITY AND EXPERIMENTATION

A number of different types of validity exist, but only the two major varieties are considered here: internal and external. Internal validity has to do with whether the independent variables that were manipulated caused the changes in the dependent variable or whether other factors involved also influenced the dependent variable. Internal validity has many threats. Some of the major threats are considered here.

1. *History.* During the time that an experiment is taking place, some events may occur that affect the relationship being studied. For example, economic conditions may change, new products may be introduced, or other factors may change that alter the results.
2. *Maturation.* Changes may also take place within the subject that are a function of the passage of time and are not specific to any particular event. These are of special concern when the study covers a long period of time, but may also be a factor in tests that are as short as an hour or two. For example, a subject can become hungry, bored, or tired in a short time and this can affect response results.
3. *Testing.* When pretreatment and posttreatment measures are used, the process of taking a test can affect the scores of a second measurement. The experience of participation in the first

measurement can have a learning effect that influences the results on the second measurement.

4. *Instrumentation.* This threat to internal validity comes from
changes in measuring instruments or observers. Using different
questions or different observers or interviewers is a validity
threat.

5. *Selection.* One of the more important threats to internal validity
is the differential selection of subjects to be included in experimental and control groups. The concern is over initial differences that exist between subjects. If subjects are randomly assigned to experimental and control groups, this problem can be
overcome.

6. *Statistical regression.* This potential loss of validity is of special
concern when subjects have been selected on the basis of their
extreme scores. For example, if the most productive and least
productive salespeople are included in an experiment, the average of the high scores may decline and the low scores may increase.

7. *Mortality.* Mortality occurs when the composition of the study
groups changes during the experiment. Subjects dropping out of
an experiment, for example, cause the makeup of the group to
change.

Although internal validity concerns whether experimental or nonexperimental factors caused the observed differences, external validity is concerned with whether the results are generalizable to other
subjects, stores, or areas. The major threats to external validity are:

1. *Subject selection.* The process by which test subjects are selected for an experiment may be a threat to external validity. The
population from which subjects are selected may not be the
same as the target market. For example, if college students were
used as subjects, generalizing to other types of consumers may
not be appropriate.

2. *Other factors.* The experimental settings themselves may have
an effect on a subject's response. Artificial settings, for example, can give results that are not representative of actual market
situations. If the subjects know they are participating in a price
experiment, they may be more sensitive to price than normal.

FIELD VERSUS LABORATORY EXPERIMENTS

Experiments are conducted in two types of settings—field and laboratory. Field experiments result in an experimental setting that is more realistic in terms of modeling actual conditions and is therefore higher on external validity. These experiments are carried out in a natural setting with a minimum of artificial elements in the experiment. The downside of field experiments is that they usually cost more, have lower internal validity due to lack of control over variables that influence the dependent variable, and also may alert competition to changes a company is contemplating in marketing their products.

Laboratory experiments are experiments conducted under artificial conditions, such as testing television ads in a movie theater rather than in buyers' homes. However, such experiments usually are lower in costs, have higher internal validity due to more control of the experimental environment, and provide greater secrecy of potential marketing actions. It is also possible to use more elaborate measurement techniques in a laboratory setting than in field experiments.

Disadvantages of laboratory experiments include loss of realism and lower external validity due to the artificial conditions used in the experiment. For example, an experiment where people are given play money and asked to shop in a laboratory setting may reveal a great deal about some aspects of consumer behavior but there would be great difficulty in trying to generalize the findings to the purchase environment encountered in the marketplace.

The type of information to be generated from the experiment and its intended use dictate which type of experimental setting is more appropriate in a given situation. It is even possible to use both—a laboratory experiment followed by a field experiment—to validate the findings of the laboratory study under actual market conditions.

EXPERIMENTAL DESIGN SYMBOLS

Certain symbols help describe experimental designs. These symbols are used because they help in understanding the designs. They include:

- X = exposure of a group of subjects to an experimental treatment or a level of an independent variable (e.g., to a particular ad or product price, etc.). If different levels are used, then such as $X_1, X_2, X_3, ..., X_n$ are used.

- O = observation or measurement of the dependent variable in which the researcher is interested.
- R = random assignment of people to groups or groups to treatments.

Other notions are also helpful. The left-to-right notation indicates the time sequence of occurrence of events. Thus the notation

$$RO_1XO_2$$

would mean that subjects were randomly assigned to this group (R); a before measure (O_1) was taken; the subjects were then exposed to the treatment (X); and then an after measure (O_2) was taken.

All the notations on a single line refer to a single group of respondents, and notations that appear together vertically identify events that occurred at the same point in time. Thus,

$$O_1X_1O_2$$
$$X_1O_3$$

refers to two groups of subjects, one of which received a pretest measure and a posttest measure (O_1 and O_2), whereas the other received only a posttest measure (O_3). Both groups were exposed to the same treatment (X_1) and that the treatment and posttest measures occurred at the same time for both groups.

ETHICS AND EXPERIMENTATION

Over the past few years, concern for protecting the rights of subjects used in research projects has increased. It is a potential problem in all studies involving human subjects. The researcher should give careful consideration to the potential negative effects on those participating in an experiment to avoid violating the subjects' rights and deflect potential lawsuits. Luckily, most marketing research experiments are not likely to involve negative effects, but the possibility of such effects should be carefully evaluated.[1]

EXPERIMENTAL RESEARCH DESIGNS

Many possible experimental designs are available to choose from and they vary widely in terms of both complexity and effectiveness. The most widely accepted classification of designs are: (1) preexperiments, (2) true experiments, and (3) quasi-experiments. Although a complete coverage of experimental designs is beyond the scope of this book, a brief explanation and examples of these three designs are presented in the following.

Preexperimental Designs

Preexperimental designs are designs that are weak in terms of their ability to control the various threats to internal validity. This is especially true with the one-shot case study.

One-Shot Case Study

This design may be noted as:

$$X_1 O_1$$

An example of such a study would be to conduct a sales training program without a measure of the salespeople's knowledge before participation in the training program. Results would reveal only how much they know after the program but not how effective the program was in increasing knowledge.

The One Group Pretest-Posttest

This design can be represented as:

$$O_1 X_1 O_2$$

This improves on the one-shot case study because of the addition of the pretest measurement, but is still a weak design in that it fails to control for history, maturation, and other internal validity problems.

The Static Group Comparison

This design provides for two study groups, one of which receives the experimental treatment and the other serves as a control. The design is:

$$X_1 O_1$$
$$O_2$$

The addition of a control group makes this design better than the previous two. However, ensuring that the two groups were not different before the introduction of the treatment is not possible.

True Experimental Designs

The major deficiency of the previous designs is that they fail to provide groups that are comparable. The way to achieve comparability is through the random assignment of subjects to groups and treatments to groups. This deficit is overcome in the true experimental designs discussed in the following.

Pretest-Posttest Control Group

This design is shown as:

$$RO_1 X_1 O_2$$
$$RO_3 \quad O_4$$

In this design, most internal validity problems are minimized. However, some difficulties are still there. For example, history may occur in one group and not the other. Also, if communication exists between the groups, the effect of the treatment can be altered.

Posttest-Only Control Group

Pretest measurements are not used in this design. Although well-established in experimental research design, such measurements are not really necessary when random assignment to groups is possible. The design is represented as:

$$RX_1O_1$$
$$R \quad O_2$$

The simplicity of this design makes it more attractive than the pretest-posttest control group design. Internal validity threats from history, maturation, selection, and statistical regression are adequately controlled by random assignment. This design also eliminates some external validity problems as well. How does this design accomplish such notable achievements? We can think of the O_1 observation as a combination of the treatment effect (e.g., a change in price, or the advertising campaign we ran, or a change in package design, etc.), plus the effect of all the extraneous variables (i.e., history, maturation, testing effect, instrumentation, selection, statistical regression, and mortality). However, since O_2 will theoretically be subject to all the same extraneous variables, the only difference between what we observe between O_1 and O_2 (e.g., a measure of sales at two stores) will be the fact that O_1 (e.g., sales at store #1) was measured after the treatment X_1 (e.g., where prices were lowered), and O_2 (e.g., sales at store #2) did not receive the treatment. Therefore, all the other extraneous variable effects "wash" or cancel out between the two observations, so any difference in the observations must be due to the treatment. These results are dependent, however, on the random assignment of multiple units (stores in this example) to either the test or control conditions. Sample sizes for each of the test and control conditions must be large enough to approach a "normal distribution" of stores so that we can assume that the only difference that we see between O_1 and O_2 is the result of the treatment, and not due to some extraneous variable differences between the test and control stores.

Quasi-Experiments

Under actual field conditions, one often cannot control enough of the variables to use a true experiment design. Under such conditions, quasi-experiments can be used. In a quasi-experiment, comparable experimental and control groups cannot be established through random assignment. Often the researcher cannot even determine when or to whom to expose the experimental variable. Usually, however, it is possible to determine when and whom to measure. The loss of control over treatment manipulation (the "when" of the experimental variable exposure) and the test unit assignment (the "who" of the experimental variable exposure) greatly increase the chance of obtaining confounded results. Therefore, we must build into our design the ability to account for the possible effects of variables outside our control in the field, so that we can more safely conclude whether the treatment was, in fact, the thing that caused the results we observed.

A quasi-experiment is not as effective as a true experiment design, but is usually superior to available nonexperimental approaches. Only two quasi-experiment designs will be discussed here.

Nonequivalent Control Group

One of the most widely used quasi-experimental designs, this differs from true experimental design because the groups are not randomly assigned. This design can be represented as:

$$O_1 X_1 O_2$$
$$O_3 \quad O_4$$

Pretest results are one indicator of the degree of comparability between test and control groups. If the pretest results are significantly different, there is reason to doubt the groups' comparability. Obviously, the more alike the O_1 and O_3 measures are, the more useful the control group is in indicating the difference the treatment has made (i.e., comparing the difference in the O_2 to O_1 with the difference between O_4 to O_3). Close similarity allows for control over the extraneous variables of history, maturation, testing, instrumentation, selection, and mortality. However, statistical regression can be a problem if either the test or control group has been selected on the basis of extreme scores. In such a case, the O_2 or O_4 measures could be more the result of simply regressing back from the extreme to the average score, rather than the result of anything that intervened between the first and second observation of either group.

Separate Sample Pretest-Posttest

This design is most applicable in those situations where we cannot control when and to whom to introduce the treatment but can control when and whom to measure. The design is:

$$R \ O_1$$
$$R \ X_1 O_2$$

This design is more appropriate when the population is large and there is no way to restrict who receives the treatment. For example, suppose a company launches an internal marketing campaign to change its employees' attitudes toward customers. Two random samples of employees may be selected, one of which is interviewed regarding attitudes prior to the campaign. After the campaign the other group is interviewed.

LIMITATIONS OF CAUSAL RESEARCH

Managers are naturally attracted to the results that can be gained from doing experimentation. After all, are we not often looking to know what really causes the effects we see such as satisfied customers, rising (or falling) sales, motivated salespersons, etc.? However attractive causal research may be, managers should recognize the following limitations.

1. Field experiments can involve many variables outside the control of the experimenters, resulting in unanticipated differences in conditions surrounding treatment groups.
2. It may be difficult or expensive to gain the cooperation of retailers and wholesalers when setting up the experiment.
3. Marketing personnel may lack knowledge of experimental procedures, reducing the chance of results that demonstrate causality.
4. Experiments are notoriously expensive and time-consuming.
5. The experimenter must be careful not to introduce bias into the experiment by saying or doing something that may consciously or unconsciously affect the behavior of the test participants.[2]

EX POST FACTO RESEARCH

Ex post facto (after the fact) studies try to discover a causal relationship without manipulation of the independent variable or control over respondent exposure to treatment conditions. These studies are characterized by an observance of an outcome followed by attempts to find the causal factor that caused the observed outcome. Consider this example:

> A research manager for a regional bank was concerned with assessing customer images of their various branch locations. A mail survey asked whether they were satisfied with the services provided by the branch location that they used. Each respondent rated his or her branch location on a number of attributes: for example, friendliness of bank personnel, convenience of location, parking facilities, and so forth. After receiving the questionnaires, the manager divided the sample into two groups: those who expressed satisfaction with the branch location and those who expressed dissatisfaction. An analysis of these two groups revealed that compared with customers who expressed satisfaction, dissatisfied customers rated their branch location as unsatisfactory with respect to friendliness of service. The researcher concluded that friendliness of services is the primary factor leading to customer satisfaction, and, consequently, it plays an important part in the decision about which bank to use.[3]

An attempt has been made to identify a cause-effect relationship ex post facto, without manipulation of variables, assignment of respondents to treatments, or control of extraneous variables. The observed association between friendliness of service, customer satisfaction, and choice of bank may in fact be spurious and the correlation was in fact due to another variable not included in the analysis. For example, the people who rated their branch lower on the friendliness and satisfaction scales may be from an area populated by high-income households and who may have higher expectations of all aspects of service and who are more difficult to please in general. In such a case, the same level of service and friendliness of personnel among the branches is perceived differently by respondents, as is their level of overall satisfaction. Any causal inference drawn from ex post facto research, although indicating a *possible* causal relationship, must be supplemented with true experimental or quasi-experimental studies before we can draw cause-effect conclusions. However, in some cases, merely demonstrating covariation between variables of interest is sufficient for marketing planning purposes. We merely must be careful not to assume we know more than we can legitimately claim we do.

TEST MARKETING

Test marketing is the name given to a set of experimental or quasi-experimental (field) studies that are intended to determine the rate of market acceptance for (usually) a new product. A company typically would use test marketing to determine such information as:

- The sales volume and market share expectations of the new product.
- An estimate of the repurchase cycle and likelihood of repurchase.
- A profile of trier-adopters.
- An understanding of competitor reactions to the new product.
- Some feel for the effect of the new product sales on existing product sales.
- The performance of a new product package design in generating trial and satisfaction.

With the cost and likelihood of new product failure, marketers conducting test markets avoid large-scale introduction of products destined to fail. On the other hand, test marketing itself may cost millions of dollars, delay the cash flow of a successful new product, and alert competitors to your plans, so the costs may be high in either case. However, when the stakes are high and the costs of failure are very significant, test marketing may be the best of the unattractive options available. The following are several points to ponder when making the decision of whether or not to test market a product:

1. Weigh the cost and risk of product failure against the profit and profitability of success. The higher the probability of success and lower the costs of failure, the less attractive is test marketing.
2. The difference in the scale of investment involved in the test versus national launch route has an important bearing on deciding whether to test. The greater the investment called for in manufacturing, the more valuable a test market becomes in indicating the payout of such an investment before it is made.
3. Another factor to be considered is the likelihood and speed with which the competition will be able to copy the new product and

preempt part of your national market or overseas markets, should the test market prove successful.

4. Investments in plant and machinery are only part of the costs involved in a new product launch. The investment in marketing expenses and effort may be extensive, and sometimes the new product will be given space only at the retail level previously occupied by your existing products. Stock returns and buybacks for unsuccessful products likewise increase the costs of failure, not to mention the psychological impact of failing on a national scale. The higher these associated costs, the greater the potential value of test marketing in helping decision makers arrive at the best decision regarding large-scale product launch.[4]

Interestingly, A.C. Nielsen data indicate that 75 percent of products that undergo test marketing succeed, and 80 percent of products not tested fail.[5] Careful readers, however, may identify this implied causal relationship between test marketing and success as ex post facto research—we observe the relationship and identify the implied causal factor instead of conducting a controlled test to determine causality. In this case, the type of firms doing test marketing (large, big-budget firms with considerable marketing expertise), or not doing test marketing (small, low-budget firms without high-priced marketing talent), may explain more of the success rate than does test marketing itself.

We will now examine the three basic types of test markets: standard, controlled, and simulated.

Standard Test Market

In a standard test market, the firm uses its regular distribution channels and the firm's salesforce to stock the product in selected test areas. Test-site selection is an important consideration. Some criteria for selecting test sites are:

1. There should be a balance in the size of a test area between being large enough to generate meaningful results but not so large as to be prohibitively expensive (a good rule of thumb is that test areas should comprise at least 2 percent of the potential market).

2. They should provide representative media that would be used in a national launch, but be self-contained so that media in test areas will not "bleed over" into other test areas or control sites.
3. They should be similar along demographic dimensions with the full-scale market area (i.e., region or entire United States).
4. The trading area should be self-contained to avoid transshipments between test and control areas or two test areas.
5. Competition should be representative in test areas.
6. Test areas should provide for testing under different conditions that will be encountered on a national scale (e.g., both hard and soft water sites for water soluble products).[6]

Additional considerations include the measures used to indicate performance (e.g., trial rates, repeat purchase rates, percentage of households using, sales, etc.) and the length of the test (e.g., dependent upon the repurchase cycle, competitive response, and consumer response, but a minimum of ten months for new consumer brands). Standard test markets are subject to the problems associated with after-only experimental designs and are time-consuming and expensive. However, the number of product versions being tested can be reduced, thereby reducing costs, by the use of the product development research approaches described in Chapter 14.

Controlled Store Test Markets

Controlled store test markets are run by a research firm such as Audits and Surveys, A.C. Nielsen, Burgoyne, or Ehrhart-Babic, who, for a fee, handle warehousing, distribution, product pricing, shelving, and stocking. Typically, these organizations pay a fee to distributors to guarantee shelf space. Sales and other performance measures are also gathered by the research firm.

Advantages of controlled test markets are that competitors cannot "read" test results because they are available only to the research firm conducting the test and are not available through syndicated sales tracking services that would track standard test market data, they are faster to run since it is not necessary to move the product through a distribution channel, and they are less costly to operate than standard test markets. Disadvantages include use of channels that might not be representative of the firm's channel system; the number of test sites being usually fixed and limited, making projections difficult; firms not getting a read on the willingness of the trade to support the product under normal conditions; difficulty in mimicking nationally planned promotional programs; and research firms that are careful to prevent stockouts, optional shelf positioning, incorrect use of point-of-purchase materials, and other practices that may not duplicate conditions existing with the normal launch of a product. Nevertheless, controlled store test markets are often used as a check before going to standard test markets. If the results are promising, a standard test market follows. If not, the product is killed or revised.

Simulated Test Markets

A simulated test market is not conducted in the field, but rather in a laboratory setting. Firms providing such services (e.g., Burke; M/A/R/C; National Panel Data; Yankelovich, Clancy-Shulman; Custom Research, Inc.) follow a procedure that usually includes the following:

1. Respondents are recruited and screened to fit the desired demographic and usage patterns of the target market.
2. Respondents are shown ads for the tested products as well as competitive products, or are shown product concepts or prototypes.
3. Respondents are asked to record their attitudes toward the product on structured questionnaires and are either asked to indicate their purchase interest or are given a chance to buy the product or competitive products in a simulated shopping environment. For example, an aisle might be set up similar to an aisle in a drugstore with your tested cough syrup along with competitive cough syrups. Respondents can "purchase" any of the brands they desire.
4. Those who choose the tested products take it home and use it as they would under normal conditions, and are contacted after an appropriate time period and asked a series of attitudinal, repurchase intent questions, and usage-related questions.
5. Data from these steps are processed by a computer programmed to calculate estimated sales volume, market share, and other performance data based on assumptions of a marketing mix incorporated into the program.

Simulated test markets do *not* assume that the attitudes and behaviors evidenced in the simulation will be exactly duplicated in the market, but rather depend upon observed relationships that have been discovered historically between laboratory and eventual market findings. Although costing in the low six figures, simulated test markets are cheap compared to a full-blown standard test market, they are confidential, and permit easy modifications in a marketing mix to calibrate the most successful plan for introduction. The disadvantage is that they operate under a series of assumptions about what will really happen, and standard test markets *are* the real thing. Reported accuracy of simulated test markets are within 29 percent of forecast 90 percent of the time.[7]

SUMMARY

Whenever researchers must find answers to research questions dealing with cause and effect inferences they must consider the need for experimentation. Experimental designs differ from exploratory or descriptive designs in the degree of control exerted by the researcher over relevant variables. Experiments involve manipulation, control, and measurement of variables in order to allow for causal inference. In some cases such experiments must be conducted in the field, rather than in a controlled laboratory setting and are referred to as quasi-experiments. Several experimental designs were discussed, along with test marketing, one of the most commonly conducted causal experimental approaches used by marketers.

NOTES

1. For a discussion of the ethics of marketing research see N. Craig Smith and John A. Quelch. 1993. "Ethical Issues in Researching and Targeting Consumers," in N. Craig Smith and John A. Quelch, eds. *Ethics in Marketing,* Homewood, IL: Irwin, pp. 145-195.

2. Kinnear, Thomas C. and James R. Taylor. 1991. *Marketing Research.* New York: McGraw-Hill, p. 285.

3. Dillon, William R., Thomas J. Madden, and Heil H. Firtle. 1994. *Marketing Research in a Marketing Environment,* 3rd ed. Burr Ridge, IL: Irwin, p. 180.

4. These points were taken from N.D. Cadbury. 1985. "When, Where, and How to Test Market," *Harvard Business Review,* (May-June), pp. 97-98.

5. "Test Marketing: What's in Store," *Sales and Marketing Management,* 128, March 15, 1982, pp. 57-58.

6. Tull, Donald S. and Del L. Hawkins. 1993. *Marketing Research,* 6th ed. New York: Macmillan, pp. 252-258.

7. Material provided by Burke Institute on their BASES simulated test marketing program.

WORKSHEET

1. List the research objectives requiring causal research (from #11, worksheet, Chapter 2).

   Research Objectives

   _____

   _____

   _____

2. For each objective, indicate the variables to be manipulated, measured, and controlled.

   Variables

Manipulated (Hypothesized Cause)	**Measured** (Anticipated Effect)	**Controlled** (Extraneous Variables)
Ex.: Advertising____	Sales_____	Product prices_____
		Location in store____
Obj.# _____	_____	_____

3. Describe the treatments (manipulations of the variables believed to be the causal factors).

Variable	Treatment Levels
Ex.: Advertising budget____	Normal ad budget_____
	50 percent of ad budget_____

4. Describe the variables to be measured (known as the dependent or effect variables).

Variable	Units of Measurement
Ex.: Sales_____	Number of units sold per store____
	during time of test_____

5. Describe the variables to be controlled (known as the extraneous variables).

Variable	Control
Ex.: Product prices	Prices held constant during test
Location of product	Shelf level for product held constant at top shelf during test

6. Describe the experimental design.

Example

$$O_1 \quad X_1 \quad O_2$$

$$O_3 \qquad O_4$$

O_1 = Sales measured in territory A with normal rate of advertising.
O_3 = Sales measured in territory B with normal rate of advertising.
X_1 = Reduction of advertising by 50 percent.
O_2 = Sales measured in territory A after reduction of advertising by 50 percent.
O_4 = Sales measured in territory B with normal rate of advertising.

Experiment	Experimental Design
_____	_____
_____	_____
_____	_____

7. Test marketing

a. Describe the research objectives requiring a test market (from #8, worksheet, Chapter 1).

Research Objectives

_____

_____

_____

b. Plan the test market strategy.

Research Objective #1

Manufacturing decisions

_____

_____

_____

Distribution decisions

_____

_____

_____

Promotional (consumer and trade) decisions

_____

_____

_____

c. Determine test market methodology.

Research Objective	Standard Test Market	Controlled Test Market	Simulated Test Market
a. _____	_____	_____	_____
b. _____	_____	_____	_____
c. _____	_____	_____	_____

d. Select test market areas.

Research Objective	Number of Markets	Size of Markets	Representative Demographics	Test Area Selected	Isolated? (Yes or No)
1					
2					

e. Execute the plan.

Test Market   Time of Test Market

_____   _____

_____   _____

f. Evaluate the results.

Test	Awareness and Attitudes	Trial Rate	Purchase Measures	Repurchase Measures	Effect on Competition
1					
2					
3					

Chapter 4

Measurement

If a researcher measures the wrong things, or the wrong subjects, or uses inappropriate measurement and analysis procedures, then the resulting data will lack validity or reliability or both. Decisions made on the basis of such data will not be effective and may have serious repercussions on the firm's profitability and market share for years. Whereas anyone familiar with the research process knows we cannot deliver 100 percent accuracy in all research, we can certainly improve accuracy by understanding and controlling for measurement-related errors.

The major topics discussed in this chapter revolve around the following measurement issues: (1) what is to be measured, (2) who is to be measured, (3) how to measure what needs to be measured, and (4) validity and reliability of measurement tools.

WHAT IS TO BE MEASURED?

There are many different types of measures used in marketing research. However, most measures fall into one of the following three categories:[1]

- *States of being*—age, sex, income, education, etc.
- *States of mind*—attitudes, preferences, personality, etc.
- *Behavior*—purchase patterns, brand loyalty, etc.

Table 4.1 shows examples of the types of measures frequently used in marketing in consumer and industrial marketing research.

The research objectives indicate the concepts that must be measured. For example, customer satisfaction, store loyalty, and sales performance are all concepts that relate to marketing problems. How-

TABLE 4.1. Types of Measures

Measurement Type	Type of Buyer	
	Ultimate Consumers	**Industrial Customers**
States of Being	Age	Size or volume
	Sex	Number of employees
	Income	Number of plants
	Education	Type of organization
	Marital status	
Behavior	Brands purchased	Decision makers
	Coupon redemption	Growth markets
	Stores shopped	Public versus private
	Loyalty	Distribution pattern
	Activities	
States of Mind	Attitudes	Management attitudes
	Opinions	Management style
	Personality traits	Organizational culture
	Preferences	

ever, most concepts can be measured in more than one way. Store loyalty, for example, could be measured by: (1) the number of times a store is visited, (2) the proportion of purchases made at a store, and (3) shopping at a particular store first. These alternate measurement approaches are called operational definitions. An operational definition specifies how a concept will be measured.

What we really measure are characteristics or attributes of people or things, rather than the object itself. For example, we measure such attributes of a person as age, height, weight, years of education, or brand preference, rather than how much "person" is present. The same idea holds true when we seek to measure marketing-related concepts. We must measure attitudes toward a brand, for example, rather than measuring the "brand" itself. A key to proper measurement is the correct identification of the attribute of interest and the proper use of a measurement tool, which captures the appropriate unit of measurement of the attribute of interest. For example, we use a ruler, not a weight scale, when measuring length, and we must also use the proper tool when we measure attitudes, behaviors, and preferences. These characteristics or attributes are referred to as variables. A variable is a changing value. There are two types of variables: discrete and continuous.

Discrete variables are those that can be identified, separated into entities, and counted. The number of children in a family is an example of a discrete variable. Although the average may be 3.5, a given family would have 1, 2, 3, 4 or more children but not 3.5.

Continuous variables may take on any value. As a simple rule, if a third value can fall between the two other values, the variable is continuous. It can take on an infinite number of values within some specified range. Temperature, distance, and time are continuous variables, and each can be measured to finer and finer degrees of accuracy. Frequently, continuous variables are rounded and converted to discrete variables expressed in convenient units such as degrees, miles, or minutes.

WHO IS TO BE MEASURED?

The question of the object of the measurement process may appear to have obvious answers: people, stores, or geographic areas. However, more thoughtful answers would reveal a multiplicity of possible objects to be measured.

For example, the level of influence on decision making of a husband and wife depends in part upon the product or service being purchased. The resulting decision might be wife-dominated, husband-dominated, joint, or autonomic (either solitary or unilateral). Moreover, such decision-making influence can change over time, as evidenced in recent trends toward female heads of households making financial decisions.[2] Husband-wife decision making also varies from culture to culture.[3] In another study of children's influence on decision making in the family, it was discovered that about 17 percent of the nine- to twelve-year-old children surveyed considered themselves the main decision maker with regard to a decision to go to a restaurant, and forty percent thought themselves the primary decision maker in choice of restaurant.[4] Thus, collecting data from the "decision maker" does not always represent an obvious choice of respondent.

The buying center concept used in understanding organizational buying patterns provides a useful framework for other consumer and industrial purchasers. A buying center consists of everyone involved in a buying action.

Buying center participants play different roles. These roles must be identified and understood to select the type of respondents to be measured in a research project. These roles are:

- *Users*—those who actually use the product.
- *Gatekeepers*—those who control the flow of information or access to decision makers.
- *Influencers*—those who influence the choice of product or supplier by providing information.
- *Deciders*—those who actually make the choice of product and/or supplier.
- *Buyers*—those who actually complete the exchange process for a family or organization.

For some purchases, the involvement of many different people playing different roles creates a very complex buying process. One study of the purchase of a computing system yielded a complex flowchart of the buying process and the roles played by different people within the organization.

The major point of this discussion is to emphasize the need to judiciously select the respondents, stores, and areas to be measured. If we ask questions of the wrong people, we will still get answers; they just will not be meaningful and could even be misleading.

HOW TO MEASURE WHAT NEEDS TO BE MEASURED

Measurement involves a system of logical decision rules whose standard is a scale. Four scales widely used in marketing research are nominal, ordinal, interval, and ratio scales. These are listed in order of the least sophisticated to the most sophisticated in terms of the amount of information each provides. The scale classification of a measure determines the appropriate statistical procedure to use in analyzing the data generated through the measurement process.[5]

Nominal Scale

The nominal scale is the lowest level of measurement. It measures difference in kind (e.g., male, female, member, nonmember, etc.). Many people consider a nominal scale as a qualitative classification rather than a measurement. It produces categorical data rather than the metric data derived from more advanced scales. Although numbers may be used as labels (e.g., 0 for males, 1 for females), they can be replaced by words, figures, letters, or other symbols to identify and distinguish each category. Nominal scales are said to recognize differences in kind, but not differences in degree. As a result, nominal scales tend to oversimplify reality. All items assigned to the same class are assumed to be identical.

Summaries of data from a nominal scale measurement are usually reported as a count of observations in each class or a relative frequency distribution. A mode, or most frequently observed case, is the only central tendency measure permitted. Since the nominal scale does not acknowledge differences in degree, there are no useful measures of dispersion (e.g., range, standard deviation, variance, etc.). This scale calls for nonparametric statistical techniques such as chi-square analysis.

Ordinal Scale

The ordinal scale goes a step further than the nominal scale to introduce a direction of difference. If measurement can be ordered so that one item has more than or less than some property when compared with another item, measurement is said to be on an ordinal scale. Ordinal scales are frequently used in ranking items such as best, second best, etc. Such a ranking reveals position but not degree. For example, if favorite vacation destinations are rank ordered, it may be determined that Florida ranks first, the Rocky Mountains second, and New England third, but it is not clear if all three are relatively close in desirability, or if Florida is much more desirable and the Rockies and New England are a distant second and third choice.

The most appropriate statistic describing the central tendency on an ordinal scale is the median. Dispersion can be quantified using the range, interquartile range, and percentiles.

Interval Scale

Measurement is achieved on an interval scale with two additional features: (1) a unit of measurement, and (2) an arbitrary origin. Temperature, for example, is measured by interval scales. Each scale has a unit of measurement, a degree. An interval scale indicates a difference, a direction of difference, and a magnitude of difference, with the amount expressed in constant scale units. The difference between 20 and 30 degrees represents the same difference and direction as the difference between 100 and 110 degrees.

The arbitrary origin of the interval scale means there is no natural origin or zero point from which the scale derives. For example, both Fahrenheit and Celsius scales are used to measure temperature, but each has its own zero point.

The arithmetic mean is the most common measure of central tendency or average. Dispersion about the mean is measured by the standard deviation. Many researchers will assume their measures are interval level measures to permit the use of more powerful statistical procedures. Great care must be used here to avoid the use of inappropriate statistical procedures.

Ratio Scale

The most advanced level of measurement is made with a ratio scale. This scale has a natural origin. Zero means a complete absence of the property being measured. Properties measured on a ratio scale include weight, height, distance, speed, and sales. Measurement on a ratio scale is less frequent in marketing research than in the physical sciences. All the common descriptive and analytical statistical techniques used with interval scales can be used with ratio scales. In addition, computation of absolute magnitudes are possible with a ratio scale, but not with an interval scale. Therefore, although it cannot be said that 100 degrees Fahrenheit is twice as hot as 50 degrees Fahrenheit (it is not when converted to Celsius), it can be said that $2 million in sales is twice as much as $1 million in sales.

Table 4.2 is a summary of these measurement levels along with sample types of variables and questions used in their measurement.

TABLE 4.2. Scales of Measurement

Measure	Results	Sample Questions	Measure of Central Tendency
Nominal	Classification of Variables	Which brand do you own? A ___ B ___ C ___	Mode
Ordinal	Order of Variables	Rank your preference for stores. ___ First ___ Second ___ Third	Median
Interval	Differences in Variables	The salespeople were friendly. ____ ____ ____ ____ ____ Strongly Agree Neutral Dis- Strongly Agree agree Disagree	Mean
Ratio	Absolute Magnitude of Differences in Variables	What was you sales volume by store last year? Store A $_____ Store B $_____ Store C $_____	Mean Geometric Mean

Source: Adapted from Robert F. Hartley, George E. Prough, and Alan B. Flaschner. 1983. *Essentials of Marketing Research.* Tulsa, OK: PennWell Books, Inc., p. 145.

Measuring Psychological Variables

Decisions concerning the market environment are usually based on an understanding of and ultimately a desire to influence customer behavior. The study and measurement of attitudes provide indicators and explanations of behavior. Attitudes are basically mind-sets used as parameters from which the environment is perceived. As such, attitudes are guides indicating the way consumers will respond to the environment.

Attitudes are composed of several important components. The first is a person's cognitions or knowledge about an object or situation. This component usually focuses on awareness measures. Awareness levels precede evaluative beliefs, which become the basis for judgments about characteristics and attributes inherent in an object. In other words, do not measure a consumer's image of a brand unless it is known that the consumer is aware of and familiar with it. Attribute judgments might require comparisons of different products or evaluations on quality levels between two objects.

Another component of attitudes is the affective component that involves feelings toward a situation, object, person, etc. Comparative judgments of liking or disliking are standard forms of measurement for this component of attitudes. Still another is the behavioral component. This deals with individuals' expectations of how they believe they will respond to an object in the future. For example, this might involve "likelihood" of purchase of a particular object or brand. Each component of attitude builds upon the other. This is known as the hierarchy of effects of attitudes, which places the components in a hierarchical ordering beginning with cognitions or knowledge and ending with behavior.

Scaled statements are frequently used in marketing research to measure preferences, attitudes, and other psychological variables. Rating scales, such as Likert-type scales, and the semantic differential are commonly used to measure psychological variables. These are examined briefly in the following paragraphs.

Rating scales are simple, involving a set of statements that will be rated. This might include simply an agreement or disagreement with a statement about a product or there may be degrees of agreement/disagreement to achieve an ordinal level of measurement. Category scales are frequently used in marketing research and provide more information than a simple agreement or disagreement scale because they contain more categories. The following is a category scale.

How would you rate our service?

_____ Excellent _____ Good _____ Fair _____ Poor

Likert Scales

Agreement/disagreement scales such as the following examples are generally referred to as Likert or Likert-type scales. Such scales were developed by Renis Likert using a method referred to as the method of summated ratings.

In a Likert-type scale, a choice among five to seven responses is usually offered, such as: (1) strongly agree, (2) agree, (3) undecided, (4) disagree, and (5) strongly disagree. The following is an example.

The product is the best in the market.

Strongly Agree	Agree	Undecided	Disagree	Strongly Disagree
1	2	3	4	5

Numbers assigned to the degrees of agreement/disagreement indicate order and can be analyzed by comparing responses of different groups (age, sex, etc.) or different products or stores. If a set of scaled statements has been frequently used, some researchers assume an interval level of measurement has been achieved and thus use more sophisticated statistical techniques.

The Semantic Differential

Marketing researchers have found many applications of semantic differential scales. The semantic differential scale is a seven-point scale using pairs of adjectives or phrases that are opposite in meaning. Each pair of adjectives measures a different dimension of the concept. The respondent chooses one of the seven scale positions that most closely reflect his or her feelings. A large number of dimensions would be needed to completely measure a concept.

Two forms of a semantic differential scaled statement are shown in the following.

Clean ___ ___ ___ ___ ___ ___ ___ Dirty
     1   2   3   4   5   6   7

The store was clean. ___ ___ ___ ___ ___ ___ ___ The store was dirty.
               1   2   3   4   5   6   7

Again, the numbers assigned to the positions on the scale indicate order, so at least an ordinal level of measurement has been achieved, although many researchers assume interval level data are obtained through this method. Semantic differential scales can also be graphed to show comparisons by group or objects by plotting medians or means.

IMPROVING THE MEASUREMENT PROCESS

Improving the measurement process means developing measurement tools that are both valid and reliable. Validity refers to the extent to which measures actually regulate a concept while reliability has to do with the reproducibility of a measurement process.

Validity

Validity is the extent to which differences found among respondents using a measuring tool reflect *true* differences among respondents. The difficulty in accessing validity is that the true value is usually unknown. If the true value were known, absolute validity could be measured. In the absence of knowledge of the true value, the concern must be with relative validity (i.e., how well the variable is measured using one measuring technique versus competing techniques). Validity is assessed by examining three different types of validity: content, predictive, and construct.

The *content validity* of a measuring instrument is the extent to which it provides adequate coverage of the topic under study. To evaluate the content validity of an instrument, it must first be decided what elements constitute adequate coverage of the problem in terms of variables to be measured. Then the measuring instrument must be analyzed to assure all variables are being measured adequately. Thus, if people's attitudes toward purchasing different automobiles are being measured, questions should be included regarding attitudes toward the car's reliability, safety, performance, warranty coverage, cost of ownership, etc., since those attributes constitute attitudes toward automobile purchase. Content validity rests on the ability to adequately cover the most important attributes of the concept being measured. It is one of the most common forms of validity addressed in "practical" marketing research.

Predictive or *pragmatic validity* reflects the success of measures used for estimating purposes. The researcher may want to predict some outcome or estimate the existence of some current behavior or condition. The measure has predictive validity if it works! For example, the ACT test required of most college students has proved useful in predicting success in college courses. Thus, it is said to have predictive validity.

Construct validity involves the desire to measure or infer the presence of abstract characteristics for which no empirical validation seems possible. Attitude scales, aptitude tests, and personality tests generally concern concepts that fall in this category. In this situation, construct validity is assessed on how well the measurement tool measures constructs that have theoretically defined models as an underpinning. For example, a new personality test must measure personality traits as defined in personality theory in order to have construct validity.

Reliability

Reliability is concerned with estimates of the degree to which a measurement is free of random or unstable error—in other words, obtaining similar results with independent but comparable measures. There are two basic dimensions of reliability: stability and internal consistency.

A measure is said to be reliable if consistent results can be secured with repeated measurements of the same person with the same instrument. The stability of measurements in survey situations is more difficult and less attractive than for observational studies. Although a certain action can be observed repeatedly, the researcher usually can resurvey only once. This leads to a test-retest arrangement with comparisons between the two tests to determine how reliable the measurement process is for a given study.

The concern for internal consistency is to determine if a large number of items related to one subject area are all measuring elements of the same subject. In measuring attitudes, for example, several questions may be used to measure one concept. Internal consistency would be achieved if scores on subsets of the questions measuring the same concept were highly correlated with each other. Thus, if the items were randomly divided into two sets of questions, internal consistency would result in a high degree of correlation in responses between the two sets of items.

DEVELOPING VALID AND RELIABLE
MEASUREMENT INSTRUMENTS

Many concepts in marketing are easy to measure. For example, accurate measures can usually be obtained for purchase behavior and shopping patterns. However, concepts such as motivation, attitudes, and preferences are more difficult to measure. These concepts must be operationally defined by developing special measurement procedures as shown in Figure 4.1.

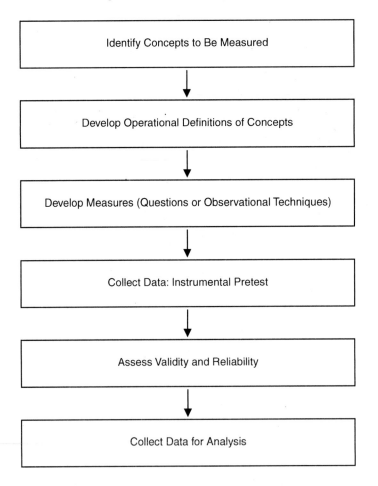

FIGURE 4.1. Measurement Development Process

The process begins with a definition of the concepts to be measured. The choice of concepts is based on the definition of the management problem and the resulting research hypotheses or objectives. The second step involves operationally defining these concepts. For example, if the concept "store loyalty" is to be measured, how will it be defined operationally? Shopping at one store first? Percent of purchases at one store?

The third step is to develop the questions or the observational techniques to be used to measure the concepts. This will be discussed in more detail in a later chapter. Next, some data are collected to pretest the accuracy of the measurement tools. This should be followed by an assessment of the validity and reliability of the instrument.[6] The final step is to use the instrument, revised as necessary, to collect data from the respondents selected in the sample for the study.

SUMMARY

The researcher must be sure that the measurement process is carefully analyzed to ensure good measurement tools are used in research. All the questions of what, who, and how to measure must be dealt with to yield valid and reliable measures of marketing concepts. Failure to exercise care throughout measurement procedures can result in misleading information and ineffective decisions. The process of developing measures to be used in research projects should constitute a substantial part of the researcher's time and effort in the planning stages of each project.

NOTES

1. Buzzell, Robert D., Donald F. Cox, and Rex V. Brown. 1969. *Marketing Research and Information Systems: Text and Cases*. New York: McGraw-Hill, Inc., p. 133.

2. Raymond, Joan. 2000. "For Richer and for Poorer," *American Demographics,* (July), pp. 58-64.

3. Ford, John B., Michael S. LaTour, and Tony L. Henthorne. 1995. "Perceptions of Marital Roles in Purchase Decision Processes: A Cross-Cultural Study," *Journal of the Academy of Marketing Science,* Vol. 23, No. 2, pp. 120-131.

4. Labrecque, J. and L. Ricard. 2001. "Children's Influence on Family Decision-Making: A Restaurant Study," *Journal of Business Research,* (November), pp. 173-176.

5. This discussion follows that of Baker, Raymond. 1983. *Marketing Research: Text and Cases.* Reston, VA: Reston Publishing Company, Inc., pp. 181-185.

6. A comprehensive discussion of validity and reliability testing procedures is beyond the scope of this book. An excellent reference for such a discussion can be found in Kerlinger, Fred. 1986. *Foundations of Behavioral Research,* 3rd ed. Fort Worth, TX: Holt, Rinehart and Winston.

WORKSHEET

1. What are the relevant concepts that need to be measured?

   a. _____   h. _____

   b. _____   i. _____

   c. _____   j. _____

   d. _____   k. _____

   e. _____   l. _____

   f. _____   m. _____

   g. _____   n. _____ .

2. Who should be measured? (Not just people, stores, or areas, but specific types of people, stores, or areas.)

   a. _____   f. _____

   b. _____   g. _____

   c. _____   h. _____

   d. _____   i. _____

   e. _____   j. _____

3. How will the concepts be measured? What scales are appropriate for each variable?

   Key variables: Measurement scale:

   a. _____   a. _____

   b. _____   b. _____

   c. _____   c. _____

   d. _____   d. _____

4. What measures will you attempt to validate?

Concepts: Validation assessment
                                        techniques:

a. _____   a. _____

b. _____   b. _____

c. _____   c. _____

d. _____   d. _____

5. How will you assess the reliability of measures?

Concepts: Reliability assessment
                                        techniques:

a. _____   a. _____

b. _____   b. _____

c. _____   c. _____

d. _____   d. _____

Chapter 5

Introduction to Data Collection

In previous chapters we have discussed how to translate a management problem into a research purpose and objectives, use the research objectives to formulate a research design, and how the research design permits measurement of variables of interest to us.

No matter whether the research design is exploratory, descriptive, or causal, its basic purpose will be to gather useful information that can be classified, compared, and analyzed in order to solve the original problem that initiated the research process. Data analysis and interpretation will be discussed in Chapter 9. That chapter will deal with the process of taking the mass of raw data generated by the data-collection process, and show how to analyze it in a way that answers the research questions. This chapter will deal specifically with the various types of data, the sources of data, the methods of data collection, and the procedures and tactics of data collection.

SOURCES OF DATA

There is a wide variety of data sources that should be considered when seeking answers to the research questions under consideration. In order to focus quickly on the pertinent data relative to the research questions, researchers and decision makers alike should be familiar with the basic sources of information. This will ensure that time and money is not wasted in misdirected search for either unavailable or irrelevant information.

TYPES OF DATA

Generally, data are classified by being either *primary data* or *secondary data*. Primary data are those data that are collected for the first time by the researcher for the specific research project at hand. Secondary data are data previously gathered for some other purpose. The terms "primary" and "secondary" may cause some confusion. These terms have nothing to do with the relative importance of the information. Whether the data are primary or secondary is determined by whether they originated with the specific study in consideration or not.

The first tenet of data gathering among researchers is to exhaust all sources of secondary data before engaging in a search for primary data. Many research questions can be answered more quickly and with less expense through the proper use of secondary information. However, caution must be used to ensure that primary sources of secondary data are used since they are generally more accurate and complete than secondary sources of secondary data.

SECONDARY DATA SOURCES

The first problem that confronts a researcher in initiating a secondary data search is the massive amount, wide variety, and many locations of secondary data. Some method of logically summarizing the sources of secondary data is helpful. Most textbooks on the subject divide secondary data sources into two groups: *internal data sources* and *external data sources*.

Internal secondary data sources are closest at hand since they are found within the organization initiating the research process. These internal data have been collected for other purposes but are available to be consolidated, compared, and analyzed to answer the new research question being posed. This is particularly true of organizations that have sophisticated management information systems that routinely gather and consolidate useful marketing, accounting, and production information.

Specific internal records or sources of internal secondary data are:

1. Invoice records
2. Income statements (various cost information)

3. Sales results
4. Advertising expenditures
5. Accounts receivable logs
6. Inventory records
7. Production reports and schedules
8. Complaint letters and other customer correspondence
9. Salesperson's reports (observations)
10. Management reports
11. Service records
12. Accounts payable logs
13. Budgets
14. Distributor reports and feedback
15. Cash register receipts
16. Warranty cards

Even though most research projects require more than just internal data, this is a very cost-efficient place to begin the data search. Quite often a review of all internal secondary data sources will inexpensively give direction for the next phase of data collection. The internal search will give clues to what external data sources are required to gather the information needed to answer the research question.

External secondary data originate outside the confines of the organization. An overwhelming number of external sources of data are available to the researcher. Good external secondary data may be found through Web searches, libraries, associations, and general guides to secondary data. Most trade associations accumulate and distribute information pertinent to their industry. Quite often this includes sales and other information gathered from their members. The *Directory of Directories* and the *Directory of Associations* are excellent sources for finding associations and organizations that may provide secondary information for a particular industry. Published books and magazines represent hundreds of thousands of sources each year while the government at all levels produces tens of thousands of annual reports and publications. Appendix B of this book contains a listing of some of the more commonly used sources of secondary data. Some of the more frequently used sources are:

1. Government agencies and reports
2. Census data—U.S. Bureau of the Census

3. Trade association reports
4. Books, periodicals, and newspapers (*Readers' Guide,* other indexes)
5. *Dissertation Abstracts International*
6. Annual reports
7. Syndicated commercial information
    a. Moody's
    b. Standard and Poor's
    c. A. C. Nielsen
    d. Market Research Corporation of America (MRCA)
    e. Simmons MRB, Inc.—The Study of Media and Markets
    f. Mail diary services
    g. *Findex,* the Directory of Market Research Reports, Studies, and Surveys
    h. *Predicast Basebook and Forecasts*
    i. *Statistical Abstract of the United States*
8. Annual *Survey of Buying Power*
9. Standardized marketing data sources
10. Databases

SECONDARY DATA SOURCES
ON THE WORLD WIDE WEB

The Internet has become the first, and far too often, the only, source used by marketing researchers in search of pertinent secondary data. Although it is safe to say that secondary research should not use the Web exclusively, any search for secondary data is incomplete without some use of the Internet. Our objective in this section is not to inundate the reader with a long list of Web sites, but rather to focus on those "megasites"—sites with the most comprehensive information databases including links to other sites—that can be "bookmarked" and regularly used in secondary research. Perhaps the best way to conceptualize the types of secondary information on the Web is shown on the Figure 5.1.

At the top of the pyramid are the search engines that provide access to all that is on the Web. Underneath that are two types of searches: those that seek information about markets—either business-to-business (B2B) markets or business-to-consumer markets, or market-

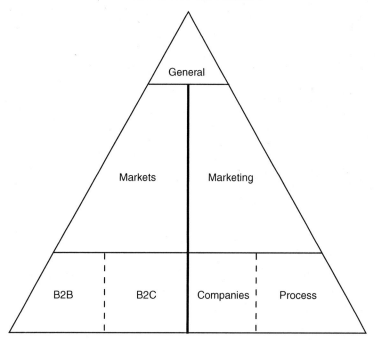

FIGURE 5.1. Categories of Secondary Information on the Internet

ing—either companies that offer marketing services, or the process of marketing itself. The following are some suggestions for Web sites of primary interest for each of these categories.

I. General search engines
   A. <www.google.com> or <www.yahoo.com>
      Although virtually everyone reading this book will have had experience using Google or Yahoo! as their portal to the Web, it bears mentioning that a well-designed search (using appropriate Boolean Logic, field searches, proximity operators, truncation, nesting, and limiting) will generate thousands of "hits" for which the object of the search appears on the Web. Readers unfamiliar with the use of sophisticated search strategies can save considerable time and frustration by learning how to do targeted search before using these engines.

B. <www.teoma.com>. Bought by Ask Jeeves in 2001, this search engine quickly finds "communities" (groups of Web sites related to the search topic) without generating unproductive links, as is sometimes the case with Google.

II. Markets

  A. Business-to-business (B2B) markets

    1. Government sources

      <www.fedworld.gov>. Links to 100 federal agencies issuing statistical data. B2B researchers will probably be most interested in information contained in the Economic Census (see <http://www.census.gov/epcd/ec02/go2items.htm>). Of particular interest will be data contained in the North American Industry Classification System (NAICS) at <www.census.gov/epcd/www.naics.html>.

    2. Commercial Sources

      <www.marketingpower.com>. The Web site of the American Marketing Association has hyperlinks to other Web sites that identify over 40,000 research reports, including many on B2B markets.

  B. Business-to-consumer (B2B) markets

    1. Government sources

      See <www.fedworld.gov> for government information about the consumer market of interest.

    2. Commercial sources

      In addition to searching <www.marketingpower.com> for reports on the consumer market of interest, commonly used Web sites for determining the size of a market would include the Survey of Buying Power at <www.salesandmarketing.com> and a similar database called Demographics USA at <www.tradedimensions.com> which offers calculation of a Buying Power Index (BPI) similar to the Survey of Buying Power, but at a more specific level (e.g., a BPI for high-tech products). Also of use to the marketer of consumer goods is the geodemographic information available at <www.claritas.com>, whose PRIZM system is perhaps the best known of the geodemographic consumer market segmentation sources.

III. Marketing
   A. Companies

      To see a directory of marketing service firms that can be used for a wide variety of marketing services (e.g., advertising, new product or brand development, research, etc.) go to <www.marketingpower.com> and see their marketing services directory.

   B. Process

      By "process" we mean the marketing process itself. That is, when you are seeking information about some aspect of marketing (e.g., sales promotion, customer satisfaction, research, etc.) that has been published in a business periodical or is otherwise available to the public. The two primary sources of information for such material are <www.dialog.com> and <ebscohost.com>, both of which cover hundreds of sources.

Appendix B gives a more comprehensive list of data sources.

YOUR LOCAL LIBRARY

One source of secondary data that should never be underestimated is a local public or college library, particularly if it is a federal depository. A well-equipped library will not only contain many of the sources previously mentioned and in Appendix B, but will have a variety of helpful indexes, directories, abstracts, and personnel who can assist in locating specific information. Any thorough search for secondary data should include a comprehensive library search. Not only is the public library an important source of information, but various institutions maintain excellent libraries in their various areas of specialization. Research foundations, financial institutions, energy companies, engineering firms, utilities, universities, and manufacturing establishments often maintain good libraries. The reference librarian can help you find your way through the maze of data sources.

Specific syndicated sources are available to provide marketing information. Several specific syndicated services are:

- *Nielsen Retail Index*—This service measures consumer activity at the point of sale. It is based on national samples of supermarkets, drug stores, mass merchandisers, and beverage outlets. The store audits track volume at the retail level such as sales to consumers, retail inventories, out-of-stock conditions, prices, dealer support, and number of days' supply.
- *Roper Reports and the Harris Survey*—These surveys deal with public opinion on social, political, and economic subjects. Both involve large national samples and are conducted approximately every month.
- *National Purchase Diary (NPD) Panel*—This diary panel of over 13,000 families provides monthly purchase information about approximately fifty product categories.
- *Nielsen Television Index*—Perhaps the most well-known service, the Nielsen Television Index measures television show ratings and shares among a panel of 1,200 television viewers who are matched according to U.S. national statistics.
- *Arbitron Radio Market Reports*—These reports, based on a representative sample in each market, provide information concerning radio listening habits.
- *Simmons MRB Media/Marketing Service*—Based on extensive data collection from a national sample of about 20,000 individuals, this service reports information concerning media exposure as well as purchase behavior about several hundred product categories. Simmons offers a software package (Choices) that allows the user to create almost unlimited comparisons and cross-tabulations of the extensive database.
- *Starch Readership Reports*—These reports provide measures of exposure to print ads in a wide variety of magazines and newspapers using a large number of personal interviews.
- *BehaviorScan*—This service, provided by Information Resources, Inc. (IRI), uses supermarket scanners to measure the consumption behavior of a panel of consumers.

Other sources of secondary information are specific associations. Trade associations and other special purpose groups gather and publish detailed information concerning their specific activities. Directories are available to help identify and locate associations of particular interest.

USES OF SECONDARY DATA

Even though the research design might require the collection of primary data, secondary data has many important uses. The most common uses and functions of secondary data are to:

1. Provide the background necessary to understand the problem situation and provide an overview of the market dynamics.
2. Provide exploratory information that can aid in the planning and design of the instruments used to gather primary data.
3. Serve as a check and standard for evaluating primary data.
4. Provide insight into sample selection.
5. Suggest research hypotheses or ideas that can be studied in the primary data phase of the research process.

The extensive use of secondary data reduces the possibility of "reinventing the wheel" by gathering primary data that someone else has already collected. In some cases, the information and insights gained from secondary data are sufficient to answer the research question.

Advantages

Secondary data are data gathered for some purpose other than the research project at hand. Consequently, researchers must understand and appreciate the relative advantages and disadvantages of this secondary information. To properly use and evaluate secondary information, its value must be assessed.

Secondary data possess the following advantages:

1. *Low cost.* The relatively low cost of secondary data is one of its most attractive characteristics. The cost of this data is relatively low when it is obtained from published sources. Only the cost of the time required to obtain the data is incurred. Even when the secondary information is provided by a commercial firm, it is normally less expensive than primary data because it is available on a multiclient basis to a large number of users rather than being custom designed on a proprietary basis for a single client.
2. *Speed.* A secondary data search can be accomplished in a much shorter time frame than can primary data collection, which re-

quires design and execution of a primary data-collection instrument.

3. *Availability.* Some information is available only in the form of secondary data. For example, census information is available only in secondary form. Some types of personal and financial data can not be obtained on a primary basis.

4. *Flexibility.* Secondary data is flexible and provides great variety.

Disadvantages

Since both internal and external secondary data were generated for some purpose other than to answer the research question at hand, care must be taken in their application. The limitations of secondary data must be considered.

Secondary data have the following potential limitations or disadvantages:

1. *A poor "fit."* The secondary data collected for some other research objective or purpose may not be relevant to the research question at hand. In most cases, the secondary data will not adequately fit the problem. In other cases, secondary data collected from various sources will not be in the right intervals, units of measurement or categories for proper cross-comparison. The secondary data may not be collected from the correct or most representative sample frame.

2. *Accuracy.* The question of accuracy takes several factors into consideration. First of all, did the secondary data come from a primary secondary source or a secondary source? Secondary sources of secondary data should be avoided. The next consideration is the organization or agency that originally collected the data. What is the quality of their methodology and data-gathering design? What is their reputation for credibility?

3. *Age.* A major problem with published and secondary data is the timeliness of the information. Old information is not necessarily bad information; however, in many dynamic markets, up-to-date information is an absolute necessity.

4. *Quality.* Information quality is sometimes unknown. The reputation and capability of the collecting agency is important to assessing the quality of the information provided. To verify the overall quality of secondary information it may be necessary to

know the sampling plan that was used, the data-collection method that was used, the field procedures that were utilized, the training that was provided, the degree of nonresponse that was experienced, and other possible sources of error.

Summary

Whenever research requirements are defined, secondary data should be exploited first to give background, direction, and control over the total research process. Beginning with a secondary data search will ensure that the maximum benefit is derived from the collection of primary data. All pertinent secondary data should be gathered before moving to the primary gathering stage because it is generally quicker and cheaper to collect secondary data. Good secondary data can be found both internally and externally. Library facilities should be used as a starting point in gathering secondary data, and the federal government is the largest single source of secondary information.

Although secondary information may answer the research question, generally it provides only the springboard for a collection of specific custom-designed information. The next section of this chapter will discuss the collection of primary data.

PRIMARY DATA

Primary data are data generated in a research project for a specific purpose in a specific format or collected from a specific population sample. This type of information can come from various sources. Some of the major sources are:

1. *The organization itself.* We generally think of the organization as a source of internal secondary information; however, the organization can also be a valuable beginning source of primary data for answering research questions (e.g., a survey of the salesforce).
2. *The environment.* The market environment includes customers and potential customers, as well as competitors. Customers are very important sources of information related to their demands and intentions. An emerging factor relative to the market envi-

ronment is the competition. This factor is increasing in importance and the next decade will be one of severe marketing warfare among competitors. Customers and even potential customers can be surveyed and information can be gathered from them much easier than from competitors. It is difficult to obtain information directly from competitors, however. Competitive intelligence and analysis is an important type of primary data.

3. *The distribution channel.* Wholesalers, retailers, manufacturers, and various suppliers and users can be vital sources of information for an organization. In fact, the role of wholesalers and retailers has increased greatly in importance in recent years in many product categories.

TYPES OF PRIMARY DATA

Primary data come in a variety of forms. Some of the more common types of primary data are briefly described in the following.

Demographic/Socioeconomic Data

Information such as age, education, occupation, marital status, sex, income, ethnic identification, social status, and the like are of interest to marketers because when combined with other types of primary data (e.g., consumption rates, attitudes, etc.) these descriptions help marketers profile target market members or other groups of interest. Consequently, through media plans, channels of distribution, and other ways, marketing plans can reflect the type of people who are our targets. In other words, this information is quite often of interest to us because the means by which we get our message and product to our target market is most often described in terms of demographic/socioeconomic data (e.g., magazine subscription lists, typical retail customers, television viewers, etc.). The equivalent of demographics for industrial marketers (e.g., sales volume, number of employees, location, North American Industry Classification System [NAICS] code, etc.) is likewise used in combination with other information for targeting purposes.

Attitudes

Attitudes refer to a person's feelings, convictions, or liking for an object, idea, or individual. Attitudes are a common object of measurement for marketing researchers because it is believed that they are precursors of behavior. Although marketers are ultimately responsible for influencing behavior, not just attitudes, we are not always able to observe and measure behaviors. For example, for a potential new product we must measure attitudes toward the product concept instead of behavior toward a product that does not yet exist. Also, attitudes help us to understand why people behave as they do, and marketers always want to know *why* behavior occurs, in addition to the frequency with which it occurs. Chapter 6 discusses some of the more common means of measuring attitudes.

Psychographics/Lifestyle Data

This type of data is concerned with people's personality traits, what interests them, how they live, and their values. It is sometimes referred to as a person's AIO—activities, interests, and opinions. Although empirical evidence linking someone's personality with their purchase and consumption behavior is weak, marketers find that combining psychographics and lifestyle information with demographics provides a "three-dimensional" perspective of a target market, permitting a much better focus to a marketing program.

Intentions

Intentions refer to the anticipated future behaviors of an individual. This is a subject of interest to marketers who factor the planned behavior of their consumers heavily into marketing plans. Intentions may be specific to the research project under investigation, or may be the kinds of purchase intentions routinely measured by such organizations as the Survey Research Center at the University of Michigan. Although some disparity will always be between what consumers say they will do, and what they actually do, marketers feel that obtaining some measure of planned future behavior is useful in distinguishing the potential of several alternative offerings.

Awareness/Knowledge

Referring to what subjects do or do not know about an object of investigation, awareness, and knowledge is of interest to marketers who wish to distinguish the image, experience, feelings, etc., of consumers who are familiar with a product from those who are not. If I am interested in determining my brand's image, for example, I want to first determine which consumers are aware of and knowledgeable about my brand. Other areas for determining awareness (unaided or aided) and extent of knowledge are advertisement recall, retail store familiarity, manufacturers, country of product origin, and so on.

Motivations

Motives consist of inner states that direct our behavior toward a goal. Other terms used to describe motives are needs, wants, urges, drives, or impulses. Our concern with motives centers on an interest in why people act as they do. When we ask respondents to indicate how important each of several product attributes is in influencing their choice we are attempting to identify what motives are influencing their behavior. Other ways of assessing motives include projective techniques (see Chapter 2), open-ended questions asking why people acted as they did, and a variety of other exploratory, descriptive, or even causal techniques intended to probe the needs that channel a person's actions.

Behaviors

Here we are tracking the actual actions taken by respondents. Marketers may have an interest in any number of specific behaviors enacted by selected groups of respondents, but typically purchase and consumption behaviors are of significant interest. Obtaining information about a person's behaviors might be accomplished through either self-report (e.g., asking someone to indicate how often he or she consumes a particular product) or through observation, either disguised or undisguised, of a subject's behavior as it occurs.

METHODS OF COLLECTING PRIMARY DATA

The research design of any research project is developed to obtain answers to the research questions/objectives of the study. This research design will call for specific types of information and also indicate specific methods of gathering the data. The primary methods of collecting primary data are *communication* and *observation*. Communication includes various direct approaches of asking questions of respondents either by personal interview, telephone survey, or mail questionnaire. Observation, on the other hand, involves the process of viewing market situations either in the field or in laboratory settings. In this method of data collection, an observer records predetermined activities of the entity being observed, either in a structured (descriptive or causal research) or unstructured (exploratory) fashion. Sometimes the actions of interest are recorded by mechanical devices instead of an observer. Those observations in a laboratory setting are generally considered of causal design and are experimental in nature.

PROCEDURES OF THE COMMUNICATION METHOD

Communication is the most commonly used approach to gathering primary data. Interviewing is frequently used because it is a flexible way of gathering information about people, their actions, attitudes, motivations, and intentions. In most cases communication survey research involves the use of a questionnaire or discussion guide. The specific type of survey method (mail, telephone, or personal interview) should match the information requirements of the study design.

PERSONAL INTERVIEWING

This face-to-face method is employed when the survey may be too long to conduct over the telephone or there might be material to show the respondent. Personal interviews are effective when the interviewer is placing a product in a home or office, the respondent is tasting a product, the sample necessitates contacting homes in a specific manner, such as every fourth home or going to every home until an interview is conducted, then skipping a specified number of homes before attempting the next contact as well as other applications. Personal interviewing allows for more in-depth probing on various issues.

The advantages and disadvantages of personal interviewing include:

Advantages

- Exhibits such as ads, packages, or pictures can be shown.
- Flexibility and versatility.
- Speed can be accomplished with multiple interviews being completed in multiple locations.
- Sampling can be done in a very representative way.
- Observation of the respondent allows for viewing behavior as well as asking questions.

Disadvantages

- Cost.
- Interviewer bias.
- Administration/execution problems.

The most common varieties of personal interviews are discussed in the following text.

Door-to-Door Interviewing

In door-to-door interviewing, the client or field service director will assign an interviewing location and often the exact address at which to begin. The interviewer then takes a specific direction in order to contact respondents according to the sample pattern that is specified to be followed. He or she will ask the questions and record the respondent's answers either during the interview or immediately afterward.

Central Location/Mall Interviewing

The use of a central location or mall area is effective in instances where respondents will taste a product, look at a package design, view a commercial, or listen to a recording or view a videotape and report their impressions. Shopping malls are frequently used because of their high volume of traffic. Other central locations such as a church meeting hall, hotel, or other facility might be used to conduct a large number of personal interviews. When this method of personal interviewing is used, the respondents are generally recruited in advance. Shopping malls may be used as locations for prearranged interviews or involve "intercepts" where shoppers are recruited in the mall for the interviews.

Vendor/Dealer/Executive/Professional Interviewing

This type of interviewing can also be conducted on the telephone, but it is usually done face-to-face when it is necessary to probe deeply about specific information in regard to specific aspects of a particular field of inquiry. An interview with an expert in a particular area is an excellent way to produce exploratory information. This information can then be used to form the basis of questionnaire design to be used to collect quantitative information. Good background and exploratory research leads to good questionnaire design, which in turn leads to good descriptive research.

Focus Group Interviewing

One of the most popular exploratory research techniques, focus group interviewing consists of a small group of people (usually 8 to 12) assembled for the purpose of discussing in an unstructured spontaneous manner topics introduced by a group moderator. The objective of conducting focus groups is *not* to accomplish the goals of a survey, but at a lower cost. In fact, focus groups, as an exploratory research technique, cannot be substituted for descriptive research's survey design. Focus groups are such a popular technique because when appropriately used they can effectively and efficiently achieve the goals of exploratory research, which are to:

- generate new ideas, or hypotheses that can be tested in later phases of the research study
- clarify concepts, actions, or terms used by consumers
- prioritize issues for further investigation

- provide an opportunity for management to see how their "real" consumers think, feel, and act
- obtain an "early read" on changing market trends

Focus groups are good at accomplishing such objectives because their relatively unstructured approach permits a free exchange of ideas, feelings, and experiences to emerge around a series of topics introduced by a moderator. The moderator works from a topic outline that covers the major areas of interest to the client firm, but because each group session consists of different individuals with their own feelings, desires, opinions, etc., no two sessions with the same agenda will be exactly the same in conduct or findings. The term "focus group" is used because the moderator focuses the group's attention on the predetermined subjects, without letting the discussion go too far afield. However, it is considered unstructured in the sense that a good moderator will consider the particular dynamics of each group when introducing these topics and the order in which they are brought up for discussion. Because they are so frequently used in marketing research, several books have been exclusively devoted to a discussion of how to conduct and analyze focus group sessions.[1] We will confine our discussion here to a few of the more important aspects of using focus groups as a qualitative exploratory research approach.

Why Conduct Focus Groups?

The standard reasons for conducting focus groups include:

Idea Generation

Consumers or knowledgeable experts may provide a good source of new products or other ideas in the fertile environment of a group setting.

Reveal Consumers' Needs, Perceptions, Attitudes

Probing consumers on why they think or act the way they do may reveal less obvious, but no less important, reasons for their behavior.

Help in Structuring Questionnaires

Hearing the way consumers think and talk about a product, activity, or consumption experience not only generates hypotheses that might be tested in a descriptive research design, but also informs the researcher about how to word questions in ways directly relevant to the consumer's experience.

Some less-frequently mentioned reasons for conducting focus groups include:

Postquantitative Research

Focus groups are most often mentioned as research done prior to a survey, but they might be of equal value in helping researchers to "put flesh on the bones" of quantitative research. Discovering that a certain percentage of consumers behave in a particular fashion may make it desirable to probe a group of those consumers in some depth to discover why and how they came to act in that manner.

Making the Abstract Real

One of the most memorable qualities of focus groups is their ability to make "real" what was heretofore only considered in a very abstract manner. For example, it is one thing for a product manager of a brand of dog food to know that many dog owners really love their dogs. It is quite another for that product manager to see dog owners in a focus group take obvious delight in recounting their Ginger's latest adventure with a raccoon, or grow misty-eyed in remembering Jason, now dead ten years, or hear the soft lilt in their voice as they describe the relationship they have with Kate and Bailey, their golden retrievers. Attendance at a focus group can infuse lifeless market data with new meaning and make its implications more memorable and meaningful. One checklist for management using focus groups to obtain a more "three-dimensional" understanding of their actual customers includes the following advice:

1. Do not expect your customers to look like the models in your ads. Fitness seekers do not all look like the aerobic instructor on the video—they are *trying* to.
2. Do not expect your customers to like you. Sitting behind the mirror can be blitz group therapy. Your ego and your company's ego are in the hands of a few customers. It can be upsetting and anger-provoking to hear what they have to say. Be prepared.
3. Do not expect consumers to care as much about your product as you do. It represents only a small part of their lives.

4. Do not expect your customers to be people just like you—or, on the other hand, to be unlike you.

5. Do not expect people to be consistent, and do not label them as hypocrites when they are not.

6. Use your qualitative researcher as a consultant to put the study in context. Are these customers satisfied or dissatisfied, compared to what the researcher has seen in other categories?

7. Remember, if they buy your product, they *are* your customers— whether or not you like the way they look, talk, think, or feel about you.

8. Be honest about your expectations. There is no clean slate. Everyone has preconceptions about their customers. Ask where your expectations come from—research, or prejudice.[2]

Reinforcing Beliefs

Judith Langer recounts a focus group experience by The Gillette Company that illustrates the ability of focus groups to convey a message much more powerfully to employees than repeat admonitions by management:

> The Gillette Company asked us to conduct research on "quality," a major issue to consumer companies. What does quality mean to consumers; when do they and don't they look for it; how do they recognize it? A focus group with women showed that consumers are more demanding and "educated" about quality than in the past. This comment was typical:
>
> "I think as consumers we're becoming more aware of what goes into a product. For myself, I have become more aware of the ingredients—food or clothing or whatever. I feel that I'm not the same shopper I was perhaps six years ago. That was just fad buying. Now I look at something."
>
> Marketing, market research, and research and development people observe the group; the videotape of the session has since been shown to others in the company. Hans Lopater, Gillette's research director, says that the focus group made what top management has been saying more tangible and believable.

This wasn't another generalized corporate lecture. These were real people who cared, who could tell the difference, who shopped what they believed. Understanding the importance of quality in today's competitive marketing environment, one can argue, can affect not only a company's attitude, but ultimately its bottom line.[3]

Early Barometer

Focus groups may provide an early warning system of shifts in the market. Probing consumers on lifestyle changes, consumption patterns, opinions of new competitive entries, etc., may reveal threats and opportunities entering the market long before they might be revealed in a large-scale survey. Keeping an open mind and maintaining an active curiosity allow for researchers to see the far-reaching significance of seemingly innocuous observations made by focus group participants.

Focus Group Composition

Conventional industry wisdom suggests that focus groups should consist of 8 to 12 people selected to be homogeneous along some characteristic important to the researcher (e.g., do a lot of baking, own foreign luxury cars, manage their own retirement account with more than $100,000 invested, etc.). Usually recruitment of focus group participants strives to find people who fit the desired profile but who do not know each other—thus reducing the inhibitions of group members to describe their actual feelings or behaviors. Typically, group sessions last from ninety minutes to two hours. Going against such conventional wisdom may be necessary in some cases. For example, one of the authors conducted research for a food company that wanted a few direct questions asked prior to presenting participants with prepared versions of their food products, as well as their competitor's. Although not a taste test per se, the client wanted to hear the subject's reactions to the products and a discussion of the circumstances under which the products would be used in their homes. For this study a series of one-hour group sessions were run with five people per group. The more structured discussion and the desire to query each participant made the shorter time and smaller group more conducive to achieving the study's objectives.

Selection and Recruitment of Group Participants

The research objectives and research design will indicate the types of people to be recruited for a focus group. If a facility especially designed for focus group use is contracted with, the management of the facility typically will conduct recruitment of focus group members. If a marketing research firm is being hired to conduct the groups, the firm will usually reserve the facility; identify, recruit, and select the participants; moderate the groups; and make an oral and written report of the findings. Sometimes the client organization will provide a list of possible participants taken from a master list of customers, members, users, etc. It is usually necessary to provide *at least* four names for every respondent needed (i.e., approximately fifty names per focus group).

Prospective participants are screened when contracted to ensure their eligibility for the group, but without revealing the factors used to assess their eligibility. For example, if the researcher is interested in talking with people who have traveled to Europe in the past year, he or she would also ask about other trips or activities to camouflage the central issue under investigation. This deception is helpful in discouraging respondents from answering in ways strictly intended to increase or diminish chances for an invitation, and to discourage selected participants from preparing "right" answers for their participation in the group sessions. It is advisable to provide a general idea of the topic for discussion (e.g., personal travel) to encourage participation. Actual participants are usually rewarded with an honorarium (say $25 to $50 per person) for their time. The size of the honorarium depends upon the type of participant (e.g., physicians expect more than mechanics). The focus group facility management usually covers the cost of recruiting, hosting, and compensating the groups in their fee. The following are six rules for recruiting focus group members:

1. Specifically define the characteristics of people who will be included in the group.
2. If an industrial focus group is being conducted, develop screening questions that probe into all aspects of the respondents' job

functions. Do not depend on titles or other ambiguous definitions of responsibilities.

3. If an industrial focus group is being conducted, provide the research company with the names of specific companies and employees, when possible. If specific categories of companies are needed, a list of qualified companies is critical.
4. Ask multiple questions about a single variable to validate the accuracy of answers. Therefore, if personal computer users are to be recruited, do not simply ask for the brand and model of personal computer they use. In addition, ask them to describe the machine and its function; this will ensure that they are referring to the appropriate equipment.
5. Do not accept respondents who have participated in a focus group during the previous year.
6. Have each participant arrive fifteen minutes early to complete a prediscussion questionnaire. This will provide additional background information on each respondent, reconfirm their suitability for the discussion, and help the company collect useful factual information.[4]

Moderator Role and Responsibilities

The moderator plays a key role in obtaining maximum value from conducting focus groups. He or she helps design the study guide, assists the manager/researcher who is seeking the information, and leads the discussion in a skillful way to address the study's objectives while stimulating and probing group participants to contribute to the discussion. The following are ten traits of a good focus group moderator:

1. Be experienced in focus group research.
2. Provide sufficient help in conceptualizing the focus group research design, rather than simply executing the groups exactly as specified.
3. Prepare a detailed moderator guide well in advance of the focus group.
4. Engage in advance preparation to improve overall knowledge of the area being discussed.

5. Provide some "added value" to the project beyond simply doing an effective job of conducting the session.
6. Maintain control of the group without leading or influencing the participants.
7. Be open to modern techniques such as visual stimulation, conceptual mapping, attitude scaling, or role-playing that can be used to delve deeper into the minds of participants.
8. Take personal responsibility for the amount of time allowed for the recruitment, screening, and selection of participants.
9. Share in the feeling of urgency to complete the focus group while desiring to achieve an excellent total research project.
10. Demonstrate the enthusiasm and exhibit the energy necessary to keep the group interested even when the hour is running late.[5]

Reporting the Results of Focus Groups

In writing the findings of focus groups, care must be taken to not imply that results typify the target population. The groups were not formed in an effort to generate inferential statistics, but rather to clarify concepts, generate ideas and insights, make the abstract real, etc. Therefore, it is the qualitative rather then quantitative conclusions that should be the focus of the written report. Goldman and McDonald make the following suggestions about writing the report on focus group findings:

1. The report should not be a sequential summary or transcript of the sessions, but rather a "logically organized and coherent interpretation of the meaning of these events."
2. The report should begin with an introductory section that reviews the research purpose, research objectives, and a short description of the research methodology. This is followed by a report of findings, the marketing implications, recommendations, and suggestions for future research phases.
3. An "Executive Summary" at the beginning of the report should cover the major discoveries as well as the relevant marketing implications that can be justifiably concluded based on the qualitative research results.

4. The results section is not necessarily best done by following the sequence of topics covered in the discussions. It may be approached rather as focusing on marketing problems or market segments, and discussing the findings from the groups that might have been addressed in diverse order during the group sessions.
5. The written analysis should progress from the general to the more specific. For example, a report on a new snack product concept might start with a discussion of general observations about snack eating, then go to a discussion of brand image and loyalty, then address the response to the new snack concepts.
6. The marketing implications section should provide guidance for the development of marketing response to the findings without overstating the conclusiveness of the qualitative findings. Everyone, report writers and readers, should remain aware of the limited objectives for conducting the groups, as well as the limitations of this type of research method in general.[6]

Trends in Focus Groups

Several new variations in the traditional focus group approach are being successfully used by some companies. One is *two-way focus groups,* which involve conducting a focus group, then having a specific group of respondents interested in the comments of the first focus group view the video of the focus group during their own focus group session. This approach could be expanded to a three-way focus group setting. One of the authors of this text worked with a company that supplied food products to fine restaurants that used a three-way focus group approach. In this instance the first group consisted of patrons of expensive restaurants talking about their experiences at such restaurants. The video of these consumers was then viewed in a focus group of chefs and restaurant managers who commented on what they were seeing and were asked what they might do to address the needs of these consumers. The video of the chef's focus group was then observed by the food brokers used by the food service company who talked about what they could do differently to better serve the needs of the chefs. Managers from the sponsoring food service company attended all three focus groups (multiple groups of each "level" of focus groups were conducted).

Quads is another variation of focus groups that has been used. In these groups usually four respondents (hence the name quads) discuss a limited set of topics, perhaps engage in a taste test, and might complete a short evaluation of products. These take less time to complete than the usual focus group (less than one hour as opposed to ninety minutes to two hours), allowing for more of these to be conducted in an evening than traditional focus groups. The attraction of these quads is the ability to get 100 percent participation of respondents (in a ten-person focus group participation by each person is more limited) on a short, specific set of issues, allowing observers to more easily focus on the differences in responses and generate hypotheses regarding those observations. Conducting more groups allows for more "fine-tuning" of discussion questions and methodology and changes to be made from one group session to the next. Both two-way and quad variations of focus group approaches (and many more variations practiced by research firms) illustrate the *flexibility* inherent in conducting good exploratory communication research.

Internet focus groups are rapidly gaining in popularity. Internet focus groups are, as with all focus groups, an exploratory research technique that capitalizes on the efficiency afforded by the Internet to engage people in diverse geographic locations together in a discussion of a topic of interest to the researcher and participants. Such groups can be conducted within a company with employees or externally with customers or members of a target market. If confidentiality is a concern with employees, they can use a hyperlink embedded in e-mail to go to a secure Web site where they can participate anonymously.

Internet focus groups with consumers have an obvious advantage in cost savings over traditional focus groups (approximately 1/5 to 1/2 the cost) as well as allowing for greater diversity among participants. Participants may in some situations be able to enter their input and reactions to other participants anytime during the extended focus group time frame—twenty-four hours a day. Use of IRC (Internet Relay Chat) and/or Web chat sites make it easy for participants to contribute to a discussion set up at that specific site for a specific purpose. It is then possible to immediately generate transcripts of 20 to 30 pages of verbatim responses for analysis. Advantages include speed of recruitment, savings in travel costs and time away from the office, respondents are able to participate from the comfort of their own home, and anonymity of responses. Disadvantages include a loss of observable information (e.g., facial expressions, body language, sense of excitement, confusion, etc.) that veteran focus group moderators use in analyzing traditional group sessions. Also, it is not possible to ensure that the person engaging in the focus group session is really the person you wanted. It is not possible to effectively screen people for certain desirable and easily verifiable characteristics (e.g., age, gender, racial background, etc.), and be certain the person on the Internet actually fits the desired profile. Also, unless the topic is about the use of the Internet itself, the people who are available for Internet focus groups may or may not be representative of the complete target market.

Some research companies operate Internet focus groups by recruiting and building a database of respondents from screening people visiting their Web site or through other recruitment methods. These people are then profiled through a series of questions, which allows the research firm to select respondents with the characteristics desired by the client organization. Potential respondents are e-mailed, asking them to go to a particular Web site at a particular time (using a hyperlink embedded in the e-mail). The "moderator" types in questions and responds, probes, and clarifies during the session by typing in queries. For an example of a company using these types of focus groups, visit <www.greenfieldonline.com>.

TELEPHONE INTERVIEWING

Telephone interviewing is usually employed when the study design requires speedy collection of information from a large, geographically dispersed population that would be too costly to do in person; when eligibility is difficult (necessitating many contacts for a complete interview); when the questionnaire is relatively short; or when face-to-face contact is not necessary.

Specific advantages and disadvantages of telephone interviewing include:

Advantages

- Provides ease of making a contact (callback) with a respondent.
- Administration and close supervision is provided by professional staff at a central telephone center.

- Drawing representative samples of persons with telephones is relatively easy.
- Sequential disclosure and questionnaire flexibility with skip patterns, refer backs, etc., is possible.
- Speed in gathering information.
- Relatively low cost.
- Simplicity at conducting a pretest.
- Access to hard-to-reach people.

Disadvantages

- Exhibits cannot be shown unless a mail/phone or phone/mail/phone methodology is used.
- Question limitations such as limited scales.
- Long interviews are difficult to administer by telephone.

Telephone interviewing may be conducted in either of the following ways:

From the Home

In this case, interviewing is conducted directly from the interviewers' homes. They have all the materials that will be needed to complete an assignment and use the specified period (per instructions) on the telephone contacting respondents and conducting interviews.

From Central Location Phone Banks

In this method, telephones are installed in a room or several rooms in a central location. They may be installed in a permanent office (e.g., a research firm with WATS lines), or in a hotel or motel, a church basement or, if a great many phones are required, in a ballroom. Central location interviewing has many advantages. It allows for constant monitoring and supervision. If an interviewer has a problem or question, it can be handled on the spot. Mistakes can be corrected; respondents can be called back immediately if the supervisor finds that the interviewer's information is not complete. Interviews can be monitored to ensure correct interviewing procedures, techniques, and quotas are being followed.

Since telephone interviewing is the most commonly used method of data collection, a detailed discussion on the specific procedures of telephone interviewing is located in Chapter 6.

CATI Interviewing

Most market research companies now use some form of computer-assisted telephone interviewing (CATI) system. The survey instrument or questionnaire is programmed into a computer, and the "pages" of the questionnaire appear on the terminal screen in front of the interviewer. The interviewer can input the results either through the keyboard or in some cases by using an electronic light pen that can touch the appropriate response on the screen. The CATI system also provides for automatic skip patterns, immediate data input, and in some cases automatic dialing. This system promotes flexibility and simplification. In addition, increased speed and improved accuracy of the data are accomplished. Various programs of random-digit dialing can be attached to the CATI system. The computer-generated random-digit numbers can eliminate the sampling bias of unlisted numbers. Predictive dialing is another important feature that makes telephone interviewing more effective. With predictive dialing, the technology does the dialing, recognizes a voice response, and switches to the caller so fast that the interviewer virtually hears the entire "hello." The system predicts how many dials to make to keep the interviewing staff busy without spending over half of their time just making contact. The system automatically redials no-answer and busy numbers at specified intervals. Some predictive dialing systems can be set to identify answering machines automatically and reschedule those calls as well. This results in more efficient calling and higher penetration of the sample list.

Internet Research

Previously in this chapter we discussed the use of the Internet for doing exploratory research in the form of Internet focus groups. We will now discuss the use of the Internet for conducting survey research.[7] (Chapter 7 will describe a firm which specializes in Internet survey research.) Some of the newer, Internet and facsimile based approaches will now be discussed. Several reasons have been suggested for explaining the rise in the use of the Internet for conducting surveys. First, the questionnaire can be created, distributed to respondents, and electronically sent to the researcher very quickly. Since data are electronically delivered, statistical analysis software can be programmed to analyze and generate charts and graphs summarizing the data automatically. Second, Internet surveys are less expensive than using interviewers or printing, mailing, and tabulating mail surveys. Third, it is possible to create panels of respondents on the Internet and longitudinally track attitudes, preferences, behaviors, and perceptions over time. A fourth reason is that other methods are not as cost-effective as is the Internet for asking just a few questions. Another reason is the ability to reach large numbers of people globally very quickly and at low cost. Finally, Internet surveys can be made to look aesthetically pleasing and can, via Netscape or Internet Explorer or similar browsers, add audio and video to the questionnaire.

Internet surveys can either be e-mail or Web-based approaches. E-mail surveys are simple to compose and send, but are limited to simple text (i.e., flat text format) and allow for limited visual presentations (e.g., no photo or video based stimuli) and interactive capabilities, and can not permit complex skip patterns. Web surveys, in comparison, are in HTML format and offer much more flexibility to the researcher, providing opportunity for presentation of complex audio and visual stimuli such as animation, photos, and video clips, interaction with respondent, skip patterns, use of color, pop-up instructions to provide help with questions, drop-down boxes to allow respondents to choose from long lists of possible answers (e.g., "In which state do you currently reside?"). Based on answers to a set of screening questions, Web-based Internet surveys can direct respondents to customized survey questions specifically designed with those respondent characteristics in mind. These types of HTML format surveys can also be downloaded to the respondent's computer for completion and then either mailed or electronically sent to the researcher. Of course differences in monitor screen size, computer clock speed, use of full or partial screen for viewing questionnaire, use of broadband versus telephone transmission lines, etc. may result in different presentations of the questionnaire for different viewers. Also, computer navigation skills still vary widely across the population and must be taken into account when designing a Web-based survey. Designing Internet surveys adds another set of challenges to the researcher using questionnaires to collect data, and those researchers interested in using this medium should consult one of the recent publications addressing this topic.[8]

Some of the movement toward the use of the Internet for survey research is the increasing number of people with access to and amount of time devoted to being on the Web. Set up time can be as fast as or faster than CATI (computer-assisted telephone interviewing), with faster survey execution (often the targeted number of completed surveys can be reached in a few days). Also, the ability of the respondent to choose the time for completing the survey gives it an advantage over personal or telephone interviewing.

Not everything about the use of the Internet for survey research is positive, however. At present one of the issues of greatest concern is the degree to which respondents to Internet surveys are representative of a target population. If the survey is meant to be projectable onto a population with a high percentage of access to and usage of the Internet (e.g., university faculty, businesses, groups of professionals, purchasers of computer equipment), then this issue is of less concern. But when the survey is meant to be projectable to the "mass market" (i.e., U.S. population in general or a large portion of it cutting across ages, occupations, income levels, etc.), then conducting research by using the Internet exclusively is problematic. Descriptive research requires the use of probability sampling methods and not only is a large percentage of the U.S. population not reachable at home via the Internet, and is therefore in violation of the "known and equal probability" random sample selection requirement, it is also true that e-mail address directories do not provide all addresses with a known probability of being sampled. "In sum, e-mail and Web surveying of the general public is currently inadequate as a means of accessing random samples of defined populations of households and/or individuals."[9] In comparison, the sampling frame for telephone interviews is well-defined and its coverage biases are documented. With phone interviewing it is much easier to verify that the respondent is the person you targeted than it is with Internet surveys. Voluntary response at a Web site is particularly troublesome as a means of sampling a specified population with particular parameters (e.g., geographic, demographic, experience, etc. characteristics). Based on these problems, many researchers restrict Internet surveys to nonprobability sampling-based exploratory research. However, there are researchers who claim it is just as valid to use the Internet for probability sampling-based descriptive research as it is to use mall interviews or mail surveys. As previously mentioned, these claims for projectability are more valid when almost the entire target population has Internet access.

Another computer-based survey method is to put the questionnaire on a computer disk and send it by mail to the home or work location of the respondent. The computer disk contains the skip patterns for the questionnaire in its software. For example, if the question is, "Do you have a pet?" and the answer is no, the next question asked is different than if the answer was yes. Some of the same advantages and disadvantages regarding the use of graphics and other visuals, and ease of tabulating and statistically analyzing e-mail surveys are also true for computer disk by mail surveys.

A code of conduct providing guidelines for conducting research over the Internet has been developed by The Market Research Society and can be found at <www.mrs.org.uk/standards/internet.htm>. These standards, published in January 2004, include the following sections:

1. Definition of Internet research
2. Cooperation is voluntary
3. Respondents must not be inconvenienced
4. Respondents must give their informed consent
5. Researcher's identity must be disclosed
6. Respondent's anonymity must be safeguarded
7. Safeguarding data
8. Client-supplied data
9. Research with children and young people
10. Privacy policy statements

MAIL SURVEYING

Another method of data collection through communication is mail surveying. Quite often, research is conducted by sending to each potential respondent a self-administered questionnaire along with a cover letter, completion instructions, a self-addressed stamped return envelope, and in some cases, a token or incentive for the respondent to return the questionnaire. With the mail survey methodology, there is no personal interaction in most cases. However, in some cases, a telephone call or personal contact is made to obtain agreement from the potential respondent before the questionnaire is mailed or placed. Specific advantages and disadvantages of mail interviewing include:

Advantages

- Cost-effective.
- Efficiency in reaching large samples.
- Access to hard-to-reach people.
- Self-administered/no interviewer bias.
- Limited use of exhibits is possible.

Disadvantages

- Low return rate.
- Nonreturn bias; those who return a mail questionnaire may not represent the sample as a whole.
- No control of who fills out the questionnaire.
- No ability for sequential disclosure of information.
- Slow response.
- Hard to pretest.
- Question limitations.

STRENGTHS AND WEAKNESSES OF COMMUNICATION METHODS

Personal Communication

Personal interviews are the most productive, accurate, comprehensive, controlled, and versatile types of communication. There is ample opportunity for a well-trained interviewer to probe and interpret body language, facial expression, and other nuances during the interaction. Rapport can be developed that would put the interviewee at ease and gain his cooperation. The interviewer can explain any misunderstanding the respondent might have and keep the respondent on track and in sequence in responding to the questionnaire. In spite of the advantages of greater depth and productivity, the personal interview does take more time and money to administer.

Telephone Communication

Telephone interviews have the advantage of speed and relative economy compared to personal interviews. Interviews of this type are also easily validated and the personal interaction of a qualified interviewer maintains a relatively high degree of control. The proper sequencing of question response also can be maintained. Although not as flexible and productive as a personal interview, a well-designed questionnaire administered by a skilled interviewer can gather relatively comprehensive information. The interviewer also is in a position to probe at appropriate times and follow appropriate skip patterns. Weaknesses of the telephone interview are its inability to be as long or as detailed as personal interviews and its inability to show the respondent any products, pictures, or lists.

Mail Communication

Mail questionnaires allow for wide distribution. Also, the lack of interviewer/respondent interaction can give the feeling of anonymity, which can encourage accurate response to relatively sensitive questions. In theory, the respondent has time to check records or even confer with someone else to make sure reported information is accurate. Disadvantages include a low response rate that results in nonresponse error. Control of the sample is minimal. Knowing the difference in results between those who participated and those who did not is impossible. Too often participants are those who are either more interested in the subject area or who have more free time to fill out questionnaires. Also, a mail survey is slow, less flexible, and does not allow for probing. Control is lost with a mail questionnaire and sequencing is futile. Furthermore, researchers never actually know who completed the questionnaire. Many of these problems can be overcome through the use of mail surveys conducted by consumer panel organizations (see Chapter 2). Table 5.1 lists the strengths and weaknesses of the various methods of data collection via communication.

TABLE 5.1. Strengths and Weaknesses of Methods of Data Collection

	Interviewing		Questionnaire		
	Personal	Telephone	Self-Administered	Mail Back	Internet
Response Rate	Moderate to High	Moderate to High	High	Low to High	Low to High
Timing	Slow	Fast	Moderate	Slow	Fast
Cost/Coverage	High	Moderate	Low	Low	Low
Interviewer Impact (bias)	High	Moderate	Low	Low	Low
Ability to handle complex questions	High	Low	Moderate	Moderate	High
Control	High	High	Low	Low	Low
Length	Long	Short	Long	Long	Moderate to Long
Sample Control	High	High	Moderate	Low	Moderate

Internet Communication

The ability to cover a wide range of the population through the use of the Internet for surveying is improving, but is not yet equal to that provided by the other communication methods. Technology is also allowing for use of visuals, including streaming video, in the questionnaire, as well as complex skip patterns in question sequencing. Disadvantages are low response rate, control over who is completing the survey is minimal, and fatigue resulting in failure to complete entire questionnaire.

Communication versus Observation

The communication method has a number of advantages over the observation method. First of all, it is much more *versatile*. The observation method is limited by the amount of information that can be visually observed and recorded. Videotaping can assist in this process, but the observed behavior must be interpreted correctly. Consequently, direct observation is excellent at providing information about direct behavior and external characteristics; however, direct questioning can provide information on those variables as well as on an individual's feelings, intentions, motives, and other intangible attitudinal variables. Second, the communication method is generally *less expensive* and *quicker* to accomplish than the observation method. See Figure 5.2 for a decision model on the use of communication or observation for collection data.

PROCEDURES OF THE OBSERVATION METHOD

Observation involves the process of physically or mechanically recording some specific aspect of a consumer's activity or behavior. Some research designs call for this type of data. Some contend that observation is more objective than communication. However, observation, whether in a field setting or a laboratory, is not very versatile. Observation cannot answer questions concerning attitudes, opinions,

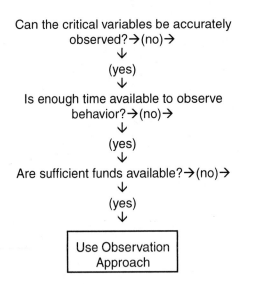

FIGURE 5.2. Checklist for Selecting Method of Data Collection

motivations, and intentions of consumers. Observation works well when measuring specific behavioral variables but is less effective measuring attitudinal variables. Often a design that starts with unobtrusive observations followed by communication to obtain information about motives, attitudes, etc., behind the observed behavior is an effective approach. *Direct observation* involves actually watching an individual's behavior. His or her purchase behavior is watched or he or she is viewed while using a specific product. Sometimes this behavior is monitored in a *natural setting* or real-life situation. Observations can also be made in an *artificial setting* that is developed by the researcher to simulate a real-life situation. Quite often a contrived store setting is established to simulate consumers' responses to products in an "actual" purchase situation. A major advantage of artificial or simulated observation is the greater degree of control offered researchers to alter specific variables.

An observation may be accomplished with or without the knowledge of the subject. Obviously, the advantage of disguised observation is that the subject has no motivation to alter his or her behavior. *Mechanical observation* is sometimes appropriate to meet the study objectives of the research design. When this is the case various mechanical devices such as cameras and counting instruments are used to make observations. Eye motion, galvanic skin response, perspiration, pupil size, and various counting devices are examples of mechanical methods of measuring and recording activity. Eye-tracking equipment can be used to measure where the eye goes in viewing an advertisement, a product package, or promotional display. A specific application of this technology would be to determine the impact of color in advertising and copy on a newspaper page. The tracking equipment records not only where the eye goes on the page but also how long it focuses on a specific area. People meters are designed to measure both the channel that is being watched as well as which person in the household is doing the watching.

SUMMARY

To this point in the book we have discovered that pursuit of answers to research objectives necessitates both a research design and data-collection methods that permit the execution of that design. "Good research" in any particular case could involve collection of information using one or more of the combinations of research design type and data-collection method. Table 5.2 illustrates that all combinations are possible. Which cell(s) a researcher should be in is a function of the research objectives, research budget, time available, and the decision maker's preferred data form for making decisions.

TABLE 5.2. Examples of Data-Collection Methods Used for Generating Exploratory, Descriptive, or Causal Research Information

Data-Collection Form	Research Design Types		
	Exploratory	*Descriptive*	*Causal*
Secondary			
Communication	Previous industry studies help to define what "customer service" means to consumers.	Annual survey revealing the number of times during the week people wash dishes by hand.	A journal article that reports on testing the hypothesis that public service advertising changes people's attitudes toward donating blood.
Observation	A *Wall Street Journal* article reporting that there are a growing number of magazines devoted to Internet usage.	Syndicated data indicating the market shares of various brands of coffee.	A report by a marketing research firm on the use of test marketing by different industries in the past year.
Primary			
Communication	A focus group of distributors that discusses trends in package-handling technologies.	A survey of salespeople to determine the frequency with which competitors have given free goods to dealers.	Running two advertisements in matched markets and determining which ad resulted in greater recall and positive attitudes toward the company.
Observation	Watching production line workers using a handheld grinder and gaining insights on products design changes.	Recording license plate numbers in store parking lot and getting R.L. Polk to generate a map showing trade area and distribution of customers.	Doing a test market for a new product and determining if sales reached objectives.

NOTES

1. Krueger, Richard A. 1990. *Focus Groups*. Newbury Park, CA: Sage Publications; David W. Stewart and Prem N. Shamdasani. 1990. *Focus Groups*. Newbury Park, CA: Sage Publications; Alfred E. Goldman and Susan Schwartz McDonald. 1987. *The Group Depth Interview.* Englewood Cliffs, NJ: Prentice-Hall.

2. Langer, Judith. 1987. "Getting to Know the Customer Through Qualitative Research," *Management Review*, (April), pp. 42-46.

3. Ibid.

4. Welch, Joe L. 1985. "Research Marketing Problems and Opportunities with Focus Groups," *Industrial Marketing Management*, (14), p. 248.

5. Greenbaum, Thomas L. 1991. "Do You Have the Right Moderator for Your Focus Groups? Here Are 10 Questions to Ask Yourself," *Bank Marketing*, (23:1), p. 43.

6. Goldman and McDonald, *The Group Depth Interview,* pp. 170-182.

7. The following sources were referred to in writing this section on Internet research: Watt, James. 1997. "Using the Internet for Quantitative Survey Research," *Quirk's Marketing Research Review*, (June/July), pp. 18-19, 67-71; Totten, Jeff W. "Pro and Con: Internet Interviewing," *Marketing Research*, Summer 1999, 11:2, pp. 33-37; Diane K. Bowers. 1998/1999. "FAQs on Online Research," *Marketing Research*, 10:4, pp. 45-49; Dillman, *Mail and Internet Surveys*, pp. 352-361.

8. See, for example, Dillman, Don. 2000. *Mail and Internet Surveys*. New York: John Wiley & Sons, pp. 361-401.

9. Dillman, *Mail and Internet Surveys,* p. 356.

WORKSHEET

1. Data collection should usually begin by searching secondary data.

Type of Data Needed (i.e., internal or external)	Data Form (e.g., sales, demographics, industry shipments, etc.)	Source(s) of Data (e.g., census, trade assoc., on-line search, etc.)	Results of Search (e.g., secondary data discovered)

2. If secondary data do not fully answer the research questions/objectives then primary data must be collected. Use the research objectives to indicate the type of primary data needed.

Research Objectives	Type of Primary Data Required (e.g., demographics, attitudes, motives, etc.)	Data-Collection Method (i.e., communication, observation, or both)
i. _____	_____	_____
_____	_____	_____
_____	_____	_____
ii. _____	_____	_____
_____	_____	_____
_____	_____	_____
iii. _____	_____	_____
_____	_____	_____
_____	_____	_____

3. For each type of primary data requiring communication, indicate the data-collection mode.

Type of Data Requiring Communication (from #2)	Data-Collection Mode (e.g., personal, phone, mail, focus group)	Identification of research client organization? (yes or no)

4. For each type of primary data requiring observation, indicate the data-collection mode.

Type of Data Requiring Observation (from #2)	Data-Collection Mode (e.g., direct, mechanical)	Degree of Disguise	Natural or Artificial Setting

5. Focus group research:

Objectives for Groups	Number of Groups	Location
_____	_____	_____
_____	_____	_____
_____	_____	_____

6. Indicate the screening criteria used in recruiting participants.

_____

_____

_____

7. Provide the topic discussion guide for the groups.

_____

_____

_____

8. Checklist for conducting groups.*

Advance Notice

_____ Recruit participants two weeks before the session.

_____ Send a letter of invitation to each participant.

_____ Provide participants with a reminder phone call twenty-four hours before the session.

_____ Overrecruit the number of participants by 25 percent.

Questions

_____ Introductory questions should be short and not identify status.

_____ Questions should follow a logical sequence.

_____ Critical issues of concern should be the focus of questions.

_____ Be sure to use probing or follow-up questions.

_____ Use "think back" questions where needed.

Logistics

_____ Give thought to the physical characteristics of the room (size, comfort, etc.).

_____ Arrive early to make any necessary changes.

---

*Adapted from Krueger, Richard A. 1988. *Focus Groups*. Newbury Park, CA: Sage Publications, pp. 89-90.

_____ Ensure tape recording is adequate.

_____ Provide name tags and/or name tents for participants (first name only).

_____ Be sure to bring extra tapes, batteries, and extension cords.

_____ Snacks should be simple and convenient.

_____ Bring extra copies of handouts and/or visual aids.

Moderator Skills

_____ The moderator should have high energy and a positive attitude.

_____ An introduction should be made without referring to notes.

_____ Questions should be asked without reading from notes.

_____ Avoid demonstrative head nodding.

_____ Avoid comments such as "excellent," "great," "wonderful."

_____ Avoid personal opinions.

Immediately After the Session

_____ A summary of key points should be provided as soon as possible.

_____ Ensure that the tape recorder captured the comments.

Chapter 6

Designing the Data-Gathering Instrument

When we use the term "data-gathering instrument" we typically are referring to using a descriptive research design data-collection method. We do not think of collecting "data" per se in exploratory research (i.e., we are generating hypotheses, ideas, insights, clarifying concepts, prioritizing objectives for the next phase of research, etc.), and although we do generate data in causal research, we tend to think in terms of putting together an experimental design rather than designing a data-collection instrument.

The quality of the information gathered is directly proportional to the quality of the instrument designed to collect the data. Consequently, it is extremely important that the most effective data-gathering instrument possible be constructed.

As mentioned in Chapter 2, it is vital to anticipate the total information needs of the project so the data-gathering instrument can be designed in such a way that it will provide answers to the research questions. The instrument must also gather the data in a form that permits processing it using the analytical techniques selected. As a result of its importance, the data-gathering instrument is the "hinge" that holds the research project together and must be done well.

GOALS OF A QUESTIONNAIRE

A questionnaire is the main type of data-gathering instrument in descriptive research designs. A questionnaire is defined in *Webster's New Collegiate Dictionary* as "a set of questions for obtaining statistically useful or personal information from individuals." Obviously, an effective questionnaire is much more than that. Since poor questionnaire design is a primary contributor to nonsampling errors, specifically response errors, the questionnaire should be well designed.

The questions should minimize the possibility that respondents will give inaccurate answers. The questions that are asked respondents are the basic essence of a research project. Inquiring by way of interrogation through specific questions forms the basic core of survey research. The reliability and validity of survey results are dependent on the way the specific questions are planned, constructed, and executed. A "good" questionnaire should accomplish the following goals.

Express the Study Objectives in Question Form

The questionnaire must capture the essence of the study objectives and ask questions that will gather the data that will provide the information needed to answer the various research questions. Quite often, a set of study objectives are adapted to an existing questionnaire that has been effective in the past. Each project with its unique set of study objectives should have a custom-made questionnaire designed especially for that project. The design of the questionnaire is the wrong place to try to economize during the research process.

Measure the Attitude, Behavior, Intention, Attributes, or Other Characteristics of the Respondent

The questions must be specific and reported in a form that will allow for comparisons to be made and results to be analyzed. The responses to the questions must provide the information that is necessary to answer the research questions and in a format that can be subjected to the appropriate analytical technique. (Techniques of analysis will be discussed in Chapters 9 and 10.)

Create Harmony and Rapport with the Respondent

A well-designed questionnaire targeted at the correct population sample should provide an enjoyable experience for the respondent. The frame of reference of the respondent must be considered in the design, wording, and sequencing of a questionnaire. Occupational jargon, cultural background, educational level, and regional differences can alter the effectiveness of a questionnaire if they are not taken into consideration. Not only should the questionnaire appeal to the respondent, it should be designed so the respondent can easily understand it, be able to answer it, and be made willing to answer it.

Provide Just the Right Amount of Information: No More, No Less

This is a trite statement, but it has much truth to it. There are often honest differences of opinion on just how much information is needed to answer a set of research questions. However, in designing a questionnaire the two basic mistakes are leaving an important question unasked, which makes the survey incomplete, and asking too many irrelevant questions, which makes the survey too long and unwieldy. A researcher must learn to economize in asking questions to avoid respondent burnout, which leads to early terminations and incomplete and inaccurate information. However, care must be taken in the design process to be sure the proper quantity of information is gathered to accomplish the research objectives. A rule of thumb in questionnaire design is "when in doubt, leave it out."

CLASSIFICATION OF QUESTIONS

Questions can be classified in terms of their degree of *structure* and *disguise*. By structure we mean the degree to which the question and the responses are standardized at some point in the data-collection process.

When a questionnaire is classified according to disguise, it depends on how evident the purpose of the question or questionnaire is. An undisguised questionnaire is one in which the purpose of the research is obvious to the respondent because of the questions asked. A disguised questionnaire obscures the purpose of the research and tries to indirectly get at a respondent's point of view. Of course the sponsor of the research may or may not be revealed to the respondent before he or she answers the questions, but this is not what is meant by "disguise."

Based on the classification of questions according to structure and disguise, the following general types emerge.

Structured-Undisguised Questions

These are the most commonly used in research today. Every respondent is posed the same questions in the same sequence, with the same opportunity of response. In most cases the purpose of the research is clearly stated in an introductory statement or is obvious from the questions asked. This type of instrument has the advantages of simplicity in administration, tabulation, and analysis; standardized data collection; objectivity; and reliability. The disadvantages include lack of flexibility in changing questions "on the fly."

Structured-Disguised Questions

These are probably the least-used questions in market research. They maintain the advantages of structuring while attempting to add the advantage of disguise in eliminating possible bias from the respondent's knowledge of the purpose of the survey. The main advantages of this type of questionnaire are ease of administration, coding, tabulating, and analysis. An additional advantage is to gain insight on a sensitive issue without "tipping" your hand to the respondent. The problem with this type of research is the difficulties encountered in interpreting the respondent's answer. An example of a structured-disguised question would be:

Which of the following types of people would eat a lot and which would eat a little hot cereal?

Eat a Lot   Eat a Little

_____   _____ Professional Athletes
_____   _____ Wall Street Bankers
_____   _____ Farmers
_____   _____ College Teachers

The structure is obvious. The disguise is related to the purpose of the questions, which is to use the responses to determine the image people have of hot cereal. It is easy to tabulate the responses but considerably more difficult to interpret what the responses mean with regard to the respondents' image of the product. For example, What does it mean that 23 percent of respondents said professional athletes eat a lot of hot cereal, and 18 percent said they eat only a little compared to 31 percent and 22 percent respectively for college teachers?

Unstructured-Undisguised Questions

This type of question is appropriate for in-depth interviews and focus group interviews. It allows the interviewer or moderator to begin with a general question or series of questions and allows the discussion to develop following a general series of questions in a discussion guide. Because of the nature of this type of question, the effectiveness of the depth or focus group interview depends largely upon the skills of the interviewer or moderator. Advantages of the method are that more in-depth and accurate responses can be obtained, particularly for complex and sensitive issues, and greater cooperation and involvement can be obtained from the respondent. The unstructured-undisguised interview is well suited for exploratory research, gaining background, and generating and clarifying research questions.

Unstructured-Disguised Questions

Unstructured-disguised questions are often used in motivation research to determine the "whys" of an individual's behavior. Projective methods are often used to get at the subtle issues that are not easily explored by direct questioning. Word association, storytelling, and sentence completion are methods that can be used to try to gain information about a subject without revealing the actual purpose of the research (see Chapter 2).

Descriptive research questionnaires largely consist of structured-undisguised questions. They are highly structured data-gathering instruments, compared to the less-structured instruments used in exploratory research's focus group or in-depth interview guides. In the descriptive research questionnaire each respondent asks a particular question, hears (or sees) the same question, and has the same response options. This is obviously true with questions such as:

Would you say you eat away from home more often, less often, or about the same as you did three years ago?

More _____ Less _____ Same _____

Here, both the question and the response categories are highly structured. Open-ended questions are structured but the response is not, at least at the point of gathering the data. An example of an open-ended question:

> [If said "less"]
> Why do you eat away from home less often than you did three years ago? [Record verbatim]

> _____

> _____

> _____

The respondent could give any explanation to the interviewer or write in any response if the respondent were completing the questionnaire alone. The responses become structured when the researcher develops categories of the answers based on the type and frequency of the responses (e.g., the number of times the researcher sees an answer such as "I work at home now whereas I used to eat lunch out every day at work" or "Our household income has decreased and we can't afford to eat out as often"). The researcher may establish a number of different categories of responses after considering all the responses and then tabulate the responses for all completed questionnaires by categories. Thus, what appears to be an unstructured question is in fact structured as a question before asked and as an answer after it has been asked.

Another way of collecting information is when the respondent hears what appears to be the same open-ended question in a phone or personal interview, but the interviewer categorizes the response into predetermined categories at the time the question is asked, such as:

[IF "LESS OFTEN" INDICATED IN PREVIOUS QUESTION, ASK]

> Why do you eat away from home less often than you did three years ago? [CHECK ALL THAT APPLY]

> _____ Economics/less money/lower income

> _____ Change in household members/circumstance

> _____ Changed jobs, etc.

_____ Other [Record Verbatim]

_____

_____

_____

Instructions to the interviewer are in brackets. In this example the interviewer exercises the judgment in categorizing the response (the respondent hears only the questions, the responses are not read). Response categories may have been established based on exploratory research or previous descriptive studies. If a response does not fit any of the given categories the interviewer is to record the verbatim response, allowing the researcher to later establish new categories to capture the unanticipated responses. The researcher must balance the ease of tabulating and lower expense of having structured responses with the flexibility and "richness" of the more expensive open-ended responses that must later be structured.

We will address the remainder of this chapter to the construction of a questionnaire that uses structured-undisguised questions to collect data.

STEPS IN DESIGNING A QUESTIONNAIRE

No single generally accepted method for designing a questionnaire is available. Various research texts have suggested procedures ranging from 4 to 14 sequential steps. Questionnaire design, no matter how formalized, still requires a measure of science and a measure of art with a good dose of humility mixed in. In designing a questionnaire, presumption must be set aside. Although for simplicity of format, the sequence for developing a questionnaire is given on a step-by-step basis, rarely is a questionnaire constructed in such a routine way. Quite often it is necessary to skip from one step to another and to loop back through a previous series of steps.

The following represent a sequential procedure that needs to be considered for the development of an effective survey instrument.

- *Step One:* Determine the specific information needed to answer the research questions.
- *Step Two:* Identify the sources of the required information.
- *Step Three:* Choose the method of administration that suits the information required and the sources of information.
- *Step Four:* Determine the types of questions to be used and form of response.
- *Step Five:* Develop the specific questions to be asked.
- *Step Six:* Determine the sequence of the questions and the length of the questionnaire.
- *Step Seven:* Predetermine coding.
- *Step Eight:* Pretest the questionnaire.
- *Step Nine:* Review and revise the questionnaire.

A brief discussion of each of the questionnaire development steps follows.

Determine the Specific Information Needed

The initial step to be taken in the design of a questionnaire is to determine the specific information needed to answer the research questions. This task can be made much easier if the earliest phases of the research process have been precisely accomplished. Clear study objectives facilitate this important decision. One of the most common and costly errors of research is the omission of an important question on the data-gathering instrument. Once the questionnaire is fielded, it is too late to go back for additional information without significant delay and additional cost. Consequently, the researcher must determine all of the information required before the questionnaire is developed. Sometimes the articulation of research objectives into specific questions by setting up dummy tables to be used when analyzing the results will trigger a new idea or research question that should be included in the survey. Every effort needs to be marshalled at this point of the design process to ensure relevant results for the analysis phase of the research process. In some cases it is advisable to conduct exploratory research to ensure that all of the relevant variables are identified. Focus groups, reviews of secondary sources of information, and some selected personal interviews are good ways of making sure that the pertinent variables are identified.

Identify the Sources

Step two involves the important aspect of identifying the sources of the information requirements determined in step one. Sample selection will be discussed in more detail in Chapter 8, however, the characteristics of the sample frame are extremely important in designing the data-gathering instrument. The sophistication, intelligence, frame of reference, location, ethnic background, and other characteristics of the potential respondents are vital to determining the type of questionnaire, the wording of questions, the means of administration, as well as other aspects of the questionnaire.

Choose the Method of Administration

Step three involves utilizing the results of steps one and two to decide whether a personal interview, telephone survey, or mail questionnaire is most acceptable. Issues such as whether a stimulus is required, the length of the questionnaire, the complexity of the questions, and the nature of the issue being researched must be considered in choosing which type of survey is best. These decisions should be made with respect to the information required and the nature of the sources of the information. Other considerations that affect this decision are the cost and time constraints placed on the research project. The time and cost advantages of the methods of administration were discussed in Chapter 5.

Determine the Types of Questions

Step four involves choosing the types of questions to be used in the questionnaire. To accomplish this the researcher must look both backward and forward. The researcher looks back to review the information required and the nature of the respondents. This can dictate various decisions concerning the types of questions selected. The researcher must also look forward to the analysis stage of the research process to ensure that the right form of data is obtained to accommodate the proper analytical techniques.

Four basic types of questions might be used in a questionnaire: open-ended, dichotomous, multichotomous, and scales. Most questionnaires have more than one type of question.

Open-Ended Questions

Open-ended questions such as "What did you like about the product?" provide an unlimited range of replies the respondent can make. The major advantages and uses of this type question are that they can be used when the possible replies are unknown, when verbatim responses are desired, and when gaining deep insight into attitudes on sensitive issues is needed. Open-ended questions are also useful to break the ice with the respondent and provide background information for more detailed questions. As discussed earlier, these questions are good for providing respondents with maximum flexibility in answering questions regarding motivations (why they behave as they do), or in explaining attitudes, behaviors, or intentions in greater depth. Their responses can be categorized by the researcher after the questionnaire has been completed, but the extra time for collecting and categorizing responses may add to the expense of the study (sometimes as much as thousands of dollars per open-ended question).

Dichotomous Questions

A dichotomous question gives two choices: either yes or no, or a choice of two opposite alternatives. These questions are preferred for starting interviews, are easy to tabulate, and can be used as a lead-in for more specific questions to a particular group. A weakness of dichotomous questions is that they can force a choice where none exists or lead to bias. Another weakness is that few questions can be framed in terms of a dichotomy, particularly more complex questions.

Multichotomous Questions

Multichotomous questions provide several alternatives to the respondent. In some cases he may be asked to select only one from a list or he may be asked to select as many as are applicable. The advantages of the multichotomous question are: ease of administration, ease of tabulation, and flexibility for factual as well as attitudinal responses. Some disadvantages exist in the length of the list of alternative responses (e.g., the list is not exhaustive, response alternatives may not be mutually exhaustive, or reading the list may lead the respondent).

Scales

Although a scale can be considered a multichotomous question, it deserves separate consideration. Scales are used to measure degrees of feelings, attitudes, interest, and intentions.

Types of Scales. In Chapter 4, scales were briefly addressed in the discussion of measurement issues; we deal with them in greater length here due to their almost universal use in structured questionnaires. Some of the frequently used scales in marketing research are: the Likert scale, semantic differential scale, and itemized rating scales. A *Likert scale* essentially asks respondents to agree or disagree with a series of attitudinal attributes using the following scale:

Strongly Disagree	Disagree	Neither Agree Nor Disagree	Agree	Strongly Agree
1	2	3	4	5

The *semantic-differential scale* is a method in which respondents are asked to indicate which cell between two bipolar descriptors best describes their opinion about an object. The following list of bipolar statements exemplifies this technique:

Inconvenient:	___: ___: ___: ___: ___: ___: ___:	Convenient
Discourteous:	___: ___: ___: ___: ___: ___: ___:	Courteous
Old-fashioned:	___: ___: ___: ___: ___: ___: ___:	Modern
Rough:	___: ___: ___: ___: ___: ___: ___:	Smooth

Many *itemized-ratings scales* are used in marketing research. An itemized scale requires a respondent to categorize an opinion by selecting one specific descriptor from among a limited number of categories that best describes the respondent's point of view. Examples of commonly used itemized scales are the purchase intention scale and the hedonic scale.

The *purchase intention scale* is commonly used to establish estimates of "trial" and "repeat" purchases. This scale generates results that are very important inputs into volume-estimation models:

Definitely Will Not Purchase	Probably Will Not Purchase	May or May Not Purchase	Probably Will Purchase	Definitely Will Purchase
1	2	3	4	5

The *hedonic scale* is used to determine what statement best describes how well someone likes or dislikes a product taking all features into consideration:

Like Extremely	Like Strongly	Like Very Well	Like Fairly Well	Like Moderately	Like Mildly	Neutral	Dislike Moderately	Dislike Intensely
1	2	3	4	5	6	7	8	9

A respondent is asked to place his or her opinion on a scale from one end of a spectrum to another. Quite often the range will be from poor to excellent, from very satisfied to very dissatisfied, from very important to not at all important, from very interested to not at all interested. The scale is often on a five-, seven-, or ten-point scale. The benefit of a scale is that it permits the objective measurement of attitudes and feelings. This allows for the identification of segments who are more favorably inclined toward a product, service, or issue. Scaling is somewhat subject to various frames of reference differences and to the halo effect. Some debate exists concerning whether scales should be balanced or unbalanced. Balanced scales have the same number of responses on the positive side of the scale as on the negative side of the scale, such as the purchase intent and value scale:

Very Good Value	Fairly Good Value	Average Value	Somewhat Poor Value	Very Poor Value
1	2	3	4	5

Unbalanced scales have more possible responses on one side of the scale then the other, usually the positive side. An example of an unbalanced scale is the hedonic scale. Some debate also exists over whether to have a neutral response. Those who feel there should be a "neutral" option believe so because they think that this is a legitimate response category and for the sake of accuracy the respondent should have that "ground to stand on." People against having a neutral response category argue that most individuals are unlikely to be authentically neutral on an issue. They consider the neutral as an easy way out or a "polite negative." Consequently they feel that it is much better to frame the issue so that the respondent is "forced" to indicate a preference, however slight.

The "don't know" or "no opinion" response should always be available to respondents. An honest expression of a lack of awareness, experience, or thought given to an issue should be allowed so that these responses are not lumped together with those people who have considered the issue and find their position is the neutral point on the scale.

Earlier we mentioned that the researcher must look ahead to the analysis stage of the research process when determining the types of questions in order to ensure that the right levels of data are obtained to accommodate the planned analytical techniques. By this we mean that the researcher who plans to use specific analytical techniques (e.g., multiple regression, multidimensional scaling, conjoint analysis, analysis of variance, etc.) to test hypotheses or determine the relationship between variables of interest (such as between sales volume and various attributes of the target market), must have collected data in the form required by the analytical technique. In other words, one cannot just use any data as an input to these techniques. They require "raw data" in very specific forms before they can be run, just as a production process requires raw material to be in a very specific form to be able to produce a product. Consequently it must be determined how to *analyze* the data even before questions are written that will *generate* the data. In the interest of simplifying things somewhat, we will confine our questionnaire design suggestions to address analytical procedures no more complicated than cross-tabulation. As will be seen in Chapter 9, that technique is the most widely used and useful approach to getting managerial answers to the research objectives.

With respect to choice of type of scale, research has shown that the type of scale used (e.g., Likert, semantic differential, etc.) does not impact the quality of data as much as the number of scale points and number of item statements. Here, more is better, obviously with diminishing returns occurring at some point. Therefore, a five-point scale is better than a three-point scale, but not as good as a seven-point or ten-point scale. Likewise, having eight attitudinal questions regarding how the target market feels about your customer service department is better than two questions, but eighteen questions may be overdoing it.

Develop the Specific Questions

Step five of the process of constructing a questionnaire is to actually write the specific questions that will be asked. The previous steps regarding the information required and the choices made relative to the types of questionnaire and questions will, to a large extent, control the content of the questions. The wording should be understandable and as explicit as possible. Questions should be worded in ways that avoid leading, pressuring, or embarrassing the respondent. The questions should avoid ambiguous words. Basic rules for wording questions are:

- Keep the questions short, simple, and to the point. Reasons for keeping the questions as brief as possible are that longer questions make the response task more difficult, are more subject to error on the part of both interviewers and respondents, cause a loss of focus, and are less likely to be clear. One question should not ask more than one thing at a time.
- Avoid identifying the sponsor of the survey. In some cases, such as customer satisfaction surveys, the researcher may want to identify the sponsor of the survey. In most cases, however, it is best to not identify the sponsor so more objective responses may be gathered.
- Keep the questions as neutral as possible. Unless a question can be worded objectively, it should not be asked. Nonobjective questions tend to be leading because they suggest an answer.
- Do not ask unnecessary questions. Always ask, "Is this question, necessary?" Each question should relate or add to a specific research objective. If the question falls in the "nice to know" but "not necessary" category, leave it out.
- Avoid asking questions the respondent either cannot answer or will not answer. Since respondents will answer most questions, it is important to determine if a respondent can be expected to know the information desired. On other occasions, respondents

will have the information required but may not be willing to divulge it. If a question appears to be sensitive it may be best to leave it out. If it is crucial to the research objective, then it is best to ask the sensitive question later in the survey after a degree of trust has been established with the respondent.

- Keep the tone of the questions positive. Generally, a positive tone will be less leading and will provide the highest level of cooperation.
- Avoid asking leading or overly personal questions. Words or phrases that show bias are emotionally charged and will lead to inaccurate results. When sensitive questions must be asked, they should be asked after a warm-up period and/or hidden within a series of less-personal questions.

Determine Question Sequence and Length of the Questionnaire

Step six can be extremely important in the completion rate of the survey. Excessive length may deter a number of respondents from completing the survey. This step can be equally important to the quality of the results acquired. The sequence of the questions should follow a logical pattern so it flows smoothly and effortlessly from one section to another. Another important consideration is to ensure that questions that build on previous questions are placed properly in the questionnaire. Generally, questions will flow from the general to the specific. This warms up the respondents and lets them reflect appropriately before being asked specific questions that require good recall and some degree of detail. Skip patterns for branching questions need to be carefully designed. Quite often, a respondent must be directed to a specific location in the questionnaire based on a previous question such as, "Have you baked brownies in the past three months?" "Yes" respondents go on to answer specific questions about the baking occasion while "No" respondents "skip" to a different part of the survey. Personal and telephone surveys lend themselves more to branching than do mail questionnaires.

Most questionnaires have three basic sections: introduction, body/content, and classification section.

Introduction

The introduction tells the respondent who the researcher is, why he or she is requesting the respondent's information, and explains what is expected of the respondent. The introduction should explain the purpose of the questionnaire and enlist the cooperation of the respondent. In the case of a mail survey this may take place in an attached cover letter. On the phone this is accomplished with a positive tone without sounding as though it is a polished sales pitch. Most people want to express their opinion as long as they know it is not a sales gimmick. The introduction should promise to keep the respondent's identity anonymous and his or her information confidential. Often the introduction will qualify the respondent in a special way to make sure that the interviewer is talking only to the right respondents. Qualification questions may include brand usage, age/sex categories, security issues such as whether the respondent or any member of his or her household works for a competitor of the client, an advertising agency, or a marketing research company.

Body/Content

The body or main content of the questionnaire provides basic information required by the research objectives. This is usually the most substantial portion of the questionnaire. If the respondent has not been qualified in the introduction, the first question of this section should identify the proper respondents and have instructions to end the survey for all others. This section should begin with easy, direct questions. Place questions that are personal or reflect a sensitive issue well toward the end of the body. Once respondents have become interested in the survey, they are more likely to respond to personal or sensitive issues.

Classification Section

The final section of most questionnaires is designed to obtain cross-classification information such as sex, income, educational level, occupation, marital status, and age. These demographic data allow for comparisons among different types of respondents. Certain market segments may emerge through the use of this cross-classification data.

Predetermine Coding

Questionnaires should be precoded so that any difficulties encountered in entering data into computer tabulation and analysis programs may be solved before the data are gathered. Once the questionnaires are completed and returned, the responses can be quickly entered into the database and results generated.

Pretest the Questionnaire

The eighth step is an essential step that should not be ignored. Following the maxim, "the proof is in the pudding," a questionnaire should be pretested before it is administered. A questionnaire may be too long, ambiguous, incomplete, unclear, or biased in some way. Not only will a thorough pretest help overcome these problems, but a pretest will help refine any procedural problems a questionnaire might have. Some of the procedural problems might be improper skip patterns and misunderstanding the interviewer. A pretest will evaluate and fine-tune the questionnaire, estimate the time required for completion of the interview, check for problems with ambiguous questions or unanticipated responses, and allow for set up of coding refinements for tabulations. The pretest should be administered under actual field conditions to get an accurate response. If significant changes result from an original pretest, it is advisable to conduct a second pretest after appropriate revisions have been made. A relatively small number of interviews are sufficient to pretest a normal questionnaire. Once they have been completed, all interviewers who participated should report their findings. They will be able to determine whether the questions work and be able to make suggestions for revision.

Revise the Questionnaire

Based on the pretest and a thorough review of all the previous steps, the questionnaire should be revised. The bottom line for an effective data-gathering instrument is the accuracy of the data collected. Everything that can possibly be done in advance should be done to ensure the accuracy of the instrument.

The steps used to design an effective data-gathering instrument need to be viewed as a dynamic outline and not a sequential step-by-step process. Each step should be applied with a sharp eye on the research objectives and the data needs they require. The finished questionnaire is the result of rearticulating the study objectives into a set of effective questions for extracting the required information from the pertinent set of respondents.

SUMMARY

No matter what the type of survey method, a data-gathering instrument is generally required to gather the data required to answer the research questions. Good data-gathering instruments should reflect the research needs by reiterating the study objectives in question form; measure attitudes, behaviors, intentions, attributes, and other characteristics of respondent accurately; be balanced in structure; create harmony and rapport with the respondent; and be concise. A questionnaire should only provide the right amount of information; no more, no less.

WORKSHEET

1. Translate your research objectives into information requirements.

   Research Objectives   Information Requirements

   _____   _____

   _____   _____

   _____   _____

2. Determine the sources of information you require.

   Information Requirements   Source (e.g., trade questionnaires, consumer questionnaire, secondary data, etc.)

   _____   _____

   _____   _____

   _____   _____

3. Choose a method of administering the questionnaire.

   _____ Personal Interview   _____ Mail

   _____ Telephone   _____ Internet

   (Some questionnaires involve a sequence of methods such as screening questions via telephone, followed by sending a mail questionnaire to qualified respondents, after which a follow-up phone questionnaire may be used. In other cases only one method is used.)

4. Design questions to get information desired.

   Information Requirements   Questionnaire Questions

   _____   _____

   _____   _____

   _____   _____

5. Make sure questions are appropriate.

   Checklist.

   _____ Is the information best asked as:

         _____ an open-ended question?

         _____ a dichotomous question?

         _____ a multichotomous question?

         _____ a scaled question?

   _____ Is the question short, simple, and to the point?

   _____ Is the question "objective" (nonbiased in wording)?

   _____ Is the respondent capable of answering such a question?

   _____ Is the question not leading?

6. Design questions to collect classification information.

Classification Information (e.g., sex, age, income, etc.)	Questionnaire Questions
_____	_____
_____	_____
_____	_____

7. Sequence the questions in the questionnaire.

   Checklist.

   _____ Introduction explains purpose of questionnaire

   _____ Ensure confidentiality

   _____ Qualify respondents

_____ General first, then specific

_____ Sensitive and classification questions at end

_____ All questions coded for computer tabulation and analysis

8. Pretest questionnaire.

   Checklist.

   _____ Use same data-collection method

   _____ Revise as needed

   _____ Pretest again as needed

Chapter 7

Fielding the Data-Gathering Instrument

Once the steps are all accomplished in the preparation of a questionnaire, it is ready for the field. The field operation phase of the research process is the time that the data-collection instrument is taken to the source of the information. The planning of the field work is closely related to the preparation of the questionnaire, which was discussed in Chapter 6, and the sample selection, which will be discussed in Chapter 8. All three of these aspects of data gathering must be well conceived, planned, and executed in order to achieve the objectives of a study. Error can occur in all of these phases, and the field collection portion is no exception. The results of any excellently conceived questionnaire drawn from a scientifically selected representative sample can be nullified by errors in the fielding of the questionnaire. Consequently, the data-collection phase of the marketing research process is extremely important. A poorly executed data-collection effort can nullify the impact of a well-designed sampling scheme and data-collection instrument.

PLANNING

To minimize total error and to gather accurate information as efficiently as possible, the field service of a questionnaire should be well planned. Time, money, and personnel must all be budgeted appropriately. Time for the field portion of a research project is extremely important, since it must fit into the overall time frame of the entire research project. The field service portion should have a realistic completion date with a little leeway built in. This will allow for timely and accurate completion. Since the field work must be done before analysis can occur, good sequencing is necessary.

Budgets

Money must be appropriately budgeted for the field service effort. Cost must be assigned to all the component activities of the field service phase. Cost estimates must be made for: (1) wages of interviewers, supervisors, and general office support; (2) telephone charges; (3) postage/shipping; (4) production of questionnaire and other forms; and (5) supplies.

Staffing

Personnel are the key to successful field service operations. Care must be taken to have the best possible personnel to accomplish the research task. There is no substitute for well-trained, experienced interviewers. Consequently, the personnel must not only be selected and scheduled for a project; they must have been trained in the techniques of interviewing. Some of the basic rules of interviewing are discussed in the "Interviewing Situation" section later in this chapter. Another important part of preparing the personnel for a specific study is to ensure they are thoroughly briefed on the specific aspects of the questionnaire that will be administered. The personnel must have a clear understanding of the data-gathering instrument and what information is desired.

GUIDELINES FOR INTERVIEWERS

The field service operation should accomplish the following responsibilities:

1. Cover the sample frame in accordance with instructions to ensure representative data. The proper areas and/or persons must be contacted.
2. Follow study procedures and administer the questionnaire as written. Be familiar with the questionnaire before beginning.
3. Write down open-ended responses verbatim. Record all other responses according to instructions in the proper terms of measurement.

4. Probe, but do not lead. If a person does not understand the question, read it again, *verbatim,* perhaps more slowly or with more inflection.
5. Establish rapport with the interviewee. Be confident in what you are doing and assume people will talk to you. Most people love to have the opportunity to say what they think. Reflect enthusiasm in what you are doing, but do not lead the respondent.
6. Accomplish a field edit to ensure that the data are being collected in appropriate form.

Personal Interviews

The requirement of personal interviews creates special problems from the field service point of view. As discussed in Chapter 5, personal interviews may be done through door-to-door, mall intercept, executive interviewing, or central location interviewing. Interviewers must be located, screened, hired, trained, briefed, and sent out in the proper geographic areas called for in the sampling plan in order to execute a door-to-door survey. A company will often hire outside field service organizations to conduct this type of interviewing. If a company has subcontracted the entire project to an outside consultant firm, it would be wise to make sure that the research firm has its own in-house field service personnel or at least has a good network of field services that it subcontracts to. Interviewers must also be well trained in the art of interviewing, but quite often they must also understand technical terms and jargon, particularly in industrial marketing research. This high degree of competence and preparation of interviewers, as well as the time and travel involved, make this door-to-door interviewing quite expensive.

Mall intercept interviewing is a very popular way to execute personal interviews across a wide geographic area. This method of survey research intercepts shoppers in the public areas of shopping malls and either interviews them on the spot or executes a short screening survey and, if respondents qualify, they are invited to a permanent interviewing facility in the mall to participate in a research study. This is an effective method because there are several hundred mall facilities spread throughout the country. Many different types of studies may be conducted in shopping malls. Concept studies, product placement/home use tests, taste tests, clipboard studies (short, simple surveys), stimulated controlled store tests, and focus groups can all be administered in a modern mall facility.

Another method of questionnaire administration that involves a personal interview approach is a recruited central location test (CLT). A CLT usually involves the need for a probabilistic sample plan or a category of respondent that has a low incidence that cannot be conveniently located by other approaches. In this type of study, respondents are screened ahead of time and invited to a location at a preset time for the actual interview. These locations may include an office, church, school, private facility, hotel/motel, or even a mall research facility.

In-store intercepts are sometimes done to personally interview survey respondents. These studies are usually accomplished in a retail establishment central to the project's objectives (e.g., in a tire store for discussion of tire purchases).

Executive interviewing is the industrial equivalent of door-to-door interviewing. This type of interviewing requires very skilled interviewers who are well versed on the subject matter of the project. Consequently, this type of research is very expensive.

Telephone Interviews

Some of the same considerations involved with the development and management of a group of personal interviewers applies to telephone interviewers. However, greater control of a telephone interviewing staff can be maintained, particularly if the work is accomplished from a central telephone location. The entire interviewing effort can be monitored by a trained supervisor. On-the-spot questions can be answered and field editing can be accomplished to allow for quick correction of any problems with the data-gathering instrument. CATI systems have greatly automated telephone survey research and allow for better supervision, sample administration, and quality control. Currently, telephone interviewing is one of the most widely utilized types of survey communication. This is true because of the time and financial advantages of the method. Callbacks can be made much more easily and many people will talk on the phone when they would not open their door to talk with a stranger. In addition, telephone interviewing can execute a study design that requires a probability sample that would be too costly to do in a door-to-door manner.

Mail and Internet Surveys

Mail and Internet surveys eliminate the problems of selecting, training, and supervising interviewers. They are convenient, efficient, and inexpensive. However, they create some of their own problems such as lack of response and coverage, inability to control the sample responding, time lags in response, inability to handle lengthy or complex material (mail surveys), and potential for misinterpretation of questions.

The procedure for mail or Internet survey administration is the same for questionnaire development—pretesting, finalization, and production. However, mail and Internet surveys eliminate the field service worker. In the place of the personal or telephone interview, there is a mailing or electronic transmission of the questionnaire. Postcard reminders, incentives, tokens, e-mails, and follow-up questionnaires could be sent at appropriate times to encourage return of questionnaires.

INTERVIEWING RELATIONSHIP

Cooperation

The *first step* in the interviewing process requires the interviewer to obtain the cooperation of the potential respondent to be interviewed and then to develop a rapport with the respondent that allows the interviewer to obtain the needed information. If the interview is on an informal, conversational basis, the respondent will be at ease, and he or she will be less hesitant to voice real opinions. To be conversational and informal, an interviewer need not lose control of the situation. A balance should be sought between the stiff, formal inquisition, in which questions are grimly read and answers methodically checked, and the situation where the interviewer is too friendly and is out of control. An interview in which twenty minutes is spent on the actual questions and twenty minutes more is devoted to irrelevancies and "conversation" is inefficient.

Rapport

The *second step* of the interviewer is to develop appropriate rapport with the respondent. Rapport is the term used to describe the personal relationship of confidence and understanding between the interviewer and the respondent; rapport provides the foundation for good interviewing. A prerequisite to good rapport is that the respondent knows where he or she stands in the interview. The interview is actually a new situation for most people, and, when it begins, the respondent does not know what is expected or how far he or she can safely go in expressing opinions. Obviously, a respondent will react more favorably and openly in a situation he or she understands and accepts. The respondent should understand that the interview is confidential, that the interviewer is a friendly person ready to listen, that he or she can discuss the interview topics in detail, and that the information being provided is important. Throughout the interview, and especially in its early stages, the interviewer should make a careful effort to establish the tone of the interview in the respondent's mind. The respondent will then have a clear idea of where he or she stands, and what roles he or she and the interviewer have. The respondent should be made to understand that there are no right or wrong answers, that the interviewer is only interested in unbiased responses to the questions. Most people like to share their opinions. Good rapport, coupled with a well-designed data-gathering instrument, should serve the goal of making the interview a very positive experience for the respondent.

INTERVIEWING SITUATION

The Approach

The approach an interviewer takes in executing a survey is extremely important. In order for the sample to be representative, it is important that potential respondents are not "lost" or passed by because of something an interviewer may do or say to cause the potential respondent to refuse to participate or be excluded from the sample.

How To, How Not To

The method of approach will vary a great deal according to circumstances. As a general rule, the following scripted approach works well:

> Hello. I'm *(Name)* from *(Agency)*. We're conducting a survey in this area on *(Subject)*, and I'd like *(your)* opinion.

Notice the introduction does not ask, "May I ask you some questions?"; "Are you busy?"; "Would you mind answering some questions?"; or "Could you spare a couple of minutes?" These are approaches that allow the respondent to say "No" easily and should be avoided.

Qualified Respondent

The interviewer should make sure that the respondent qualifies for the survey. If only certain types of people are specified for in the study, no compromise can be made.

In most surveys, only one member per household may be interviewed. Including more than one interview per household will bias the survey. The exception, of course, is when the study itself seeks to collect data from multiple members of the same household, such as hearing from both husband and wife regarding a purchase decision.

Time Factor

The respondent should not be misled about how long an interview might take. An accurate answer should be given if asked, or in long interviews it is helpful to state the time required before an interview begins. However, the interviewer need not call attention to time or the length of the interview unless the respondent asks or appears to be in a hurry. For most respondents time passes very quickly while they are engaged in responding to a survey.

Declines, "Too Busy"

Should a respondent initially decline to be interviewed, the interviewer should not give up too easily. He or she should be patient, calm, and pleasantly conversational. Often a potential respondent who has initially refused will then agree to participate. If a person is completely opposed to being interviewed, the interviewer should go on to find another respondent.

In some cases, the selected respondent *is* actually too busy or is getting ready to go out so that an interview at that time is impossible. The interviewer should give a general introduction and try to stimulate the respondent's interest to the extent that he or she will be willing to be interviewed at a later time. The interviewer may need to suggest several alternate times before a convenient time for the interview can be agreed upon. If the survey is being done by telephone, an excellent technique to obtain later cooperation is to offer the respondent the option of calling back on a toll-free 800 number at his or her convenience. Callback appointment times can be noted on the screening questionnaire/introduction page of the questionnaire.

Respondents may ask why they were selected. The interviewer should explain that they were selected as one of a very small number of people in the area to take part in the survey. The respondent should be told there are no right or wrong answers; the interviewer is only interested in candid opinions. The respondent should be told that responses are confidential, and that identity will not be disclosed since responses will be grouped or tabulated as part of a total with hundreds of other interviews.

THE ACTUAL INTERVIEW

If at all possible, the respondent should be interviewed alone. The presence of other persons may influence the respondent's answers. From time to time, the respondent may be accompanied by a friend who may begin to answer the questions with or for the respondent. The interviewer should remind them that he or she is interested in only the opinions of the respondent.

The Questionnaire

The interviewer should be completely familiar with the designed questionnaire and all survey materials before conducting an interview. Practice interviews should be conducted to assure that the interviewer will not be awkward with his or her first respondents.

The interviewer should know and follow instructions that are actually printed on the questionnaire or CRT screen in all capital letters or enclosed in parentheses. They will indicate:

1. Skip patterns (tell which questions to ask next when a specific answer to a question is given).
2. When to read or not read possible answer sets.
3. When only one answer may be recorded or when multiple answers are acceptable.

Legibility

Legibility is of paramount importance in filling out the questionnaire. Often a lot of time is wasted in the tabulation process by trying to decipher what was written. The interviewer should always take time at the end of the interview to scan the work and rewrite any words that may be difficult to read by someone else. Each interview should be checked to see that it is entirely legible and understandable.

The interviewer should always use a pencil with sufficiently dark lead to be easily read. Do not use colored pencils or any form of ink: a Number 2 lead pencil is preferable. Some forms to be scanned require blanks to be filled in with a Number 2 pencil.

Asking the Questions

Each question on a questionnaire has been designed for a specific purpose and to obtain the information required to accomplish the study objectives. If an interviewer were to record or put the questions into his or her own words, a bias would be introduced and the interviews would no longer be like those of fellow interviewers who are asking the questions as stated on the questionnaire.

In the case where a respondent does not seem to understand the question, the interviewer should repeat the question to the respondent slowly, but again, not explain it in his or her own words. If the respondent cannot answer or refuses to answer a question, the circumstances should be noted in the margin and the interviewer should go on to the next question.

Do Not Lead the Respondent

The interviewer must not "lead" the respondent. By this we mean that the interviewer should not ask the respondent anything that would direct the respondent to answer the way he or she thinks the interviewer would like. The interviewer should never suggest a word, phrasing, or idea to the respondent. An example of leading would be:

RESPONDENT: It tasted good.
INTERVIEWER: By good, do you mean fresh?
RESPONDENT: Yes.

The interviewers' correct clarification to an "It tasted good." response should be, "What do you mean by 'good'?"

Do Not Be Negative

It is human nature to ask a question in a negative way. By this we mean that instead of asking, "What else do you remember?" the interviewer may ask, "Don't you remember anything else?" or "Can't you remember anything else?" By asking a question in a negative way, the interviewer may put the respondent on the defensive, and continued negative questioning may lead to irritation and termination. In addition, the normal reply to a negative probe is a negative response . . . No.

Record the Response Verbatim

Not only should the questions be asked verbatim; the interviewer is to record the answers verbatim. The interviewer will usually be able to keep up with the respondent. If the answer rushes on, the interviewer may have to repeat each of the respondent's words as he or she writes. The respondent usually slows down when this is done. Or, the interviewer may have to say, "You were saying something about. . . ." The respondent will usually go back and cover the point again.

Another way of slowing down the respondent is by explaining that his/her answer is very important and the interviewer wants to be sure to get every word down.

The exact words of the respondent capture more of the "flavor" of the response and the respondent through the use of pet phrases and words. The interviewer must record answers in the exact words of the respondent. The interviewer must not edit or rephrase the respondent's answer. Responses are recorded in the first person exactly as the respondent states his/her answer.

"X" or Circle, Not a Check

Unless otherwise specified by specific survey instructions, closed-end responses should be noted with an "X." An "X" has been proven to be more legible than a check.

If the instructions indicate that the interviewer is to circle a specified number on the questionnaire to indicate a respondent's answer to a question, it should be neatly circled and should not extend around a second word or number. When a questionnaire uses a grid format for responses, care should be taken to circle the answer in the column number corresponding to the question number.

Interviewer Attitude

The interviewer must remain completely neutral. A respondent's answers can very easily be biased by the interviewer interjecting improper voice inflections, biasing comments, or making facial gestures.

The respondent should not be rushed. Some people just do not think or converse as rapidly as others. It should be recognized that the respondent is being asked for an opinion without prior preparation and about which he or she has had very little time to think.

When interviewing, the interviewer does not have to have an expressionless face. He or she should develop the habit of encouraging the respondent to talk, without leading, and then listen carefully to what is said. There are many ways to indicate that the interviewer is following the respondent's remarks. Sometimes the nod of the head is sufficient; sometimes unbiased remarks such as "I see what you mean," "I understand," or "That's interesting," will keep the respondent expressing ideas and thinking further about the topic without leading or biasing the data.

The Closure

After completing the interview, the respondent should be thanked. Before the interviewer leaves a respondent, he or she should review responses to all questions to be certain that they have been answered correctly and the answers are clear, meaningful, and legible. The interviewer should then leave as quickly and pleasantly as possible.

Classification, Demographic, and Statistical Information

Generally, questionnaires include some classification questions such as income, age, education level, occupation, number of children in household, and other demographic or statistical information. Most people answer such questions willingly. Refusals will be rare if these questions are asked properly in an unapologetic fashion. Respondents may also be told that the answers are tabulated by a computer and that no one answer will be looked at individually.

Validations

A validation questionnaire should be prepared for every project. This questionnaire should include the original screening questions plus standard questions on method of recruitment, acquaintance with the interviews, and participation in other studies. The validation should be completed within one or two days of the end of fielding the real survey. This important quality check on the fieldwork ensures that the interview has actually taken place. Ten to 15 percent of all respondents who were reportedly interviewed are recontacted to verify their participation. If a respondent cannot answer the verification questions satisfactorily, then the interview that he or she allegedly completed is declared "invalid" and those results not included in the aggregated tabulations. If more than one invalid survey is attributed to a specific interviewer, all of that interviewer's work is discarded.

GENERAL RULES OF FIELDING
A RESEARCH PROJECT

Security of the Survey

The questionnaires, the responses, and all materials used in conjunction with the survey are confidential and should be returned to the supervisor at the completion of interviewing. Respondents generally are not told for whom the study is being conducted. The interviewer should not discuss interviews with family, friends, other interviewers, or anyone else. Confidentiality of the client and survey content and results is of utmost importance.

Briefings

Briefings, or training sessions, will be held before each project is initiated. The entire job will be discussed, giving both the supervisor and the interviewers an opportunity to carefully study job specifications and instructions and to ask any questions pertaining to the job. Field instructions will be reviewed and practice interviews will also be conducted to familiarize interviewers with the questionnaire. Individuals will be assigned quotas or specific duties involved with the job.

Supervisor Assistance

Each research project must have adequate supervision. If a question or problem arises, the interviewer should ask the job supervisor and not another interviewer for assistance. Once called to the supervisor's attention, any questions or problems can be remedied for all interviewers on the job or can be referred to the client for resolution.

Do Not Interview Friends or Acquaintances

A friend or acquaintance of the interviewer should never be interviewed. He or she might answer the questions in a manner that he or she thought would "please" the interviewer rather than give a candid response.

Adhere to the Study Specifications

The specifications of a study have been set forth for very definite reasons, and the specifications must be adhered to, to the letter. Therefore, if the interviewing method is personal, the interviewer cannot interview a respondent on the telephone; if the interviewer is to contact only one person in the household, he or she cannot interview other family members; if the interviewer is to interview one person at a time, he or she cannot interview a group of respondents. The interviewer cannot interview the same respondent on multiple studies at the same interview. By doing any of these things, the interviewer would not be following the specifications, and the interviews would be rendered useless.

Follow All Study Procedures and Instructions

Each interview must be conducted in the same manner by all interviewers. Instructions about showing exhibit cards, posters, or keeping products concealed must be obeyed the same way in all interviews. Detailed field instructions are usually provided for each project. These instructions come in many forms. A simple study may require an administrative guide, an interviewer's guide, a tally sheet, and sample questionnaire. More complicated tests may require quota sheets, test plans, preparation instructions, product-handling procedures, exhibits, concept statements, and/or sorting boards.

The administrative guide is designed for the field supervisor of the study. It provides useful background information, a start and end date, quotas, respondent qualifications, procedures for conducting the study, personnel requirements, briefing instructions, and many other special instructions. The interviewer guide is provided for each interviewer. The interviewer guide usually has some of the same information as the administrative guide as well as specific step-by-step, question-by-question instructions about how to administer the survey questionnaire. All of the field instruction aids are designed to reiterate to supervisors and interviewers the technical aspect of executing the specific study.

Accurate Record Keeping

The interviewer is responsible for keeping accurate records of all information required by the supervisor or the survey's client. If the addition of columns of numbers is required, it is the interviewer's responsibility that the addition be correct. Information collected through use of a tally sheet is often just as important as information collected in the actual interview.

Complete Assignments on Time

Interviewers assume the responsibility of completing assignments for which they have contracted within the specified time period.

Should unforeseen circumstances prevent completion of an assignment, they should notify their supervisor immediately. In addition, the supervisor should be notified immediately if the interviewer anticipates that the assignment will not be completed within the specified time.

Work Efficiency

Two factors affecting the efficiency of work performance are speed and quality. Conducting interviews at a reasonable speed is important. However, speed for the sake of numbers should never sacrifice quality. On the other hand, gaining desired information from the respondent is critical and can be done without spending undue time on any one area or by undue conversation with the respondent.

Probing

Many questions, particularly in in-depth interviews, are open-ended and require the interviewer to coax the answers from the respondent. Getting as much information as possible from open-ended questions often requires skillful probing. The interviewer should never assume anything about what the respondent is implying, but he or she should probe to get clear and complete answers to all parts of the question in the respondent's own words. The two basic purposes of probing are to *clarify* and to *develop additional information.*

Clarify

The interviewer should get as much information as possible from open-ended questions. An answer that tells something specific is much more valuable than getting several answers that are vague. The interviewer's objective should be to clarify why the respondent gave a particular answer to one of the questions. The more concrete and specific these reasons are, the more valuable the information becomes. For example, a respondent is talking about a car that he or she believes would be "economical." What does he or she mean by economical? The respondent means that it is not very expensive to buy, that it gets good gas mileage, that it is not very expensive to maintain, that it has a high trade-in value, or something else. It is up to the interviewer to find out precisely what the respondent means by "economical."

Here is an example of how to probe for clarity.

RESPONDENT: It's not my kind of movie.

INTERVIEWER: Why do you say that?

RESPONDENT: It doesn't look interesting.
INTERVIEWER: What do you mean by "interesting?"

RESPONDENT: The thread of the picture seems difficult to follow: the action is slow and drawn out. I enjoy fast-paced action-packed movies.

Develop Additional Information

An interviewer must often get respondents to expand on an answer. "It would be true to life" or "It makes you think" and other general answers should be probed by saying "Why do you say that?" or "Tell me more about that." Many of the best probes are on key words and the interviewer may repeat the key words from the respondent's answer as a question: "True to life?" or "Makes you think?"

Here is an example of probing for additional information.

RESPONDENT: They showed a bowl of soup.

INTERVIEWER: What *kind* of soup was it?

RESPONDENT: It looked like vegetable soup.

INTERVIEWER: What *else* did they show?

RESPONDENT: A little boy eating the soup and smiling because he liked it.

INTERVIEWER: What did they *say* about the soup?

RESPONDENT: They said this soup makes a warm and nutritious meal in itself.

Technical Aspects of Probing

1. When key words are probed, the word in the respondent's answer being probed should be underlined (e.g., "I thought the soup looked *tasty*.").

2. Probing questions asked that are not tied to key words should be indicated by prefacing those questions with a "p" with a circle around it, signifying an interviewer probe.
3. Answers should always be recorded verbatim in the respondent's own words. The interviewer should not edit, or try to improve his or her English, or to put things in complete sentences for him or her. Abbreviations may be used when possible as long as they are obvious to anyone who might see them. If they are not, go back after the interview and write them out.
4. The interviewer should begin writing the minute the respondent begins to speak. Responses are much more easily recorded if started before the respondent gets underway.
5. If necessary, the interviewer may ask the respondent to stop for a minute, or to repeat something he or she missed.
6. The interviewer should never lead the respondent. Legitimate probes must be distinguished from leading questions. A leading question would be "Was it a bowl of vegetable soup?" or "Do you remember the little boy that was in the ad?" Anything that suggests something specific about the subject is inadmissible.

Probing Summary

Get specifics. Ask "what else" only *after* probing the original response. Do not just accept an adjective or a thought—*FIND OUT WHY* the respondent feels that way. Get the respondents to expand on their answers. *Details,* whether positive or negative about the subject, are *very* important. Exhibit 7.1 illustrates words to clarify and questions to help probe and clarify.

ERRORS IN DATA COLLECTION

The accuracy of any data provided in a research project depends on several interrelated things. First of all, there must have been clearly articulated research objectives. Second, correct design must have been accomplished. Third, correct sampling techniques and procedures must have been used. Fourth, the data must have been collected well, and finally, the data must be analyzed correctly. Mistakes or errors at any point can negate excellent design sampling, survey technique, and

EXHIBIT 7.1. Clarifying and Probing

Words to Clarify

All right	Different	Good/Bad	Rich
Appealing	Difficult	Homemade	Satisfying/Satisfied
Appearance	Dislike	Tastes	Service
Attractive	Easy/Hard	Interesting	Shape
Better/Best	Effective	Lighting	Size
Cheap	Expensive	Like	Smell/Odor
Cleanliness	Feel/Soft/Hard/Stiff	Many	Smooth
Color	Few	Material	Spicy/Spicier
Comfortable	Fine	Neat	Stayed in Place Better
Consistency	Fit	Nice	Sweet/Sweeter
Convenient	Flavor	Okay	Taste/Flavor
Cost	Food	Price	Texture
Crisp/Crunchy	Frequently	Protection	Variety
Decor	Fresh	Quality	Worse/Worst
Design	Funny	Quick	

Questions to Help You Clarify

Why do you feel that _____?
What do you mean by _____?
Could you explain that more fully?
Could you be more specific?
Where does that occur?
When did you notice _____?
How is it _____?
What makes it _____?
What about _____?
In what way is it _____?

Probe Phrases

What else?
What else can you tell me?
What other reasons do you have?
What else can you remember/recall?
Your ideas/opinions are so helpful; can you tell me more?
What (specific wording in question)?

Tell respondents you are writing their responses down. This will eliminate long, uncomfortable pauses.

questionnaire design. Figure 7.1 illustrates the relationship between sampling and nonsampling error.

There are many types of errors generally classified as sampling and nonsampling errors. A sampling error is the difference between the observed values of a specific variable and the average of a series of observed values over a period of time. A sample error is a statistical error resulting from the fact that any given sample has an opportunity to produce a different estimate of the parameter of a population than is actually the case. This random error results from chance variation. It is quite often expressed as the ± percent of precision surrounding any estimate obtained from a sample at a given confidence level. Sampling error gets a lot of attention and will be discussed in Chapter 8. However, nonsampling error, which results from some systematic bias being introduced during the research process, can be a bigger problem than sampling error. Nonsampling errors are not a result of sampling. They include mistakes that come from sampling frame errors, nonresponse errors, and data errors. Nonsampling errors commonly arise from errors in design, logic, interpretation, field service, or presentation.

Nonsampling errors are a numerous breed. They are pervasive in nature and are highly arbitrary. Nonsampling errors, unlike sampling errors, do not decrease with sample size. In fact, they tend to increase as sample size increases. Although sampling errors can be estimated,

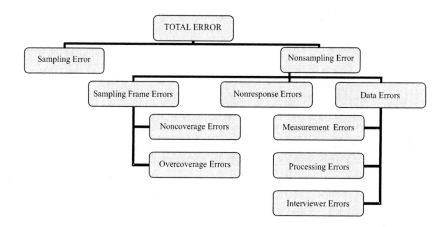

FIGURE 7.1. Sources of Research Error

their direction, magnitude, and impact are generally unknown. As a result of this, nonsampling errors are frequently the most significant errors that arise during a research project. Their reduction is not dependent on increasing sample size, but on improving methods and procedures dealing with the handling of the data itself.

TYPES OF NONSAMPLING ERRORS

There are three basic types of nonsampling errors: sampling frame errors, nonresponse errors, and data error. *Sampling frame errors* occur when certain parts of the survey population are not represented or are overrepresented in the study. This could result if part of the population of interest was not included or if some portions of the population are overrepresented. *Nonresponse errors* results when there is a systematic difference between those who respond and those who do not respond to a survey. *Data errors* occur because the information gathered is inaccurate or because mistakes are made while the data is being processed. Quite often nonsampling errors are made without the researcher being aware of them. This makes them potentially dangerous to the outcome of the project. An understanding of these types of errors will help the researcher prevent or correct them.

Sampling Frame Errors

Sampling frame errors generally consist of noncoverage and overcoverage errors. *Noncoverage errors* occur when some elements of the original population are not included in the sample. The bias from this type of error is the difference in characteristics, attributes, and opinions between those who are included and those who are not included. This is a very troublesome problem in marketing research because researchers do not know if there are significant and strategic differences between the ones who did not respond and the ones who did when there is no information on the noncovered potential respondents. Noncoverage is basically a problem with the sampling frame. The sampling frame is simply a listing of all the possible members of the population being studied. All of the basic survey methods depend on a listing of the members of the population under study. Telephone directories are not complete frames of a city's population because not every household has a number. Furthermore, of those that do, many are unlisted, and many people are in transition at any given time. Mail surveys have the same noncoverage problems, because a list that exactly includes the total population under study is rarely available. Internet surveys are even more problematic with regard to the noncoverage of people who do not have access to the Internet from their homes.

The noncoverage of sample members is as important as the noncoverage that results from not including all possible respondents in the sample frame. This occurs when the listed sample units are not contacted in both personal and telephone surveys. Quite often this situation arises when interviewers do not follow instructions or do not make the appropriate callbacks.

The most effective ways to limit the extent of noncoverage error is to recognize its existence and to take correctional measures. These measures are: improve the sample frame; establish clear instructions concerning who to interview, when to interview, and where to interview; specify callback requirements; and when possible, verify or monitor interviews.

Overcoverage errors occur when certain categories of sampling units in the sampling frame are duplicated or overrepresented. In many cases noncoverage of certain portions of the sample frame leads to overcoverage of other portions. Overcoverage can also occur when certain sample units are listed more than once. This leads to double counting and study bias.

Nonresponse Errors

Nonresponse errors occur when some of the elements of the population selected to be part of the sample do not respond. This happens most frequently among mail or Internet surveys, but can also occur in telephone surveys and personal interviews. The individuals originally chosen to be interviewed might not respond because they are not at home or because they refuse to participate.

"Not at homes" result because the potential respondent is not at home when the interviewer calls. This source of error is increasing. Included in the "not at home" category of respondents are those who are literally not at home and those who cannot be located. This includes those who use their answering machines or caller IDs to screen their calls, those gone on an extended trip, or even those who have recently moved. "Not at home" categories of respondents have different characteristics than those who are more easily located. The "not at homes" tend to be younger, better educated, more affluent, and more urban than those that are at home. Dual-career households tend to aggravate the problem. Care must be taken to account for the "not at home" factor or survey results will be incomplete and biased. The segments less likely to be home will be underrepresented and the results skewed toward the more commonly at home respondents.

Refusals occur when some respondents decline to participate or terminate prematurely after beginning the survey. The actual rate of refusal will depend on the nature of the respondent, the subject of the research, the ability of the interviewer, the length and design of the questionnaire, and the personal situation of the respondent. Mail surveys are particularly susceptible to the refusal nonresponse error. Personal and telephone interviews are also plagued with refusal nonresponse. Overall, the refusal rate appears to be increasing. More and more people are being interviewed and the novelty of being surveyed is wearing off. Because of fraud and crime, people are leery of having interviewers come into their homes. The use of the phone for telemarketing sales pitches disguised as surveys has also made legitimate surveys more difficult to complete.

Fortunately, there are many effective methods of reducing nonresponse problems. Some of the most common ones are as follows:

- Sell the respondent on the importance of his or her opinion and the value of the research.
- Notify the respondent in advance and make an appointment for a callback at a mutually agreeable time.
- Ensure confidentiality.
- Maintain contact with a callback or a follow-up mailing.
- Include return postage and envelopes for mail surveys.
- Use tokens or money incentives.
- Provide a toll-free 800 number so the respondent can callback at his or her convenience.

Careful usage of these techniques will increase the response rate of surveys and help avoid the problems associated with nonresponse error.

Data Errors

Data errors consist of interviewing errors, recording errors, coding errors, and processing errors. Usually these errors occur because inaccurate information is gathered from the respondent or the wrong information is recorded. This can result from measurement instrument bias resulting from a poorly designed questionnaire. In some cases processing error is also introduced during the editing, coding, tabulating, and processing of the data. Interviewer bias occurs due to interaction between the interviewer and the respondent. Respondents may overstate or understate certain behaviors, either consciously or unconsciously. In some ways these types of errors are the most dangerous because, unlike nonobservational error, researchers have no idea when and how observational errors might arise. Careful training, supervision, monitoring, and editing are required to minimize this type of error.

A final type of data error that should be mentioned is cheating. Cheating is the deliberate falsification of information by the interviewer. To avoid this problem, adequate control and supervision must be exercised.

SUMMARY

Once a data-gathering instrument is designed and the appropriate sample frame and size selected, it is time to field the instrument and execute the data-gathering process. To accomplish this smoothly and with a minimum of error, preplanning is a necessity. Proper budgeting and personnel recruitment lead the list of planning activities for the well-executed field service effort. Interviewers should be trained, briefed, and well supervised to obtain optimum results.

The interviewing relationship requires special attention to ensure proper rapport and understanding between the interviewer and respondent. Specific guidelines should be followed by interviewers depending on the type of interview being conducted.

General rules of interviewing must be maintained at all times. They include maintaining security of the survey, providing proper training and briefing sessions, maintaining close supervision, adhering to specific study specifications, following all study procedures and instructions, keeping accurate records, completing assignments on time, working efficiently, probing appropriately, and maintaining clarity.

WORKSHEET

Checklist

1. Budgets: Has money been appropriated for the following?

    _____ Wages of interviewers, supervisors, general office support

    _____ Telephone charges

    _____ Postage/shipping

    _____ Production of questionnaire and other forms

    _____ Supplies

2. Guidelines for interviewers: Have the following been done?

    _____ An introduction written

    _____ Interviewers know how much time the interview will take when asked by respondent

    _____ Provision has been made on the interview form for second callback appointment

    _____ Interviewer is thoroughly familiar with questionnaire

    _____ Interviewer has been trained as to the proper way to ask questions and probe for responses

    _____ Interviewer records answers verbatim in legible handwriting

    _____ Interviewer uses proper attitude in conducting interview

3. Validation

    _____ Validation questionnaire has been designed

    _____ Validation questionnaire has been used

4. Administrative Guide: The field supervisor has a guide that includes which of the following?

____ Background information on purpose and objective of the research

____ Start and end dates

____ Quotas for interviewers

____ Respondent qualifications

____ Procedures for conducting the study

____ Personnel requirements

____ Briefing instructions

5. Interviewing: Probing

____ Interviewers are familiar with when and how to probe to clarify or obtain additional information

6. Nonsampling Errors: Have the following nonsampling errors been addressed through preplanned procedures to prevent or overcome the problems?

____ Sampling frame errors

____ Noncoverage

____ Overcoverage

____ Nonresponse errors

____ Not at home

____ Refusals

____ Data errors

____ Interviewing errors

____ Coding

____ Tabulating

____ Processing

Chapter 8

Sampling Methods and Sample Size

In the course of most research projects, the time usually comes when estimates must be made about the characteristics or attitudes of a large group. The large group of interest is called the *population* or *universe.* For example, all of the registered Republicans in Jefferson County or all of the heads of households in Madison, Indiana, would each constitute a universe. Other examples of a population are all people in the United States, all households in the United States, or all left-handed Scandinavians in Biloxi, Mississippi. Once the determination of the study universe is decided, several courses of action might be taken. First, the decision might be made to survey all of the entities in the universe. If all of the members of the selected universe are surveyed, this is called a *census.* With a census, direct, straightforward information concerning the specific universe parameters or characteristics is obtained. A second course of action would be to survey a sample of the universe (population). A *sample* refers to the group surveyed any time the survey is not administered to all members of the population or universe. The process of selecting a smaller group of people who have basically the same characteristics and preferences as the total group from which it is drawn is called sampling.

WHAT IS SAMPLING?

Sampling is something everyone has some experience with. Anyone who has taken a bite of fruitcake and decided "Never again!" or any child who after a quick taste, has tried to hide his or her asparagus under the mashed potatoes has experienced sampling.

A famous quote from Cervantes states, "By a small sample we may judge the whole piece." Most of our everyday experiences with sampling are not scientific. However, our satisfaction with the results of our decisions, based on sampling, depends on how representative they are. In marketing research the goal is to assess target segments efficiently and effectively by designing and executing representative sample plans.

Sampling consists of obtaining information from a portion of a larger group or population. Making estimates from a sample of a larger population has the advantages of lower cost, speed, and efficiency, but it is not without risk. However, fortunately for researchers, this risk can be set very low by using probability sampling methods and appropriate estimating techniques, and by taking a sufficiently large sample. Thanks to the European gamblers of several centuries ago who were eager to establish the odds on various games of chance, some of the best mathematical minds of the day were dedicated to the task. This effort led to the fascinating branch of mathematics known as probability theory. Development in this area laid the foundation for modern scientific sampling.

Why Sampling?

There are many reasons for selecting a sampling technique over a census. In most cases the study objects of interest consist of a large universe. This fact alone gives rise to many advantages of sampling. The most significant advantages are:

1. *Cost savings*—Sampling a portion of the universe minimizes the field service costs associated with the survey.
2. *Time economy*—Information can be collected, processed, and analyzed much more quickly when a sample is utilized rather than a census. This saves additional monies and helps ensure that the information is not obsolete by the time it is available to answer the research question.
3. *More in-depth information*—The act of sampling affords the researcher greater opportunity to carry the investigation in more depth to a smaller number of select population members. This may be done in the form of focus group, panel, personal, telephone, mail, or Internet surveys.
4. *Less total error*—As already discussed, a major problem in survey data collection comes about as the result of nonsampling errors. Greater overall accuracy can be gained by using a sample administered by a better trained, supervised field service group.

In fact, the Bureau of the Census used sampling (as opposed to a census) in the year 2000 to improve the accuracy of their data.

5. *Greater practicality*—A census would not be practical when testing products from an assembly line, when the testing involves the destruction of the product, such as durability or safety tests or when the population is extremely large. The U.S. government has great difficulty accomplishing the U.S. Census every ten years.

6. *Greater security*—This is particularly true if a firm is researching a new product or concept. Sampling would be preferred to keep the product or concept a secret as long as possible.

SAMPLING DECISION MODEL

Sampling involves several specific decisions. This section briefly discusses the steps of a sampling decision model.

Define Population or Universe

Once the researcher decides to apply sampling techniques rather than a census, he or she must make several important sampling decisions (see Figure 8.1). The first decision is to define the population or universe. Since sampling is designed to gather data from a specific population, the universe must be identified accurately. Often this universe is called a *target population* because of the importance of focusing on exactly who the study objects are and where they are located. Usually any effort expended to do a first-rate job of identifying the population pays generous dividends later in terms of accurate and representative data. The definition of the population of interest should be related directly back to the original study objectives. Clues to identifying the target population can be found in the statement of research purpose. The research questions and research hypothesis generated from the research purpose should refine the definition of the target population. The sample must be reduced to the most appropriate common denominator. Do the research questions require selecting as sample elements individuals, households, purchase decision makers, product users, or what? Defining a population improperly can introduce bias into the study. Professional staff experience and insight are required to properly specify the target population.

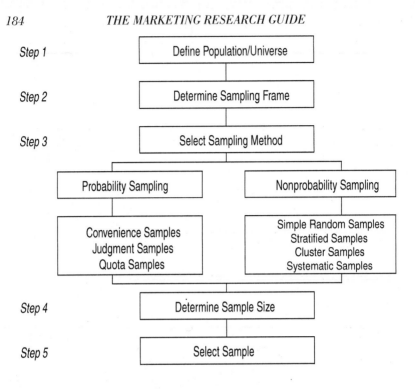

FIGURE 8.1. Sampling Decision Model

Determine Sampling Frame

The second step in the sampling decision model is to determine the sampling frame. The *sampling frame* is a listing of the members of the target population that can be used to create and/or draw the sample. It might be a directory, subscribers list, customer list, or membership roster. In some cases, the sampling frame coincides with the target population and includes everyone in the population and includes them without duplication. However, this ideal situation seldom exists in actual experience. It has often been said that "Only a divine being can select a truly random sample." Sampling lists or frames can be purchased from third-party companies specializing in sample preparation, or they can be put together by combining several sources. Because of the incompleteness of sampling frames, several discrepancies develop. In some cases, the sampling frame is made up of the subjects of interest but is smaller than the total population. As a result, certain elements of the population are omitted from the survey. In other cases, the sampling frame includes all members of the population but is larger than the population. Duplications or inappropriate units are included in the survey in these situations. A third situation occurs when some elements of the population fall in the sampling frame and some elements of the sampling frame are not of the population. In this case, both omissions and undesired inclusions occur.

For general population surveys, a traditional sampling frame has been the telephone directory. In the United States, 95 percent of potential respondents can be reached by telephone. However, the telephone directory is an incomplete sampling frame because in some metropolitan areas almost two-thirds of the telephone subscribers have unlisted numbers. Not only does this condition cause a large number of people to be left out of the directory, the omission of elements is not proportional across geographical areas. As a result, random-digit designs, where phones are programmed to dial random digits, are often used to overcome the exclusion bias inherent in directory-based sampling designs. There are numerous sources of computer-generated random-digit sampling frames for commercial use.

The goal of developing an appropriate sampling frame is to get a listing of elements of the target population that is as inclusive and proportionally representative as possible with a minimum of duplication.

Select Sampling Method

The third step in the sampling decision model is to *select the sampling method*. This decision logically follows the decisions to determine the target population and to define the sampling frame. The initial consideration in the selection of a sample is whether or not to employ a probability sampling procedure or a nonprobability sampling procedure.

Probability Sampling

Probability samples are simply those samples where each element has a known chance to be included in the sample. With nonprobability samples a way of estimating the probability of any given element being included in the sample is not known. With probability sampling a random or a systematic, chance-based procedure is utilized to select the study elements. The researcher preselects the respondents in a mathematical way so that persons in the universe have an equal or known chance of being selected. From a statistical point of view, probability sampling is preferred because it allows a calculation of the *sampling error.* Probability sampling procedures tend to be more objective and allow the use of statistical techniques. Although nonprobability sampling introduces certain biases, from an operational perspective, it offers the advantage of being less expensive and quicker to implement. However, the fact that a sample is a nonprobability sample does not mean that the sample must be less *representative* than a probability sample. The problem is, with nonprobability samples we cannot *compute* the degree to which they are representative, and therefore they cannot be used to generate such desirable statistics as confidence intervals (i.e., we cannot say such things as, "We are 95 percent confident that 45 percent ± 2 percent of the respondents say they will definitely buy formulation A.").

The most commonly used probability samples are simple random samples, stratified samples, cluster samples, and systematic samples.

Simple Random Samples. A simple random sample is a technique that allows each element of the population an *equal* and *known* chance of being selected as part of the sample. The implementation is often accomplished by the use of a table of random numbers. Computer and calculator random numbers can also be generated to assist in selecting random samples. A common analogy for a random sample is the traditional drawing of a sample from a fishbowl containing slips of paper with the names of the elements of the sampling frame.

Stratified Samples. When subgroups of the population are of special interest to the researcher, a stratified sample may serve a better purpose than a simple random sample. A stratified sample is characterized by the fact that the total population is (1) divided into mutually exclusive subgroups (strata), and that (2) a simple random sample is then chosen from each subgroup. This is a modified type of random sample. The method of creating a stratified sample ensures that all important subgroups are represented in the sample. The stratified random sampling technique is good for classifying consumers by various demographic factors. The stratified samples can be divided into proportionately stratified samples or into disproportionately stratified samples. A proportionately stratified sample allows for a breakdown where the number of items randomly selected in each subgroup

is proportionate to their incidence in the total population. A disproportionately stratified sample is a sample where the allocation of
sample elements is not established according to relative proportion.
This may result in an equal number of elements per subgroup or it
may result in the greater sampling of the subgroups that have the
greater potential for variability. This, however, requires prior knowledge of the characteristics of the population. Just as with a simple
random sample, there can be no stratified sample if there is no available sampling frame of elements of the population that breaks down
the population into the appropriate subgroups.

Some specific reasons for choosing to stratify a population sample
include:

1. A desire to minimize variance and sampling error or to increase
   precision. If a population is segmented into strata that are internally homogeneous, overall variability may be reduced. The required sample size for a well-designed stratified sample will
   usually be smaller than for a well-designed unstratified sample.
2. A desire to estimate the parameters of each of the stratum and
   have a "readable" sample size for each one.
3. A desire to keep the sample element selection process simple.

Cluster Samples. In some cases when stratified sampling is not
possible or feasible, cluster sampling can be utilized. The first step in
selecting a cluster sample is the same as in a stratified sample: the
population is divided into mutually exclusive subgroups. However,
the next step involves the selection of a random sample of subgroups
rather than a random sample from each subgroup. Cluster sampling
may not be as statistically efficient as a stratified sample; however, it
is usually more procedurally efficient in terms of cost and time. Cluster sampling is often associated with area sampling. In area sampling,
each cluster is a different geographic area, census tract, or block.

Systematic Samples. A fourth technique of probability sampling is
called systematic sampling. In this method of cluster sampling, every
element has a known but not equal chance of being selected. Systematic sampling is an attempt to increase the efficiency of the sample at
favorable costs. A systematic sample is initiated by randomly selecting a digit, *n,* and then selecting a sample element at every *n*th interval, depending on the size of the population and the sample size re-

quirement. This method is often used when selecting samples from large directories. Some loss of statistical efficiency can occur with systematic samples, particularly if there are hidden periodic sequences that cause some systematic variances to occur at the intervals selected. A systematic sample may be more representative than a simple random sample depending on the clustering of objects within the sample frame. The ideal list will have elements with similar value on the key defining characteristics of the sample close together and elements diverse in value in different locations of the list.

Nonprobability Sampling

Nonprobability samples are defined as any sampling techniques that do not involve the selection of sample elements by chance. The choices are made by convenience, expert judgment, or other criteria. Consequently, an estimate of the sampling error cannot be made. The most commonly utilized nonprobability sampling techniques are convenience samples, judgment samples, and quota samples.

Convenience Samples. The least expensive and least time-consuming of sampling techniques is generally considered to be a *convenience sample*, which is any process that quickly and easily selects sample elements. The sample element close at hand is chosen and surveyed in the application of this technique. Man-on-the-street interviews are examples of this type of sampling. The greatest problem with convenience sampling is the inability to know if the sample is representative of the target population. Consequently, one cannot generalize from the sample to the target population with a high degree of confidence.

Since the convenience sampling technique follows no predesignate method, the sampling error cannot be calculated. Consequently, specific precision and confidence level estimates cannot be made. Even with the drawbacks of convenience sampling, it is frequently used, particularly for exploratory research.

Judgment Samples. The representativeness of a *judgment sample* obviously depends on the skill, insight, and experience of the one choosing the sample. Although a judgment sample is a subjective approach to sampling, the knowledge and experience of a professional researcher can create a very representative sample. This is particularly true in industrial studies where a knowledge of the industry dynamics and decision-making procedures is necessary in identifying the correct respondents. In the area of polling "expert opinion," judgment samples can be very effective. Even though judgment samples are more restrictive and generally more representative than convenience samples, they have the same weakness that does not permit direct generalization of conclusions derived to a target population. In the final analysis, representativeness of a judgment sample depends on the experience, skill, knowledge, and insight of the person choosing the sample.

A particular kind of judgment sample is the "snowball" sample. This type of sample relies on the researcher's ability to locate an initial group of respondents with the desired characteristics. Additional respondents are identified on a referral basis relying on the initial set of respondents to identify other potential respondents.

Quota Samples. Quota sampling is the third type of nonprobability sampling; it is similar in some respects to stratified and cluster sampling. In quota sampling, the researcher divides the target population into a number of subgroups. Using his or her best judgment, the researcher then selects quotas for each subgroup. The quota method takes great effort to obtain a representative sample by dividing the population and assigning appropriate quotas based on prior knowledge and understanding of the characteristics of the population. Quite often the subgroups of the population are divided into strata or categories such as age, sex, occupation, or other known characteristics. Usually quotas are assigned based on known proportions for these characteristics such as provided by the U.S. Census. In this way, a quota sample can be drawn to represent the population based on the defining characteristics selected. An example could be to establish quotas based on age/sex proportions provided by the census and known product usage patterns. Although this would not ensure a representative sample, the researcher would know that the respondents come in the same proportion as the total population among product users and nonusers.

The problems with quota sampling are the same as for other nonprobability sampling methods. The sampling error cannot be calculated and projection to the total population is risky. A quota sample might be very representative of the quota-defining characteristics; however, another characteristic may be supremely important in defining the population that is not used to establish quotas. Consequently, this characteristic may be disproportionately represented in the final sample. It is impractical to impose too many cell categories on a quota sample. Despite some of its drawbacks, quota sampling is often used in market research projects.

Determine Sample Size

This section of the sampling model will also provide tables that allow selection of sample size for situations in which attitudes or variables are measured at various levels of confidence.

The size of the sample will be a function of the accuracy of the sample. Two criteria are used in measuring accuracy: the margin of error and the level of confidence. The first is determined as the tolerated error range (also known as sample precision) and the second is the probability that the sample will fall within that tolerated error range. A margin of error of 3 percent, for example, means that out of all possible samples of a certain determined size of coin flips, 95 percent will differ from the actual population by no more than three percentage points.

Sample size determination ultimately is a reflection of the value of the information sought. Scientific journals require that reported results must fall in the 95 to 99 percent confidence levels. When the risk involved in the decision alternatives is high, 95 to 99 percent confidence levels will be required. However, the sampling of well-known TV ratings is at the 66 percent confidence level. Even though the margin of error in these ratings is far greater than most scientific research, many advertising decisions are based on this result. Even low-budget studies, with low-risk decision alternatives that serve as a glimpse into the market environment, should usually not consider a confidence level of less than 80 to 90 percent. The 95 percent confidence level is suggested for most research.

The procedures in Appendix D will give greater definition to developing accurate sample sizes for different populations. However, Table 8.1, based on many studies from many research institutions, provides guidelines for determining sample size from different types of populations. The number of subgroups required for a sample may be known or may require some preliminary investigation or pretesting to determine.

TABLE 8.1. Typical Sample Sizes for Consumer and Institutional Population Studies

Number of Subgroups	Consumer or Households		Institutions	
	National	Regional or Special	National	Regional or Special
0-4	850-1,500	200-500	50-500	50-200
5-10	1,501-2,500	501-1,000	350-1,000+	150-500
Over 10	2,500+	1,000+	1,000+	500+

Source: Adapted from Sudman, Seymour. 1976. *Applied Sampling,* Academic Press: New York.

A subgroup in Table 8.1 might be any particular category of respondents of interest in the analysis stage, such as males verses females (i.e., two subgroups), or four income levels for households. The use of statistical calculations to determine the appropriate sample size is discussed in Appendix D.

Nonprobability Sample Size

The statistical methods of establishing sample size discussed in Appendix D apply only to probability samples. In the case of the nonprobability samples mentioned earlier in this chapter, the chance of any element of the population being chosen for the sample is unknown. Consequently, the principles of normal distribution and the central limit theorem do not apply. This eliminates the possibility of being able to use the formulas discussed in this chapter to establish sample size.

The choice of sample size for a nonprobability sample is made on a subjective basis. This should not concern the researcher too much because many of the estimates made to calculate sample size for probability samples were also made on a subjective basis. In nonprobability samples, size is determined by the insight, judgment, experience, or financial resources of the researcher. Remember, the important thing about a sample is that it should be representative—not that it be statistically derived. A number of rules of thumb are: "You reach diminishing benefits with samples greater than 300," "No sample should be smaller than forty," "A good sample is about 10 percent of the population," or "Choose a sample as large as your budget will allow." However, the final decision about the final sample size depends on whether it is believed by the researcher or sponsor to be representative of the population.

Besides judgment, available funds, and rules of thumb, other methods of determining sample size exist. One is the anticipated cross-classification to which the data will be subjected. If several demographic attributes or variables are going to be utilized, then concern must be given to the size of the cells of the cross-tabulation tables. The more cells in the tables, the larger the sample size must be (see Table 8.1). Another consideration related to sample size is the form of analysis that the data will undergo. Certain types of analysis, such as multidimensional scaling, will require larger sample sizes. Also, the nature of the research being conducted must be considered. Exploratory research will generally require smaller samples than descriptive research. Another consideration is the expected completion rate of the survey. The lower the expected completion rate, the larger the sample size must be.

Select Sample

Once the target population has been identified, an appropriate sampling frame determined or compiled, all sampling procedures selected, and a sampling size determined, it is time for the final step in the sampling decision mode. The sampling process should be executed in an efficient and professional way. Whether a sample is a probability sample or a nonprobability sample, the important aspect is to obtain as much representative information and eliminate as much sampling and nonsampling error as possible. Generally speaking, the sampling size should be increased whenever the population exhibits high variability or whenever high levels of confidence and precision are required.

WHAT IS A "SIGNIFICANT" STATISTICALLY SIGNIFICANT DIFFERENCE?

Henry Clay once said, "Statistics are no substitute for judgment." Just because two values can be adjudicated as statistically different does not mean that they are substantively different, and the reverse is also true. *Substantive* significance refers to the strength of a relationship or the magnitude of a difference between two values. Does the difference imply real-world practicality? If a very large sample is used, very small differences may be concluded to be statistically different; however, they may not be different in any substantive way. On the other hand, the difference between two values in a research project may not test as being statistically significant at a given level of confidence, but if the difference holds up in the real world it could be substantively significant.

SUMMARY

This chapter has presented the important aspects of sampling. The nature of the research project determines the type of sample, the sample size, the sample frame, and the method necessary to correctly draw/select the sample. In some projects, sampling consideration is a critical decision area because of the impact on costs and the need to draw inferences about the population from which the sample is drawn. Once the data have been collected, they must be analyzed to get meaning out of the raw data. Chapter 9 discusses the basics of data analysis.

WORKSHEET

1. Look at your research objectives to determine which population must be surveyed to answer those objectives.

   Research Objectives   Population(s) to study

   _____   _____

   _____   _____

   _____   _____

2. Indicate the sampling frame (either a list of the population members or a procedure to be used such as interviewing every fifth couple passing a point in a shopping mall) that will be used to select a sample of the population of interest.

   Population(s)   Sampling Frame

   _____   _____

   _____   _____

   _____   _____

3. Is your sample to be selected using a probability or nonprobability sampling method?

   _____ Probability

   _____ Nonprobability

4. If you are using a probability sample, select the sampling approach:

   _____ Simple random

   _____ Stratified random

   _____ Cluster

5. If nonprobability, select the sampling approach:

_____ Convenience

_____ Judgment

_____ Quota

6. Select a method for determining sample size and set the size of the sample:

Method   Sample Size

_____   Using formula: _____

_____   Using Table 8.1:   _____

_____   Using table or chart: _____

_____   Using a "rule of thumb":   _____

_____   Specify: _____

                                            _____

7. Indicate the exact procedure that will be used to select the sample of set size from your sampling frame:

_____

_____

_____

Chapter 9

Analyzing and Interpreting Data
for Decisions

Hamlet: Do you see yonder cloud that's almost in shape of a camel?

Polonius: By the mass, and 'tis like a camel indeed.

Hamlet: Methinks it is like a weasel.

Polonius: It is backed like a weasel.

Hamlet: Or like a whale?

Polonius: Very like a whale.

Hamlet, Act III, Scene ii

Data, as with cloud formations, can be made to appear to support any number of conjectures. The fertile mind of the analyst can "see" conclusions to the data that may be more the creation of the imagination than an objective reading of the information generated by the research. This gives pause to the researcher/analyst, because it implies that, although there may be an ultimate truth, the analyst's personal agenda, perceptual inclinations, experience, and even personality can influence the interpretation of the research study's results. Nevertheless, we must use all the means at our disposal to arrive at the most objective, concise, but also thorough analysis possible of the data generated by the research. However, the same observation of objective data may be subject to multiple interpretations. Consider the following apocryphal story:

An American shoe company sent three researchers to a Pacific Island to see if the company could sell its shoes there. Upon returning they made a presentation to management. The first researcher summed up the findings this way. "The people here don't wear shoes. There is no market." The second researcher said: "The people here don't wear shoes. There is a tremendous market!" The third researcher reported: "The people here don't wear shoes. However, they have bad feet and could benefit from wearing shoes. We would need to redesign our shoes, however, because they have smaller feet. We would have to educate the people about the benefits of wearing shoes. We would need to gain the tribal chief's cooperation. The people don't have any money, but they grow great pineapples. I've estimated the sales potential over a three-year period and all of our costs including selling the pineapples to a European supermarket chain, and concluded that we could make a 30 percent return on our money. I say we should pursue the opportunity."[1]

Here the three analyses reported the same results, but with different implications. The term "data analysis" covers a huge number of techniques, statistical programs, and processes that can be applied to the results generated by the data-collection instrument(s) used in our research. These can range from interpreting respondents' reactions to projective research (see Chapter 2), or the conclusions drawn from conducting focus groups (see Chapter 5), to sophisticated multivariate statistical techniques used to manipulate large databases. It is beyond the scope of this book to address these extremes of the data analysis continuum. The reader interested in such analytical processes should read material that specifically addresses those topics.[2] The discussion in this chapter will be limited to data analysis "basics" that will permit the researcher/analyst to successfully draw useful information out of the types of data generated via a descriptive research survey format.

FROM DATA TO DECISIONS

The manipulation and analysis of data generated by research becomes a "value-added" management activity when it takes place within a series of tasks leading to management decisions and, ultimately, to a market's reaction to those decisions. Figure 9.1 suggests that the output of data analysis is to always lead to better decision making than could have been done without having conducted the re-

Research	⟶	Analysis	⟶	Decision Making	⟶	Evaluation
DATA BITS {	Information Piece	Implication Statement	Alternative	Decision	Result
	Information Piece	Implication Statement	Alternative	Decision	Result
	Information Piece	Implication Statement	Alternative	Decision	Result

Tools	Tools	Tools	Tools
Surveys Experiments	Univariate and Multivariate Techniques	Models and Simulations	Data-Based Management
Observations,	— Cross Tabs	Management Judgment	
etc.	— Factor Analysis		
	— ANOVA		
	— etc.		

FIGURE 9.1. Overview of the Data Analysis/Management Decision-Making Relationship

Note: Results are data bits that, along with other new data bits from research, become information that leads to implications, etc., or that suggests new research.

search. This is consistent with the philosophy about the value of research presented throughout this book.[*]

An example may help to elucidate the process shown in Figure 9.1.

Worthington, now owned by Kellogg, a company that markets egg substitutes (e.g., Scramblers, Better 'n Eggs) conducted survey research that in part, sought answers to these research objectives:

1. Why do people control their cholesterol?
2. How did people who use egg substitutes first hear about them?
3. What is the trial-to-usage ratio for those cholesterol controllers who have tried a brand of egg substitute?

---

[*]It should be noted, however, that there is definitely a place for research findings that may not lead to an immediate decision, but that educate decision makers in a more general way. Well-informed, knowledgeable decision makers are valuable by-products of the analysis of decision-oriented research information. Therefore, researchers would not fail to report findings that may not in themselves suggest a decision, but that serve to edify management in important ways about the company's markets, customers, or significant trends in the environment.

A phone survey of a demographic cross section of the adult U.S. population was conducted (2,000 respondents). Once respondents passed a set of screening questions identifying them as cholesterol controllers they were asked to respond to these and other relevant questions:

1. What is the primary reason you are controlling your cholesterol intake? (check one response)
2. Which of the following brands of egg substitutes have you ever tried? Which do you currently use?
3. From which of the following sources did you first hear about egg substitutes?

The following is a sampling of the data bits generated from these questions:

1. Reason for controlling cholesterol:
   On doctor's orders   36%
   Family history of cholesterol problem 11%
   Concerned about future levels   53%
2. Percentage of all cholesterol controllers trying and using egg substitutes brands:

	Tried	Currently Use
Egg Beaters	72%	25%
Scramblers	12%	7%
Second Natures	4%	1%
Eggs Supreme	1%	—

3. Source of "first heard" for egg substitute triers:
   TV ad   13%
   Physician   10%
   Friend or relative   26%
   Magazine ad   24%
   Hospital   2%
   Saw product in store   7%

Each of the numbers listed in these sample tables represents a "data bit." Obviously, even a short phone survey can generate thousands of these bits of data. Although interesting by themselves, they become of even greater value when combined with each other to generate "information." For example, if we know the number of people who have tried a particular egg substitute brand (*a data bit*) and which of these same people currently use that brand (another data bit), we can determine that brand's retention ratio, the percentage who have tried and still use, or the brands rejection ratio, the percentage who tried and no longer use (i.e., *information pieces*).

Moreover, when multiple *pieces of information* are combined, some important *implications* can be drawn. Consider, for example, what is learned when information is combined about the primary reason for controlling cholesterol with usage or nonusage of egg substitutes:

	Egg Substitute	
Reason for controlling cholesterol:	Users	Nonusers
On doctor's orders	61%	32%
Family history	12%	11%
Concerned about future levels	27%	57%
Total	100%	100%

Here, the *implication* may be drawn that users of egg substitutes are much more likely to be under physicians' orders to control cholesterol than are nonusers. Looking at the data from another angle, of all the cholesterol controllers under physicians' orders to control cholesterol, the vast majority are users of egg substitutes (74 percent of all those under physicians' orders to control cholesterol are users of egg substitute brands).

	Egg Substitute		
Reason for controlling cholesterol:	Users	Nonusers	Total
On doctor's orders	74%	26%	100%
Family history	20%	80%	100%
Concerned about future levels	31%	69%	100%

Another related implication comes from combining information about how respondents first heard about egg substitutes with their retention/rejection information.

	% of Egg Substitute Triers		
First heard of egg substitutes from:	Rejectors	Continuing to Use	Total
TV ad	58%	42%	100%
Magazine ad	45%	55%	100%
Friend or relative	38%	62%	100%
Physician	18%	82%	100%

The implication from this table is that those who first hear about egg substitutes from a physician are more likely to continue using them after trial than those who first hear of them from other sources.

Combining these and other implications about usage and information sources leads to *decision alternatives* regarding the allocation of resources among TV media, magazine ads, coupons, in-store promotions, and calling on physicians. When the company conducting this research did a subsequent cost-benefit analysis of promoting directly to physicians, they determined that it was to their advantage to begin to pursue that course of action.

This illustration shows how data bits are combined into pieces of information that are combined into implications, which suggest decision alternatives, which lead to *decisions.* In this case, the decision to make physicians aware of the egg substitute brand and give their high-cholesterol patients a coupon for a free package of that brand was based on research findings which demonstrated that getting trial usage from that source was much more likely to result in continued usage than if trial was gained from other sources. Monitoring the *results* of this change in the allocation of promotional resources showed that the efforts with physicians were very cost-effective in increasing sales. Thus, these decisions led to results that became data bits, which ultimately resulted in future decisions (continued promotion to physicians).

This example also demonstrates that data analysis goes beyond merely determining answers to research questions. The analytical aspects of this case did not stop with reporting answers to the original three research objectives, but rather sought to reveal the *association* that might exist between the three questions. That is, the *implications* drawn between the information pieces were what added real, significant value to the research findings. The research analyst is acting as more than a reporter of findings; he or she is seeking to know the answer to such provoking questions as:

- What does it mean that *this* (e.g., why they control cholesterol) and *this* (e.g., a difference in retention rate) are both true simultaneously? and
- What does it matter that the researcher has discovered this association? *Answer:* It suggests physicians could play an important gatekeeping role in generating product trial for people who may

prove to be brand-loyal heavy users. Not reported in this example, but true for the research, was the discovery of a direct correlation between egg substitute usage rate and physician involvement.

Therefore, the researcher/analyst's job is only half over once the research is finished. The real value-added activities come with the data analysis performed on the gathered data.

We will now discuss the means by which such data analysis can be conducted.

DATA SUMMARY METHODS

Developing a Plan of Analysis

For the purposes of this discussion we will assume that the researcher/analyst has successfully coded and entered data into the computer and now desires printouts that can be analyzed and interpreted.

The first step in generating summary data to be analyzed is to prepare a plan of analysis. Actually, the genesis of such a plan was started in the discussion in Chapter 1 concerning how to state research questions and hypotheses, and was further developed in the Chapter 2 discussions of dummy tables. Therefore, the heart of a plan of data analysis consists of:

- How to obtain answers to research questions.
- How to test hypotheses to determine if they are supported by the data or must be rejected.
- The execution of the dummy tables that were used early in the research design process to alert the researcher to the type and form the descriptive survey data should take.

However, as demonstrated by the egg substitute research example at the beginning of this chapter, it may be necessary to go beyond obtaining answers to the research questions, testing existing hypotheses, and filling out dummy tables. In that example, a new hypothesis was generated during the data analysis. The new hypothesis was that retention rates of egg substitute usage would vary by reason for controlling cholesterol and by source of first mention of egg substitutes. Such a hypothesis could very well have been generated at the time the research purpose and objectives were stated at the very start of the research process. However, it is inevitable that some hypotheses or specific tabulations or analytical outputs will be initiated during data analysis and not before.

Frequency Distributions

May researchers generate a set of frequency distributions that indicate how respondents answered the survey questions. For example:

Q: What is the primary reason you are controlling your cholesterol intake?

	Number	Percentage
On doctor's orders	651	36%
Family history	199	11%
Future concern	959	53%
	1,809	100%

Note that of the 2,000 respondents surveyed, only 1,809 answered this question. The remaining 191 were omitted for the usual reasons (spoiled questionnaire, refusal to answer, etc.). The percentage is best computed as 100 percent for those respondents who did answer the question, rather than based on the full 2,000 respondents. However, the researcher may wish to know why the 191 subjects were not included. If many could not easily choose a primary reason (they were controlling cholesterol for two or three reasons), or were controlling cholesterol for reasons not given as a response option (e.g., because their spouse was controlling and prepared meals with reduced cholesterol), then the researcher would want to know this so he or she could revise the question in the future to make provision for such problems. Hopefully, exploratory research done before the survey would reveal most or all of the response categories needed. Also, offering a fourth option:

Other [Record]: _____

is an expensive, but effective means of learning of other reasons respondents control cholesterol. Nevertheless, if the analyst is primarily concerned with how the target population is distributed among these three reasons, then the percentages should be computed based on the 1,809 respondents instead of 2,000.

If the question had been phrased differently a different-looking frequency distribution might result:

Q: Why are you controlling your cholesterol intake? [Check all that apply]

	Mentions	
	Number	Percentage
On doctor's orders	702	39%
Family history	295	16%
Future concern	1,120	62%
	2,117	117%

Here it is obvious we have multiple reasons given by some of the 1,809 respondents and the percentages are computed based on the number of respondents instead of number of responses. The percentages may be interpreted as follows: "thirty-nine percent of the respondents mentioned that they controlled their cholesterol because of a physician's orders; sixteen percent mentioned controlling...." We might be interested in asking this question both ways, with "check all that apply" asked first, followed by the "primary reason" question. Researchers should be cautioned to carefully consider why they are asking such questions and how they plan to analyze the results before assuming automatically that it would be best to always ask both questions. Time is valuable and only a limited amount of it will be given by respondents. If the researcher uses it up by asking these two questions it means he or she will not be able to ask some other important question within the time frame.

Percents cannot be averaged unless the percentage is weighted by the size of the sample responding to the question. For example, consider the following frequency distribution:

	Egg Beaters		Scramblers	
Usage rate:	Number of Users	Percent	Number of Users	Percent
High	250	50%	75	37.5%
Medium	100	20%	100	50%
Low	150	30%	25	12.5%
	500	100%	200	100%

It would be incorrect to say that an average of 35 percent of users of these two brands are medium users (i.e., 20% + 50% = 70% ÷ 2 = 35%), when actually medium users represent 28.6 percent of the two brands' usage rate (i.e., 100 + 100 = 200 ÷ 700 = 28.6%).

Do not refer only to percentages when the base of their computation is very small. For example, although the following percentages may be accurate, be careful not to misrepresent the data by referring to just the percentages:

	Male Respondents	
Reason for controlling cholesterol:	Number	Percentage
On doctor's orders	7	70%
Family history	2	20%
Future concern	1	10%
	10	100%

Dealing with "don't know" or "no opinion" responses is a matter of analyst judgment. Usually it is best to include them as a legitimate answer to knowledge or attitude-type questions and record the response rate such as:

Q: Which do you believe would be higher priced, Egg Beaters or Scramblers?

Egg Beaters	65%
Scramblers	30%
Don't know	4%
No opinion	1%
	100%

Researchers should be aware that it is standard operating procedure for marketing research firms using phone or personal interviewers to push for responses other than "don't know" or "no opinion" when asking a knowledge or attitude question, and recording a "don't know" response only when, after unsuccessful prodding, the respondent insists on maintaining that answer. Therefore, the "don't know" and "no opinion" responses will almost always be underrepresented in the final data. Although in many cases that is desirable, in some cases it may grossly distort the truth.

As an illustration of such a danger, consider results generated by research that asked triers of multiple brands of egg substitutes which brand had a higher fat content. The results (simplified here for discussion purposes) were as follows:

	Percent Mentioned As High Fat
Brand A	17%
Brand B	13%
Don't know	70%
	100%

This distribution actually was a test of the researcher's hypothesis that the low involvement of people in purchasing a product such as an egg substitute brand would be reflected in their lack of knowledge about such attributes as fat levels for the brands they had purchased. Consequently, interviewers were instructed to record the first response of the subjects and not to use standard operating procedure (SOP) to push for an answer other than "don't know." The results supported the hypothesis and suggested that altering some product attributes would have a limited effect on brand demand. Therefore, researchers should consider how they wish to deal with the "don't know" and "no opinion" response percentages.

Central Tendency and Dispersion Measures

As discussed in Chapter 4, the measures of central tendency that can be used to describe the data depend upon the type of data we have generated (nominal, ordinal, interval, ratio). The frequency distribution discussion in the previous section is pertinent to each of these four types of data.

The measures of central tendency and dispersion that can be computed for the data types can be displayed as

Nominal	Mode
Ordinal	Mode, Median
Interval	Mode, Median, Mean, Standard Deviation
Ratio	Mode, Median, Mean, Standard Deviation, Geometric and Harmonic Mean

The most commonly used measures are defined in the following and will be discussed in this section of the chapter.

- Mode = The most frequently occurring response.
- Median = The response that separates the top half of response frequencies from the bottom half.
- Mean = The average of the responses computed by summing all responses and dividing by the number of responses.

When the question involves indicating the frequency with which something occurs (e.g., the number of times a person eats at a fast-food restaurant in a typical week) the frequency is multiplied by the number of respondents checking that answer, those numbers are summed, and the mean is computed by dividing that sum by the number of total respondents. (For an example, see Table 9.1.)

Here, a judgment was made regarding how to code a range of responses. Since people are being asked to give an estimate of their behavior instead of requiring them to keep a diary or an accounting of their actual behavior, researchers are dealing with approximate responses instead of documented frequencies. Consequently, the coded midpoint of the range (e.g., two to three times per week coded as 2.5) is an estimate, and the mean of 1.85 times per week is also an approximation. Researchers should not forget this fact later when they are using this number in calculations and when drawing implications from such calculations.

TABLE 9.1. Determining Mean

(1) Number of times eat at fast-food restaurants/wk	(2) Number of Respondents	(1) x (2)
Less than once a week (coded as .5)	100	50.0
Once or twice a week (coded as 1.5)	250	375.0
Two or three times a week (coded as 2.5)	175	437.5
More than three times a week (coded as 4)	50	200.0
TOTAL	575	1,062.5
Mean = 1.85 times per week (1,062.5 ÷ 575)		

The mean's ability should be assessed to accurately reflect the sample respondents' responses by calculating a standard deviation for the responses.

> **Standard deviation:** Representing the degree of "spread" of responses among the response categories, it tells us the range of answers which includes roughly 70 percent of the sampled respondents.*

So, for example, if the mean is 1.85 times/week and the standard deviation is .32, then roughly 70 percent of respondents (and hence the population universe) eats at fast-food restaurants between 1.53 and 2.17 times per week (1.85 − .32 = 1.53; 1.85 + .32 = 2.17). Obviously, the smaller the standard deviation is, the closer are the actual responses to the mean. If the standard deviation is large relative to the range of responses, then the mean is not a very good measure to use in understanding the data. For example, if in the illustration in Table 9.1 the standard deviation is 1.70, it is almost half of the range (4 times/wk minus .5 times/wk = 3.5). The mean of 1.85 is relatively meaningless, since answers in this case are spread widely throughout the range of responses, and few people are actually near the mean. This could be an important observation when dealing with a highly segmented population. Consider Figure 9.2, which illustrates this idea.

In this case the market in question consists of five market segments. Graphically depicted is a mean which is the computation of the responses from the segment members, but, as seen here, no segment of respondents is at the mean. The mean in this hypothetical example represents no one and is therefore highly misrepresentative of the data. Consequently, considering the standard deviation along with the mean as a measure of central tendency helps inform the analyst of the dispersion of the data and what precautions to take when reporting the results.

---

*We will assume that the researcher/analyst has a computer printout that shows both the mean and standard deviation (and standard error of the mean) for the intervally scaled questions in the survey. Readers who desire more information on how to compute and interpret standard deviations and other descriptive or inferential statistics are referred to any of the standard statistical texts such as the Kachigan or Brightman books listed in endnote 2.

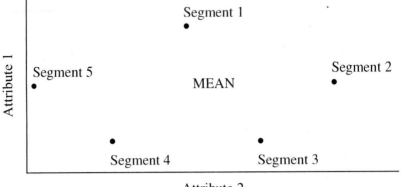

FIGURE 9.2. Segmented Populations

CROSS-TABULATION

Virtually all sets of marketing data will reveal only a fraction of the possible significant findings if viewed only in terms of frequency distributions and measures of central tendency and dispersion. As seen in the egg substitute market data, more is revealed about the underlying relationship between variables of interest when two or more variables are considered simultaneously. Cross-tabulation, probably the most often used analytical technique in marketing research, involves examination of one variable "crossed" by one or more other variables. In the egg substitute example trial-to-usage or retention rates were examined for egg substitutes crossed by reasons for controlling cholesterol. Several observations about the use of cross-tabulations will help the analyst achieve maximum benefit from the use of this analytical tool.

Setting Up Cross-Tabulation Tables

We usually think of a cross-tabulation table as looking at two or possibly three variables simultaneously. This is most often the case when a firm conducts the research project itself, including processing the data and using some software program such as SPSS or Mini-Tab to run each cross-tabbed table. If the researcher has contracted with an independent marketing research firm to do the survey (i.e., send out and receive the mail questionnaires or do the phoning of respondents), they will likely be doing the data processing, including setting up the cross-tabs per the researcher's instructions. If they are responsible for the data collection and processing, then they will probably include as part of the contracted price what will be referred to as an "eighteen-point" or "twenty-point" (or some other number) "banner" (see Figure 9.3 as an example).

This means they will provide a set of computer printout pages that are eighteen- or twenty-columns wide for every question in the survey. Each question in the survey would appear down the side of a page, called the "stub." For example, in a series of Likert-scaled atti-

	Grand Total	Gender		Region				
Page 1 I like the taste of the egg substitute brand I usually eat		%	&	S	N	E	W	Etc.
Strongly Agree 5								
Agree 4								
Neither Agree nor Disagree 3								
Disagree 2								
Strongly Disagree 1								
Page 2 Household Income	Grand Total	%	&	S	N	E	W	Etc.
More than $40K								
$35,0001 - $40,000								
$25,001 - $35,000								
$15,000 - $25,000								
< $15K								
Page 3 Control Cholesterol	Grand Total	%	&	S	N	E	W	Etc.
Yes								
No								

FIGURE 9.3. Sample Printouts

tude questions, demographic questions, and other types of questions, each question would have a separate printout.

The appeal of banners is obvious—they provide a simple way to look at survey questions crossed by the most important variables the researcher is interested in exploring (e.g., gender and region in this example).

An eighteen-point banner means any combination of column headings that total eighteen can be used. It is usual practice to devote the left-most column to "Grand Total," which in effect gives the frequency distribution for each question. So, this column on Page 1 of the example in Figure 9.3 indicates the total number and percentage of people who answered Strongly Agree, Agree, etc., for that question. The remaining seventeen columns may be divided in any combination of columns desired. In Figure 9.3 a set of two columns is devoted to gender, followed by four columns for region of the country. How are the column headings selected? In a single cross-tabulated table such as education level by income the "independent" variable would normally be placed across the top and the "dependent" variable down the side (see Figure 9.4).

We are maintaining that income "depends upon" education, so income is the dependent variable and education is the independent variable. An easy way to identify the independent and dependent variables in any situation is to ask the question:

Does A depend upon B?
A = Dependent variable
B = Independent variable

		Education Level						
Income	Grand Total	<HS	HS	Some Coll.	Col. Grad.	Some Grad.	Grad. Degree	Etc.
$25K+								
$20-25K								
$15-20K								
< $15K								

FIGURE 9.4. Single Cross-Tabulations

So, if the researcher is wondering about the relationship between age and attitude toward pop music, it makes sense to ask:

Does *your attitude toward pop music* depend upon *your age*?

The converse question:

Does *your age* depend upon *your attitude toward pop music*?

is obviously illogical—I cannot expect that my attitude will influence what my age is.

It is customary to have the banner headings consist of *independent* variables that the research purpose, questions, and hypotheses suggest are most likely to be influencing the dependent measures of interest (such as attitudes, consumption rate, likelihood of purchase, membership or nonmembership, etc.). However, this is not an inviolate rule since the researcher may wish to examine some categories of dependent variables for numerous questions in the survey. The researcher may want to see how heavy users, light users, and nonusers differ from each other in terms of their attitudes, demographics, behaviors, etc., and would therefore use those three categories of a dependent variable (rate of consumption) as a set of three columns in a banner. If you include some dependent variables as banner points use two banners—one eighteen- or twenty-point banner with all independent variables and a second eighteen- or twenty-point banner with dependent variables. This will help prevent confusion of what the data are revealing, as will be shown shortly.

Another common practice in setting up a banner heading or single cross-tabbed table is to consistently move from low to high moving from left to right in the banner, and from high to low moving down the stub. Therefore, a banner heading for income would look similar to this:

< $15K $15-20K $20-25K $25K+

and a stub heading for income would look like this:

Income

$25K +
$20-25K
$15-20K
< $15K

An easy way to remember this structure is to envision a graph, which is set up the same way:

High ┤
     │
     │
     │
     │
     │
     │
     │
Low └─────────────────────────────
                                  High

If the variable is not a quantifiable number but is rather one of an expressed intensity of feeling, the same rule holds, such as in Figure 9.5 (i.e., more positive as move left to right or bottom to top).

Agreement with Statement	Attitude Toward Product		
	Unfavorable	Neutral	Favorable
Strongly Agree			
Agree			
Neither			
Disagree			
Strongly Disagree			

FIGURE 9.5. Cross-Tabulations of Nonquantifiable Values

Choosing Variables for Cross-Tabulations

It might be tempting to ask the data processors to "cross everything by everything" so that a cross-tabled table for every combination of two questions in the survey is available. That way, no matter what the issue, one or more tables are available to look at to help the researcher determine the relationship between the variables of interest. Such a temptation should be resisted because it both fails to recognize all the valuable thinking about the project prior to this point, and it also generates a surprising number of tables (e.g., fifty variables generate 1,225 two-way cross-tab tables, 100 variables generate 4,950 two-way tables). Having a request for "everything crossed by everything" delivered as a four-foot stack of computer printouts is a sure way to dissuade the start of an analysis of the data! Considerable thought has already been given to the variables of interest as delineated in the research questions, hypotheses, and dummy tables. In fact, a cross-tabbed table is merely inserting data into a dummy table, so the plan of analysis primarily consists of determining which variables (i.e., questionnaire questions) should be simultaneously examined for possible relationships to get answers to questions, test hypotheses, or fill in dummy tables. As previously mentioned, the researcher will think of relationships he or she wishes to examine during the analysis and not before, and at some point the researcher must get on with the implications and alternative decision suggestions, which is the purpose of the research and its analysis. It is easy to become distracted by the almost infinite number of possible relationships so that one avoids drawing the conclusions necessary to move through the process shown in Figure 9.1. Finding some balance between focusing only on the original objectives of the research and adding to those objectives as the analysis progresses must be achieved if conclusions are to be reported in a timely fashion.

Interpreting Cross-Tabulations

To this point, tables have been set up and a determination made concerning some finite number of relationships between variables to explore. It is now necessary to discuss some important considerations involved with their interpretations. First, if the tables have been set up as suggested, it is possible to analyze the pattern of percentages from left to right to see if there is a positive or negative relationship between the independent and dependent variables. If the percentages increase moving left to right, the variables have a positive relationship. If the percentages decrease, then the relationship is negative. For example, in Table 9.2 there is a positive relationship between willingness to pay more to get the favorite brand of egg substitutes and consumption rate.

Note that in this case it is merely being observed that a positive relationship exists between a willingness to pay more to get the favorite brand and consumption rate without trying to make a claim that one variable *causes* the other. In fact, causal relationships cannot be determined from cross-tabulated data, even if the demonstrated relationship is statistically significant (to be discussed shortly). That is true even if computing a correlation coefficient that determined a very strong positive relationship between two intervally scaled variables. Although too involved to discuss in depth here, the reader should understand that evidence of a positive *relationship* between variables does not provide evidence that the variables should be thought of as *causally* related. This is not necessarily a major problem in the analysis, however, since it may in many cases be sufficient for managers to know that a relationship exists to choose among alternative decisions (see discussion in Chapter 3). Evidence of causality does not necessarily alter the conclusions drawn nor the resulting decision. Knowing that high consumers of our brand of egg substitutes believe it is worth paying more to get our brand has managerial significance apart from the issue of whether consumption rate causes attitude or attitude

TABLE 9.2. Positive Relationship Between Variables

I will pay up to 25¢ more to get my favorite brand of egg substitute.	Egg Substitute Consumption Rate					
	Low		Medium		High	
	#	%	#	%	#	%
Strongly Agree or Agree	113	34	239	54	308	67
Neither Agree nor Disagree	107	33	108	24	101	22
Strongly Disagree or Disagree	108	33	98	22	54	11
TOTAL	328	100	445	100	463	100

causes consumption. One additional conclusion that might come from such an observation is that it is necessary to look more closely at the way the variables are related. This leads to the next issue in analyzing data via cross-tabulations.

Three-Way Cross-Tabulations

Researchers who see a positive relationship between two variables of interest, such as previously shown, might wonder if a third variable is possibly related to both of these two variables and that may actually explain more about the existence of this relationship. In this example, the researcher might wonder if household income explains both attitude (willingness to pay more to get their brand) and usage rate (low, medium, high). These suspicions may be explored by conducting a three-way cross-tabulation (see Table 9.3).

It appears that both agreement with the statement (see percentage of agreement varies by consumption rate) and consumption rate (see column totals for number or respondents) vary with income, which mitigates the conclusion that agreement is related to consumption rate (i.e., there is a stronger relationship between income and agreement than consumption rate and agreement, or, the relationship between consumption rate and agreement depends upon income). These observations reveal an important caveat to analysts using cross-tabulations as their primary analytical tool—sometimes cross-tabulations may in fact be showing a *spurious* relationship between variables. A spurious relationship disappears when another variable enters the analysis. Figure 9.6 graphically illustrates this.

TABLE 9.3. Three-Way Cross-Tabulation

I will pay up to 25¢ more to get my favorite brand of egg substitute.	Income											
	Low Consumption Rate						High Consumption Rate					
	Low		Medium		High		Low		Medium		High	
	#	%	#	%	#	%	#	%	#	%	#	%
Agree	84	30	62	32	20	32	29	60	177	71	288	72
Neither Agree nor Disagree	98	35	54	28	21	34	9	19	54	22	80	20
Disagree	98	35	78	40	21	32	10	21	20	8	33	8
Total	280	100	194	100	62	98	48	100	251	101	401	100

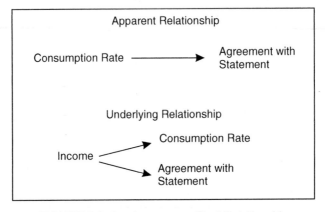

FIGURE 9.6. Spurious versus Real Relationship

How can the researcher avoid basing conclusions, and ultimately decisions, on spurious relationships? The only real answer is that the savvy analyst maintain a certain skepticism about what he or she can legitimately conclude from the data and comes to an implication only after carefully examining the data from several angles. No single procedure or tool of analysis will avoid all erroneous conclusions. A healthy dose of skepticism is the analyst's best defense against future regret and recrimination. As Thomas Huxley said: "Skepticism is the highest of duties, blind faith the one unpardonable sin."

One sure way to fall prey to spurious relationships and at the same time become distracted from the objectives of the analysis is to indiscriminately generate cross-tabulations and begin to examine them for "meaningful relationships." The danger is that the analyst might encounter some table where there is a strong relationship between two variables that he or she would not ordinarily examine or predict to have such a relationship. Fertile imagination then takes hold and very plausible-sounding explanations are devised for what is in reality a spurious and meaningless association between variables. This leads to the sort of fanciful conclusions that Hamlet and Polonius engaged in as quoted at the beginning of the chapter. The analyst's best "friend" in this case is the "theories" (research questions, hypotheses, relationships of interest) that originated at the beginning of the research. Analysts would do well to remember that logic should drive data, not data drive logic (i.e., let hypotheses, which are based on logical expectations, be tested by the data; do not let a "blind empiricism" of indiscriminate data analysis determine what is "logical"). This is not to say that data that is inconsistent with presuppositions should be ignored. Rather, it argues that our "theories" of how consumers behave and the market operates, etc., are altered only after multiple findings consistently and persuasively suggest our old theories are wrong and new ones must be developed to explain the findings.

Statistical Significance in Cross-Tabulations

Analysts of cross-tabulated data do not have to wonder whether they are looking at relationships that might or might not be statistically significant. A statistical test called *chi-square* will reveal whether the differences noted in the table are "real" or could be merely due to chance. Readers interested in how chi-squares are calculated are referred to relevant works on the subject.[3] For our purposes here, most software programs such as SPSS that perform cross-tabulations will print chi-square statistics indicating whether the relationship between the table's variables is "statistically significant" or could have occurred by chance due to sampling variations. It should be noted here that chi-square tests require data that are categorical rather than continuous (i.e., low, medium, high consumers instead of one, two, three, four, five, etc., times per week), the numbers analyzed must be counts and not percentages, and there must be at least five or more "counts" in each cell. (Other requirements are necessary, but these are the ones of primary interest to readers of this book.) Although useful in helping to determine if the observed relationship is statistically significant (e.g., there really is a difference in the rate of agreement with the statement between high, medium, and low egg substitute consumers), the chi-square statistics will not inform the analyst if the statistically significant relationship is spurious or not. The use of statistical tests *increases* rather than *decreases* the need for theory, predetermined hypotheses, and common sense.

ADVANCED ANALYTICAL TECHNIQUES

Cross-tabulations are a very useful and commonly used place to begin an examination of data beyond what can be done by frequency distribution and measures of central tendency. However, as has been seen, they are not trouble-free as an analytical technique. Moreover, they cannot reveal all that there is to know about the relationship between variables in the data set. It is beyond the scope of the following discussion to describe these other techniques in any depth, but other techniques will be briefly explained that may be useful when analyzing research results.

Correlation

Correlations establish a relationship between any two intervally scaled variables. Variables can be negatively and positively correlated. Correlation scores range from +1.00 to −1.00 with 1.00 (or −1.00) indicating a perfect relationship and 0 indicating no relationship at all. Generally (depending on sample size), two variables are said to be slightly correlated when the correlation scores are between .21 and .35. Moderate degrees of correlation are generally associated with scores of .36 through .55. High degrees of correlation would be .56 through .75. Extremely high degrees of correlation would be associated with the scores .76 through .99. When two variables are positively correlated, it means that when one variable tends to increase in value (importance, preference, etc.), the other will likewise tend to increase. When two variables are said to be negatively (or inversely) correlated, it means that when one variable tends to increase in value, the other decreases and vice versa. One example might be that the purchase selection factor of the importance of product quality is inversely correlated to the importance of cost savings. This would mean that as the quality of the product increased, the importance of cost savings to the consumer would decrease.

SUMMARY

Up to the point of data analysis, the research that has been conducted to address a management problem has merely generated costs, with no return. It is only with the advent of data analysis that research begins to generate a return against those costs. Therefore, it is critically important to the success of the project that the researcher/analyst use all appropriate means of extracting valuable insights from the data. Although a "toolchest" of sophisticated statistical programs may be necessary in getting the most from a data set, it is also true that many of the research objectives and hypotheses that drove the research can be addressed with techniques as simple as cross-tabulations. Another valuable "tool" of data analysis is the analyst's reluctance to draw implications and make decisional recommendations until he or she is convinced, by looking at the data from a variety of perspectives, that the information truly suggests the validity of those implications and recommendations.

NOTES

1. Adapted from Kotler, Philip. 1994. *Marketing Management,* 8th ed. Englewood Cliffs, NJ: Prentice-Hall, p. 24

2. Some reference works for those readers interested in a more in-depth discussion of analysis include: For analysis of qualitative research see Miles, Matthew B. and A. Michael Huberman. 1994. *Qualitative Data Analysis.* Thousand Oaks, CA: Sage; Norman K. Denzin and Yvonna S. Lincoln, eds. 1994. *Handbook of Qualitative Research.* Thousand Oaks, CA; Harry F. Wolcott. 1990. *Writing Up Qualitative Research.* Thousand Oaks, CA: Sage. For statistical analysis, including multivariate statistical techniques see Sam Kash Kachigan. 1986. *Statistical Analysis.* New York: Radius Press; Joseph F. Hair, Ralph E. Anderson, Ronald L. Tatham, and William C. Black. 1995. *Multivariate Data Analysis,* 4th ed. Englewood Cliffs, NJ: Prentice-Hall; Harvey J. Brightman. 1986. *Statistics in Plain English.* Cincinnati: South-Western Publishing Co.

3. See, for example, Kachigan, *Statistical Analysis,* pp. 342-356.

WORKSHEET

1. Write down the research questions the research was intended to answer and the questions in the questionnaire that addressed some aspects of these questions.

   Research Questions   Questionnaire Questions

   _____   _____

   _____   _____

   _____   _____

2. Indicate how you will use a cross-tabulated table(s) to obtain answers to your research questions.

Research Question	Questionnaire Questions (Set up cross-tab table)	Logic (How you will interpret table to answer questions)
_____	_____	_____
_____	_____	_____
_____	_____	_____

3. Write down the hypotheses the research was intended to test and the questions in the questionnaire that addressed some aspects of these hypotheses.

   Hypotheses   Questionnaire Questions

   _____   _____

   _____   _____

   _____   _____

4. Indicate how you will use a cross-tabulated table(s) to obtain answers to your research hypotheses.

Research Hypotheses	Questionnaire Questions (Set up cross-tab table)	Logic (How you will interpret table to answer questions)
_____	_____	_____
_____	_____	_____
_____	_____	_____

5. Fill in data for dummy tables set up when designing descriptive research.

Dependent Variable	Independent Variables				
_____	___	___	___	___	___
_____	___	___	___	___	___
_____	___	___	___	___	___

6. Indicate use of other analytical tools needed to analyze data.

Statistical Technique	Why Needed?	Results of Application (Findings)
_____	_____	_____
_____	_____	_____
_____	_____	_____

Chapter 10

Advanced Data Analysis

After you have collected data through descriptive or causal research and run the descriptive statistics and cross-tabulations described in Chapter 9, you may wish to conduct some of the statistical analyses described in this chapter. But first we will discuss how marketing researchers approach the use of statistical tests in analyzing data.

MARKETING RESEARCH
AND STATISTICAL ANALYSIS

Marketing research is conducted to help reduce the uncertainty in decision making. If we could be certain of making the correct decision without conducting research, why would we ever want to do research? Marketing research in such cases would not reduce uncertainty because there would be no uncertainty. You would always know which decision would be best. However, we all know that managers are more often unsure which of several possible decisional alternatives is best. Consequently, we conduct research to help determine which alternative should be selected, given what we discover is the nature of the market from conducting the research.

Statistics help us to better understand the significance of marketplace characteristics. We should distinguish between managerial and statistical differences, however:

> *Statistically significant differences:* When a difference (e.g., between two market segments, attitudes, likelihood of purchase between two products, etc.) is big enough that it is unlikely to have occurred due to chance, then it is statistically significant.

Managerially significant differences: When any observed difference in findings is considered significant enough to influence management decisions. For example, some statistically significant differences are considered inconsequential to management, and some that do not cross a certain statistical threshold to be considered statistically significant may influence management decisions.

So, marketing researchers run statistical analyses on the data they have collected in order to be able to reduce the uncertainty of management decisions by identifying those measured variables that are managerially significant and also statistically significantly different from one another. For example, statistical analysis of marketing research data may reveal that a market consists of five consumer segments that differ from one another in ways significant to marketing managers making targeting and positioning decisions. Without the use of statistical analysis we would not have been able to identify or define these segments or the important differences among them upon which marketing decisions will be based.

Before we begin a discussion of the kinds of statistical analytical procedures of value to researchers, let us briefly review how we arrived at this point of the research process, for we arrive at this point because of the research decisions we previously made.

Readers will remember that we devoted considerable time and effort to developing a statement of the management problem/opportunity, identification of the research purpose (which required stating the decision alternatives and criteria), and the research objectives (research questions and hypotheses), which have driven all of our subsequent research decisions. Our research design, data-collection methods, measurement tools and methods, and data-collection instruments were all selected and developed as the most effective and efficient means possible of answering our research questions and testing our hypotheses, which allow us to achieve our research purpose and thereby solve our management problem or capitalize on our management opportunity. The statistical process we use at the analysis stage is merely another step along this same path, leading from management problem to data to decisions to problem solution. We emphasize this interconnectedness of the steps because it is easy for the novice researcher to become so overwhelmed by the variety and complexity of the statistical procedures that he or she fails to keep the "big picture" in mind. We are analyzing data for a reason, which is to allow us to choose the best among the decisional alternatives that helps solve our problem. Statistical analysis merely aids in that choice. Our discussion of statistics in this chapter is no substitute for the kind of coverage you get in a statistics course, but rather covers the main topics of interest to marketing researchers seeking to reduce the uncertainty of management decision making.

HYPOTHESIS TESTING

As we noted in Chapter 1, hypotheses are speculations regarding specific findings of the research. When researchers discuss "hypothesis testing" they are referring to any means used, such as the use of cross-tabulated tables in Chapter 9, to determine if the hypotheses stated at the early stages of the research are supported by the evidence (e.g., H: First time home buyers spend more time researching how to determine construction quality than people buying for the second, third, etc. time). When researchers speak of "hypothesis testing" they are referring to a particular process and set of statistical tools used to determine the probability of observing a particular result from the research if the stated hypothesis were actually true.

We have hypotheses because we *suspect* our results will reveal some characteristic of the population under study. If we already *knew* the results would be a particular way we would not need to do the research. So, we approach the testing of a hypothesis the same way we do research in general: we are not out to prove (or disprove) anything, but rather seek to discover, test, and learn the "truth." So we are testing our hypothesis to determine whether it should be accepted as a statement accurately portraying the population's characteristics, or rejected because the observed difference is likely due to sampling error and there really is no difference as we hypothesized existed. The underlying rationale for testing the hypothesis is that we will make different decisions based upon whether the results of the statistical tests lead us to conclude the hypothesis is supported or not. For example, if our hypothesis is that there is no difference between males and females in their preference for product design A or B, and that hypothesis is rejected (i.e., the results indicate the preferences for males is A versus females for B are "real" and unlikely due to chance), then we would make different decisions on which product design to introduce and how to target our marketing programs for the product.

Hypothesis testing involves five steps:

1. The hypotheses are stated, with decisions identified for the outcome of the hypothesis test.
2. Determine the "costs" related to the two types of errors arising from your decisions.
3. Select the significance level (the alpha) you will use to determine whether to reject or fail to reject (FTR) the null hypothesis.
4. Collect the data and conduct the appropriate statistical tests.
5. Compare the results to your null hypothesis and make your decision.[1]

We will use an example to illustrate how marketing researchers could use these steps to help marketing managers make better decisions.

Assume you work for a company that manufactures lightbulbs. Your R&D (research and development) department has developed a new lightbulb (named the Longlast bulb), which they claim lasts much longer than traditional bulbs, but could sell for only a 50 percent premium over traditional bulbs. The marketing manager believes this bulb could have a competitive advantage in the market, but to attract consumers the company will need to provide a money-back guarantee for the minimum life expectancy of the bulb—if it does not last at least thirty-six months you the consumer receives a full refund. The company needs to know if such a guarantee makes economic sense, since they have decided that if the average life of the bulb does not exceed thirty-six months it is not going to market the bulb (not enough of a competitive advantage). The decision is then to either market the bulb with the guarantee or not market the bulb.

Step 1: Stating the Hypotheses and Decisions

Hypotheses are stated in two forms:

Null hypothesis is stated in terms that indicate you expect to find "no difference" or "no effect."

Alternative hypothesis states that you expect to find a difference or effect.

In our Longlast lightbulb case these hypotheses and the resulting decisions would be:

Null hypothesis: The unknown mean (average) life of our Longlast bulb population is less than or equal to thirty-six months.

Decision: If we accept (or more appropriately fail to reject) the null hypothesis we will not market the bulb.

Alternative hypothesis: The unknown mean life of our Longlast bulb population is greater than thirty-six months.

Decision: If we accept the alternative hypothesis we will market the bulb.

The statement of a null hypothesis is in keeping with the "healthy skepticism" mentioned in the previous chapter. That is, while our R&D people claim the Longlast bulb will last more than thirty-six months ("Oh, no problem. Piece of cake. Easily last more than thirty-six months," as they put it.), you retain a healthy dose of skepticism and the null hypothesis reflects that skepticism. We assume the null hypothesis is true until evidence suggests otherwise. The alternative hypothesis says what you hope will be true, that the R&D claims are correct. These are competing hypotheses—only one can be true.

Step 2: Determine the Costs of Decision Errors

Because we are going to collect a sample of lightbulbs and determine the average life of the lightbulbs in the sample instead of testing every lightbulb produced (which would not leave us any to market!), we are going to draw inferences from our research sample to the entire Longlast bulb population. These inferences can either be right or they can be wrong. Table 10.1 illustrates the possible combinations of inferences made about the null hypothesis.

Type 1 error: We reject the null hypothesis when it is actually true.

Type 2 error: We accept the null hypothesis when it is actually false.

When testing a hypothesis in any particular study we can make either a Type 1 error or a Type 2 error (or no error), but not both a Type 1 or Type 2 error. Table 10.2 shows how this table looks for our Longlast example.

We all know (or at least suspect if we have not had personal experience) that making the wrong marketing decisions incurs costs. In the Longlast case both Type 1 and Type 2 errors are costly, but in different ways. If we decide to market the bulb because the average life of our sample (which we thought would also be true of the population) was longer than thirty-six months, but its life was actually shorter than thirty-six months (a Type 1 error), we will discover our error when people begin to return expired bulbs and get their money back in perhaps twenty-four or thirty months from when they were first marketed. Lots of Longlast bulbs have been sold in the past twenty-four to thirty months. The *Wall Street Journal* runs a "page 1" story of how we are flooded with returned bulbs and requests for refunds,

TABLE 10.1. Null Hypothesis Inference Combinations

Based on the sample evidence we decide to	The Truth About the Population Parameter	
	Null is true	**Null is false**
Accept the null (FTR the null)	Correct decision	Type 2 error
Reject the null	Type 1 error	Correct decision

TABLE 10.2. Null Hypothesis Inference Combinations for Longlast Example

Based upon the sample evidence we decide to	The Truth About the Longlast Bulb			
	Thirty-six months or less			**Over thirty-six months**
Not market the bulb	Correct decision	1	2	Type 2 error
Market the bulb	Type 1 error	3	4	Correct decision

consumer confidence in our other products begins to slip, we have trouble recruiting good marketing people who do not want to be associated with such "losers," and other unpleasantness occurs.

A Type 2 error would occur when we decide not to market a bulb whose actual life is more than thirty-six months, but the lifetime of our sample was less than thirty-six months. We had a winner on our hands but did not capitalize on the opportunity. Depending on the number of people who would have been interested in our competitive advantage, we might have missed out on a golden opportunity.

Step 3: Setting a Significance Level

No one wants to have significant bad decisions on their career track record, but there always is the possibility that when we make decisions based on inferring from a sample to our population we were wrong. In hypothesis testing the significance level is the maximum risk you will accept of making a Type 1 error (marketing the lightbulb when you should not have). It now becomes clear why Step 2 is so important:

> We must consider how significant the costs are to making a mistake by marketing the lightbulb when we should not have in order to know how low to set our *maximum* risk of making such an error of judgment.

or

> The greater the costs associated with a Type 1 error, the lower we should set our maximum risk.

Some guidelines help us determine how to set the level of significance:

1. If costs associated with a Type 1 error are high and a Type 2 error is not costly, set the level of significance (i.e., the chance of making a Type 1 error) very low—at .05 or below.
2. If costs associated with a Type 1 error are not very high, but making a Type 2 error is costly, set the level of significance much higher (perhaps at .25 or above).

3. If both Type 1 and Type 2 errors are costly, set the level of significance very low and increase the sample size, reducing the chance of a Type 2 error (however, this does increase the cost of the research).

In the Longlast lightbulb case the potential costs associated with making a Type 1 error are of sufficient magnitude to justify setting the level of significance very low (say, .01). This means if you reject the null hypothesis (i.e., decide to market the lightbulb) the chance that you made a Type 1 error (decided to market it when you should not have because the average life expectancy was actually less than thirty-six months) is only one chance in a hundred. In other words you can be 99 percent confident that you made the right decision.

Step 4: Collect the Data and Conduct Statistical Tests

This is the step where the research is designed, data are collected, and the appropriate statistical tests are used to analyze the data. Our research design in this case would involve descriptive research since exploratory is not used to collect data per se, and our hypothesis does not involve cause-effect relationships. The research could run internal (within the company) tests of a sample of lightbulbs, or we could conduct in-home tests, where consumers agree to try the product in their homes in typical consumer usage situations. This approach provides researchers with information about the product's performance under actual market conditions and the subsequent research that tests consumers' opinions, perceived benefits received, problems, future purchase intent, and the like provides valuable marketing targeting and positioning information.

In this case we will assume we select a random sample of 1,000 lightbulbs (we use *probability* sampling since we are doing descriptive research) for an internal test and use a special testing technology which "speeds up" time so that we do not have to wait thirty-six months for the results of our test of the bulbs' lifetime. So, we run our test of 1,000 lightbulbs and determine the average simulated lifetime of the bulbs in months. We discover the following:

Sample mean (written as) = 37.7 months

Standard deviation (written as) = .42 months

We use a *t*-test in this case to determine if the null hypothesis should be rejected or accepted (fail to be rejected) because we do not know the population's standard deviation. However, because the sample size is so large, the *t* value is the same as the *Z* value.

A *t*-test is constructed as follows:

$$t = \frac{\text{Sample value} - \text{hypothesized population value}}{\text{Standard deviation of the sample value}}$$

In our case the calculation would be

$$t = \frac{37.7 - 36.0}{.42} = 4.05$$

See Table 10.3 for the appropriate statistical tests for the different types of hypotheses.

TABLE 10.3. Statistical Tests for Hypothesis Testing

Types of Hypotheses	Number of Subgroups or Samples	Scale of Data	Test	Requirements
Hypotheses about frequency distribution	One	Nominal	Chi-square X^2	Random sample
	Two or more	Nominal	Chi-square X^2	Random, independent samples
	One	Ordinal	Kolmogorov-Smirnov	Random
Hypotheses about proportions (percentages)	One (large sample)	Interval or ratio	Z-test for one proportion	Random sample of thirty or more
	Two (large sample)	Interval or ratio	Z-test for two proportions	Random sample of thirty or more
Hypotheses about means	One (large sample	Interval or ratio	Z-test for one mean	Random sample of thirty or more
	One (small sample)	Interval or ratio	t-test for one mean	Random sample of thirty or more
	Two (large sample)	Interval or ratio	Z-test for two means	Random sample of thirty or more
	Three or more (small sample)	Interval or ratio	One-way ANOVA (one independent variable)	Random sample

Source: Adapted from Carl McDaniel and Roger Gates. 1999. *Contemporary Marketing Research.* Cincinnati, OH: South-Western, pp. 516-517.

Step 5: Compare Results to Null Hypothesis and Make Decision

Looking at a *t* distribution table we see that the *t* value for n-1 degrees of freedom (999 in our case, but "infinity" on the table) and for an alpha (the level of significance, which was .01 in our case) in a "one-tail" test (on a normal curve, the area under the curve at only one end of the curve rather than both ends) was 2.326. Since our *t* value of 4.05 exceeded this 2.326 value we can say we are *more than* 99 percent confident that our sample mean of 37.7 months is drawn from a population whose mean is more than 36. Or, in other words, the chances that our sample mean would be 37.7 when the actual population mean is thirty-six months is very, very unlikely (less than one in a hundred). Because the odds of the null hypothesis being true (i.e., that our population mean is thirty-six months or less) are so small, it is much more reasonable to assume that the reason our sample mean was 37.7 months is that the null hypothesis should be rejected and our alternative hypothesis should be accepted (i.e., that the population mean is greater than thirty-six months).

In Step 1 we established a decision rule that said if we reject the null hypothesis and accept the alternative hypothesis we will market the Longlast lightbulb, so that is what we should do. Referring to Table 10.2, this decision means we either will make the correct decision (cell 4), or will be making a Type 1 error (cell 3). The actual chance that we are making a Type 1 error is called the "*p*-value," which in this case would be the likelihood of getting a sample mean of 37.7 months if the null hypothesis were true. This is very remote (less than one chance in a hundred), which is very reassuring of the correctness of our decision.

Although our null hypothesis was stated as a test of means (i.e., Was our sample's average of 37.7 months statistically significantly different from the hypothesized population's average of thirty-six months?), we could state hypotheses as frequency distribution, differences between subgroups (e.g., men versus women), or proportions (e.g., percentages of college educated versus noncollege graduates intending to buy our product). Table 10.3 shows the appropriate statistical tests for different forms of hypotheses. Once you set up the hypothesis and go through the steps outlined here, a statistical software program such as SPSS can be used to conduct the appropriate

TABLE 10.4. Statistical Software on the Internet

Software	Web Site	Description
SPSS	www.spss.com	A popular, comprehensive statistical package with links to other sites and data sets.
Stata	www.stata.com	Stata software for Windows, Apple, DOS, and UNIX operating systems.
UNISTAT	www.unistat.com	Comprehensive package compatible with Windows Excel. Data handling, analysis, and graphic presentation.
StatSoft	www.statsoft.com	Presents the STATISTICA range of statistical analysis products. Easy to use yet powerful statistical package.

statistical tests. Otherwise, the same process (the five steps) is followed to arrive at a decision based on the marketing research results. See Table 10.4 for a list of statistical software sites on the Web.

Concluding Thoughts on Hypothesis Testing

Hypothesis testing is very decision-oriented, as demonstrated in this discussion. In fact, the underlying reason for testing hypotheses is to get to the point (Step 5) where you can determine how confident you can be in choosing between two previously identified decision alternatives (e.g., to market or not market the Longlast lightbulb). Some other thoughts on hypothesis testing are listed below.

1. As described in Chapter 2, we use exploratory research to *generate* hypotheses; we use descriptive or causal research to *test* hypotheses. Although the exploratory research "detective work" may allow us to "check out our hunches" by looking at secondary data and doing exploratory communication or observation, and even provide us with enough information that we are willing to make a decision without further research, we cannot claim we have "tested hypotheses" by doing exploratory research. This is true even if we conduct an exploratory survey of thousands of people. The reason is that true hypothesis tests, as described here and listed in Table 10.3, all demand probability

samples that are the province of descriptive and causal research. If we have not obtained our sample using a probability sampling approach (simple random, stratified, systematic, or cluster sampling methods), the plain fact is that we cannot conduct these hypotheses tests, no matter how large our sample. This is not to say that we cannot use exploratory survey results to make decisions. We simply cannot arrive at those decisions through statistical tests of our hypotheses.

2. Two types of errors are possible when conducting tests of hypotheses. We must determine their respective costs and then set the level of significance consistent with the costs of making a Type 1 error. In doing this we must understand that we do not want to automatically set the significance level very low (e.g., .05 or less) so we will not make a Type 1 error. Such fear of making a Type 1 error is only justified when the costs of a Type 1 error are very high. Sometimes the costs of a Type 2 error (e.g., *not* marketing the Longlast bulb when we should have in our example) may be high as well and must be factored into our decision. As described in Step 3, when Type 2 error costs are high relative to Type 1 error costs, we should set our level of significance much higher (e.g., .25 or higher).

3. Doing causal research also may involve hypothesis testing. Although beyond the scope of our discussion, one typical statistical test used in determining the difference between experimental treatments is the ANOVA test (analysis of variance, see last entry in Table 10.3). For example, we can use an ANOVA test to determine if a statistically significant difference is present in the sales of a cereal brand that was tested in an experimental design with three coupon levels: 35¢, 50¢, and 75¢. ANOVA is not used exclusively with experimental data (it can be used with descriptive survey results), nor is it the only way to analyze experimental data, but it is a commonly used statistical test for experimental data.

MEASURES OF ASSOCIATION

Marketers frequently want to know how variables are associated with each other. For example, Levi's wants to know what types of people are interested in a more formal, dressy line of pants, <iVillage.com>

wants to know the lifestyle characteristics of the women who visit their Web site so they can change its content to satisfy customer needs, IBM wants to know which characteristics best describe their top salespeople. In such cases marketers are interested in using statistical analysis to determine the degree to which two or more variables are associated with each other. Our discussion of cross-tabulation in Chapter 9 was an example of looking for associations. In this chapter we will examine other statistically measurable means of determining association among variables. We will examine bivariate (association between two variables) and multivariate (between three or more variables) techniques.

Bivariate Association

The association between two variables can be graphically described in a variety of ways (see Figure 10.1):

- *Nonmonotonic:* The association or relationship between the two variables has no discernable direction, but the relationship exists.
- *Monotonic:* The association between the two variables has a general direction.
- *Curvilinear:* The association between the variables can be described by a curved line.
- *Linear:* A straight line can be drawn to describe the relationship between the variables.

We will restrict our discussion to associations between variables that can be described as linear. Linear relationships may either be positive or negative in nature. In Figure 10.2a we see a positive relationship: as variable A increases (say, education) so does B (say, income). This association does not have to be perfect. Examples include people with little education but very high income, and people with very high education but modest incomes, but in general the relationship is positive.

In Figure 10.2b we see a negative relationship: as variable A increases (say, price), variable B declines (say, sales of cellular phones).

As mentioned, marketers are very interested in determining the association between variables so they can use this information in mak-

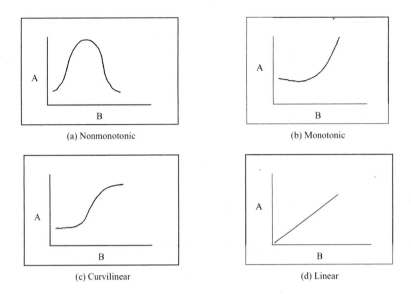

FIGURE 10.1. Graphic Representation of Association Between Two Variables

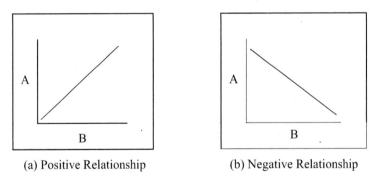

FIGURE 10.2. Linear Relationships

ing decisions. If buyer loyalty for a personal computer manufacturer as measured by repeat purchase behavior is associated with a buyer's satisfaction with the company's toll-free help line, and satisfaction with the helpline is associated with number of trained customer service agents, the company may decide to hire and train more customer service agents. If the association between two variables is strong, you can predict one variable by knowing the other one. But first you must be able to measure the degree of association. We will discuss the primary statistical procedures used for measuring association. Readers wishing for a more comprehensive discussion of these and other statistical measures of association should consult one of the standard works on the subject.[2]

Types of Bivarate Measures of Association

The choice of bivariate measures of association depends upon the scale of the data being analyzed. Table 10.5 describes several common measures. Many others are available, but we will confine our discussion to those listed in Table 10.5.

Pearson Product Moment Correlation. The Pearson product moment correlation measures the degree to which two variables are correlated or associated with each other when both of those variables are *metric* (i.e., either intervally or ratio-scaled data). The output of running this statistical analysis on two variables is a single number called a *correlation coefficient,* which can range from -1.00 to +1.00. The closer the correlation coefficient is to -1.00 or +1.00, the stronger the association is between the variables. Two variables are perfectly inversely correlated when the coefficient is -1.00 and perfectly positively correlated when it is +1.00. A correlation coefficient of 0.00 indicates that no statistical association is present between the two variables. Statistical software packages such as SPSS will compute both the Pearson product moment correlation coefficient (referred to as the r) and the statistical significance statistic (referred to as the p) for two sets of metric-scaled data. The r measures the strength of the association on the -1.00 to +1.00 scale, and the p indicates the likelihood that the association is due to chance (i.e., that the null hypothesis of no association between the two variables is supported).

TABLE 10.5. Bivariate Measures of Association

Type of Data	Measures
Interval or ratio	Pearson product moment correlation
Ordinal	Spearman's rank-order correlation
Nominal	Chi-square analysis

A *p* = .05 says that the chance we would be seeing the strength of the *r* (i.e., the association or correlation between the two variables) as what we see it for our sample data when in fact there is no association (i.e., *r* = 0.00) between the two variables is only five chances in 100. So, a *p* of .05 or lower would indicate that the degree of association between the variables as measured by the *r* is "real" and unlikely due to chance. Once we see that the *p* indicates that we are looking at a statistically significant association, we can look at the *r* to determine the strength of the association. Physicists expect to see perfect (or darn near) correlations between the physical materials they study. Marketers, as behavioral scientists, realize that people are far from "perfect" and so the correlations we measure between variables related to the behavior of consumers are not going to be -1.00 or +1.00. Marketers measuring and correlating such variables of interest as:

Consumption Rate	correlated with	Satisfaction with Product
Attitude Toward Product	correlated with	Intention to Buy
Household Size	correlated with	Frequency of Usage

and many other correlations involving metric data of interest are looking at correlations revealing various degrees of less than perfect association. Table 10.6 suggests some general rules of thumb for correlation coefficients and implied strength of association.

Spearman's Rank-Order Correlation. Marketing researchers may find that they seek to know the association between two variables that are ordinally (i.e., rank-ordered) rather than intervally or ratio-scaled. In such cases we should use the Spearman's rank-order correlation

TABLE 10.6. Correlating Coefficients and Implying Strength of Association

Range of Correlation Coefficient	Strength of Association
Greater than .80	Very Strong
.61 to .80	Moderate to Strong
.41 to .60	Weak to Moderate
.21 to .40	Weak
.00 to .20	Nonexistent to Very Weak

rather than the Pearson product moment correlation. For example, we might want to know if any association exists between the way people rank-ordered brands of automobiles based on "sportiness" and "like to be seen driving." The resulting correlation coefficient, r_s, and the measure of statistical significance are interpreted in the same way as we do for the Pearson product moment correlation. That is, a higher r_s indicates higher degrees of association (or stronger inverse association if the coefficient is a negative value).

Chi-Square Analysis. As shown in Table 10.5, chi-square tests are run when we are conducting hypothesis tests for nominally scaled variables. Chi-square tests are run on cross-tabulated data when we want to determine if the frequencies we see in each cell of a cross-tabbed table fit an "expected" (i.e., hypothesized) pattern. Since the null hypothesis states that we expect not to find an association between the two variables, the chi-square tests tells us whether we should accept the null hypothesis or not. So, for example, if we want to know if an association is present between the preferences of males versus females for new product concept A or B, our cross-tabulated data may look similar to this:

Preference for New Product Concept	Males	Females	Total
A	199	18	217
B	40	43	83
TOTAL	239	61	300

The decision we want to make is whether or not to target the two new products to consumers on the basis of gender. The question of the statistical analysis then becomes, "Is there a statistically significant difference in the preferences between males and females for the two new product concepts?" The null hypothesis for the chi-square test is then

H_0: No relationship exists between gender and new product concept preference.

And our alternative hypothesis is

H_a: A significant relationship exists between gender and new product concept preference.

When you enter the data in the cross-tabulated table (which must be in "counts" not percentages, and at least five or more counts must be in each cell of the table) into a statistical program such as SPSS, the program then calculates the probability you would find evidence in support of the null hypothesis if you repeatedly collected independent samples and got these results. So, if the chi-square test showed a .01 probability for the null hypothesis, the conclusion would be that you would get these results only one time in 100 occasions if the null hypothesis were true. That is highly unlikely, so the null is rejected and the alternative hypothesis is accepted: A relationship exists between gender and product concept preference. Chi-square does not tell the researcher the nature of the association (e.g., whether males prefer A and females B), only that the association exists by illustrating the probability of seeing such results if the null hypothesis were true. Researchers would then need to study the association between the variables more closely to discern the nature of the association between the variables and ultimately, along with other research findings, what decisions should be made about marketing the new products.

Multivariate Association

Multivariate (multiple variable) analysis refers to the statistical methods that simultaneously analyze multiple measurements of attitudes, attributes, or behavior. Multivariate techniques are simply extensions of univariate (analysis of single variable distributions) and bivariate techniques (two variable methods such as cross-tabulations, correlations, and simple regression). For a research project to terminate prior to employing multivariate techniques assumes that the purpose of the research was only to identify the variables, or that the importance of the results for the decision information required would need no more than the establishment of the associations between two variables. Multivariate techniques serve to determine the relationships that exist between multiple sets of variables. Multivariate methodologies are sometimes needed to examine the multiple constraints and relationships among pertinent variables to obtain a more complete, realistic understanding of the market environment for decision making.

Description and Application of Multivariate Techniques

The satisfactory utilization of multivariate methods assumes a degree of understanding of the market dynamics or market behavior in order to conceptualize a realistic model. The identification of the variables whose relationships are to be measured is foundational to an incisive multivariate approach. The nature and number of variables to be examined will determine what type of multivariate method will be utilized.

The first commonly used method is known as *multiple regression.* Multiple regression allows for the prediction of the level or magnitude of a phenomenon such as market size or market share. The objective is the identification of the optimum simultaneous relationship that exists between a dependent variable and those of the many independent variables. For example, frequency of listening to a particular radio station may well be a function of a number of marketing mix variables such as the type of programming, listener loyalty, community promotionals, billboard advertising, disc jockey personality, and tastefulness of the commercials.[3]

Another method is *multiple discriminant analysis.* Multiple discriminant analysis has as its objective the identification of key descriptors on which various predefined events will vary. It might be learned from a discriminate analysis that middle-income families who work in a downtown area and who have school-age children might be expected to be the first to move into a new, rural, totally planned community housing development.

Canonical correlation analysis allows for the establishment of a predictive model that can simultaneously forecast or explain several phenomena based on an understanding of their correlates. The canonical correlation analysis differs from multiple regression analysis in that more than one dependent variable exists. Whereas family income and family size might be used to predict the number of credit cards a family might have (by using a multiple regression technique), the canonical correlation analysis would also be able to predict the average monthly charges on all of their credit cards.[4]

One of the more popular of the multivariate techniques is *factor analysis.* Kerlinger states that the factor analysis might be called the queen of analytic techniques because of its power and elegance. He describes factor analysis as a method for determining the number and nature of underlying variables among larger numbers of measures. It also serves to reduce large groups of complex variables to their underlying and predictive entities. Factor analytic techniques first gained prominence in psychological and psychiatric studies. For example, verbal ability, numerical ability, memory, abstract reasoning, and spatial reasoning have been found to underlie intelligence in some studies.[5]

The applications for factor analysis have been used extensively for behavioral and attitudinal studies used in the marketplace. For example, a recent study that measured a large group of variables related to job satisfaction and morale among a certain group of engineers revealed the ability to grow professionally was the single most important factor in morale and job satisfaction. This was followed closely by self-esteem as it related closely to the type of firm they work for. The analysis revealed five central factors, which in general terms, fit closely to Maslow's hierarchy of organizational needs, except that the order of prominence for each of Maslow's needs was found to have a different sequence for the engineers surveyed. Factors identified by this technique, therefore, have served as a new dimension of segmentation that focuses on shared agreement among respondents as the differentiation among the segments.

Multidimensional scaling addresses the problem of identifying the dimensions upon which customers perceive or evaluate phenomena (products, brands, or companies). Multidimensional scaling techniques result in *perceptual maps* that describe the "positioning" of companies or brands that are compared relative to the "position" they occupy in the minds of customers according to key attributes. These "maps" allow the decision maker to examine underlying criteria or dimensions that people utilize to form perceptions about similarities between and preferences among various products, services, brands, or companies. The question of positioning, as viewed by multidimensional scaling (MDS) and perceptual mapping, deals with how a firm compares to its competitors on key attributes, what the ideal set of attributes sought by the customer might be, or what positioning or repositioning strategy should be developed for a specific sector of the marketplace.[6] A medium-sized bank might learn, for example, that the most effective way to compete for commercial loan business with larger, more prestigious banks with a wider range of services, is by focusing on the genuine concern communicated by loan supervisors as well as the expertise they develop in their knowledge of their client's subsector of industry (see Figure 10.3).

Cluster analysis allows for the classification or segmentation of a large group of variables into homogeneous subgroups based on similarities on a profile of information. Cluster analysis enables the description of topologies or profiles according to attitudes toward preferences, appeals, and so on that might also include psychographic data. For example, this analysis might be used to describe psychographic profiles and interest in new transactional services among savings and loan customers.

The last major technique to be explained is *conjoint analysis*. Conjoint measurement, also known as trade-off analysis, is used for eval-

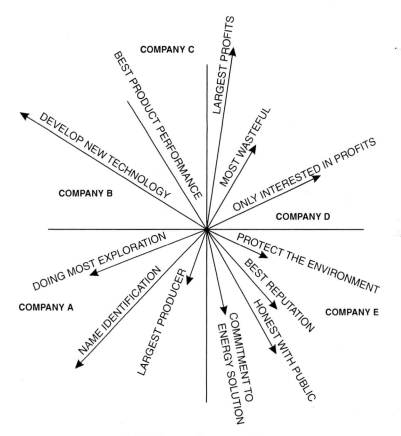

FIGURE 10.3. Perceptual Map

uating judgmental data where choices between attributes are involved. It is more commonly used in measuring the trade-off values of purchase selection factor attributes. Specifically, conjoint analysis is concerned with the joint effect of two or more independent variables on the ordering of a dependent variable. In essence, this method allows a determination of how consumers value various levels of purchase criteria and the extent to which they might tend to forgo a high level of one attribute in order to obtain a high level of another attribute. The trade-off values of holding power, scent, nonstickiness, brand name, and price for hair spray might be cause for a conjoint evaluation, for example.[7]

SUMMARY

Marketing researchers use statistical analysis of association to know how to interpret data describing the relationship between two or more variables. Ultimately, as suggested in Chapter 9, such analysis of data needs to provide us with answers to our research questions and lead us to choices among our decision alternatives. Statistical analysis gives us a window with which we can view the results of our research, which helps us to see which decisions would be best. The appropriate statistical analytical procedures must be used, or the window we are looking out of can give us a distorted view of reality and our decisions based on that distorted view could be ill-chosen.

NOTES

1. Much of this discussion of hypothesis testing is adapted from Brightman, Harvey. 1986. *Statistics in Plain English.* Cincinnati, OH: South-Western Publishing Co., pp. 160-173.

2. See, for example Newbold, Paul. 1991. *Statistics for Business and Economics.* Englewood Cliffs, NJ: Prentice-Hall.

3. Kerlinger, Fred N. 1986. *Foundations of Behavioral Research*, 3rd ed. New York: Holt, Rinehart and Winston, Inc.

4. Hair, Joseph F., Rolph E. Anderson, Ronald L. Tatham, and William C. Black. 1995. *Multivariate Data Analysis,* 4th ed. Englewood Cliffs, NJ: Prentice-Hall.

5. Kerlinger, *Foundations of Behavioral Research.*

6. Aaker, David A. and George S. Day. 1980. *Marketing Research: Private and Public Sector Dimensions.* New York: John Wiley & Sons, Inc.

7. Hair et al., *Multivariate Data Analysis.*

WORKSHEET

1. Write down the hypotheses that you will be testing and the decisions based on the hypotheses.

Null Hypotheses	Null Decision	Alternative Hypotheses	Alternative Decision
H_1		H_1	
H_2		H_2	
H_3		H_3	
H_4		H_4	
H_5		H_5	

2. Determine the "costs" of making decision errors.

Costs of a Type 1 Error

Costs of a Type 2 Error

H_1 _____

H_1 _____

H_2 _____

H_2 _____

H_3 _____

H_3 _____

H_4 _____

H_4 _____

H_5 _____

H_5 _____

3. Set the significance level for the hypotheses by considering the costs of making a Type 1 or Type 2 error.

H_1 _____

H_2 _____

H_3 _____

H_4 _____

H_5 _____

4. Collect the data and conduct the correct statistical tests.   .

Statistical test (from Table 10.3)   Results of test (e.g., *t* scores, etc.)

H_1 _____   _____

H_2 _____   _____

H_3 _____   _____

H_4 _____   _____

H_5 _____   _____

5. Compare results to null hypotheses and make a decision.

Reject	Fail to Reject	Marketing Decision Null	Marketing Decision Alternative
H_1		H_1	
H_2		H_2	
H_3		H_3	
H_4		H_4	
H_5		H_5	

6. Identify the other tests to be run for measures of association.

Research Questions	Measure of Association Tests	Results
_____	_____	_____
_____	_____	_____
_____	_____	_____
_____	_____	_____
_____	_____	_____

Chapter 11

The Research Report

This chapter discusses the essentials of preparing the research report. The basic purpose of the research report is to communicate the results, conclusions, and recommendations of the research project. (If a project encompasses several phases or a long period of time, progress reports are normally sent to the purchaser or user of the research to inform him or her of the progress to date on a given project.) The key word in the preceding statement of purpose is *communicate*. The report must be an effective tool of communication not only to accurately present the findings and conclusions, but also to stimulate the reader to some managerial action. The research project was predicated on the need for information to aid in the decision-making process. Now the cycle has been complete and the report must address that decision and recommend a course of action in view of the research findings. The user or purchaser of the information must decide whether or not to heed the advice given in the recommendation of the report, but the actions recommended by the researcher must be communicated.

TYPES OF WRITTEN REPORTS

We will discuss two basic types of research reports: technical and popular. Each type of report makes some assumptions about the interest and background of the potential readers. The type of report prepared, then, should be based on an analysis of the audience for which it is designed.

Technical Report

A technical report assumes the readers have a background in research methodology and are interested in the detail of the research design, sampling design, statistical methods, etc. The readers are interested in a full presentation and a detailed discussion of each of the steps in the research project. They have the knowledge to be able to evaluate the appropriateness and accuracy with which each step was carried out. The writer can assume that the technical language of research design and analysis will be understood by the reader.

If a technical report is prepared, then it should present a detailed account of each step in the project including copies of questionnaires and perhaps computer printouts of results. This would be especially needed where statistical tests were performed on the data. This type of report is most likely to be used when it is going to become a part of a series of studies (referred to as tracking studies) so the methodology can be duplicated in subsequent projects.

Popular Report

The popular report is designed for a different audience. The assumption is made that the readers are not interested in details about the research techniques and are mainly interested in the findings. This report is the most typical type of report read by business executives. The major interests of this type of reader are the findings and the application of the findings to the decisions to be made in a given situation.

The writing style is designed for rapid reading and comprehension of the key findings of the research. The report is nontechnical and normally makes more use of pictures and graphs and less use of detailed tables. Short, precise statements of findings, conclusions, and recommendations are used along with hyphens, asterisks, and numbers to emphasize important points.

REPORT FORMAT

Although no standardized reporting format is used in all research reports, the following elements are normally included.

1. Title Page
2. Tables of Contents, Charts, and Illustrations
3. Introduction and Objectives
4. Executive Summary or Highlights
5. Conclusions and Recommendations
6. Complete Findings of the Study
7. Supporting Charts and Tables
8. Appendixes

Title Page

The title page should tell the reader four things: (1) the subject of the study, (2) who it was prepared for, (3) who it was prepared by, and (4) the date of the study. This title page may also bear the logo of the preparing organization if the project is completed by an outside organization.

Table of Contents

A good rule to follow for including a table of contents, charts, and illustrations is to base the decision on the length of the report. If the report is less than twelve pages long, then a table of contents is not necessary. For longer reports, a table of contents, charts list, and illustrations list are usually included to enable the readers to locate the sections or illustrations in the report that they want to refer to at a given time. The table of contents should be detailed enough to serve as a guide to locating specific sections in the report. Thus, subheadings should be listed if the sections are long and contain many different subsections. This is especially true of the findings section.

Introduction and Objectives

The introduction should refer the reader to the basic purpose of the research and the specific objectives that were agreed upon in the research proposal. It will usually contain statements of limitations and a brief statement of research methodology, such as who the data were collected from, when, how, and how many respondents were surveyed if primary data were collected. The introduction, in effect, sets forth the information needed to help the reader understand the context in which the data were collected.

The objectives should be the same as those in the research proposal. This will remind the reader of the previously agreed upon objectives.

Executive Summary

The executive summary presents the highlights of the research report in a straightforward and precise manner. This summary is usually organized by topics investigated or by questions that must be answered before a decision is made.

This may be the only section read by some executives, so enough detailed statements of major issues must be given to arm them with the basic facts that emerged in the study. It should be strong enough to permit the reader to get the essence of the findings without assuming that careful reading of the entire report will be made by *every* reader.

The summary should take the form of a detailed abstract in describing purpose, methodology, and findings. Usually two or three pages is the maximum length for a good summary.

Conclusions and Recommendations

As mentioned earlier, the culmination of the research deals with the statements given in reference to the decisions to be made based on the results of the research. This material could be given in the summary but it will have more impact on the reader if it is separated into a new section. The researcher's role is not just to present the facts, but to draw conclusions on the basis of the findings and to make recommendations on the basis of the conclusions. The reader should be presented a set of conclusions and recommendations for managerial action. Although no researcher can force a manager to act on a set of recommendations, he or she should know enough about the decision and the data collected to recommend a course of action. That is what the researcher is being paid for! To simply "present the facts" and offer no recommendations is to lose the advantage gained by having someone who is not responsible for making the decision to at least suggest *some* alternative actions. The decision maker still has to "drive the car," but the one who just reads the "road map" can surely offer some suggestions about which direction to go!

Findings

This section of the report contains the detailed findings of the study. A great deal of detail is given in this section with supporting graphs and charts included as both references and sources of support for the statements that are made in the narrative of this section. This section is normally the largest section of the report and should be organized in a logical way. A topically organized format lends itself to both ease of preparation and reading. The major topics related to each research objective are presented so that the reader is taken in a step-by-step progression through all of the findings of the study. This also ensures that all the objectives are covered in the write-up of the findings.

Supporting Charts and Tables

Since many computer services offer reductions of computer print-outs, they are often included in a section of the report. The reader can then examine all the data analyzed through the computer program for a more detailed study of the findings. This also permits validation of the conclusions and recommendations made by the researcher.

Many statistical packages provide all of the accompanying analysis in the output such as cell frequencies, probabilities of occurrence under a null hypothesis, standard errors, etc. These can be examined for appropriateness of use in subsequent analyses if they are included in the report.

The report and/or oral presentation can be greatly improved through the use of presentation software. Computerized presentation packages provide a great deal of flexibility in preparing tables and include symbols and drawing capability to improve visual impact.

Appendixes

The appendixes can be used to present copies of questionnaires used in the study, more detailed secondary data, or any other type of data or material that might be helpful to the user of the report. In one study of a new outdoor recreational concept, articles on innovative recreational concepts that had been previously introduced were given. This is only one example of how appendixes can be used. The researcher should avoid any attempt to "pad" or build up the size of a report through the use of appendixes. This only takes away from the communicative force of the body of the report.

However, detailed statistical analysis or even computer printouts can be included in an appendix. This material can also be provided in a separate volume for those who will make a detailed study of the report. We also recommend that the final report be bound. This is a relatively inexpensive way to add value to the report and at the same time provide evidence of professionalism and pride. Copies of such reports may be used for years and binding adds protection to the contents. In general, a good rule of thumb to use when considering what to say and where to say it in the written report is to ask this question: "If someone totally unfamiliar with this research project were to take this report out of a file a month from now, would the report be complete enough to give him or her enough information to make decisions in this area?"

ORAL REPORTS

Another effective way to present the results of a study is in an oral presentation. The authors *do not* recommend this as a substitute for a written report, but as a supplement to the written document. The written report should be seen as an archival document, and not just a cryptic written presentation for those people thoroughly familiar with the project. If the oral presentation is effectively done, it becomes a communication tool to reinforce what is given in the written report. In many cases it becomes a technique to communicate results to key executives who might not otherwise have interests or access to those who have been collecting data outside the organization.

With today's audiovisual technology, no researcher should fail to use these aids in the oral presentation. We remember more of what we *see* and *hear* than of what we read only. Slides and transparencies can be prepared at modest costs for most research budgets and greatly add to the impact of the presentation. Again, computerized presentation graphics are easy to use and enable the researcher to customize the graphics used in the oral presentation by including company logo, industry symbols, etc. Short excerpts from videotaped focus group sessions can be very effective in demonstrating with a specific example the broader findings and conclusions that the tape segment is intended to illustrate. Remember, people are more likely to recall and use in formulating their own conclusions those bits of information presented in graphic or visual form rather than as tables or numbers.

PRESENTING STATISTICAL DATA

Two methods can be used to present statistical data: tables and graphs. Both of these methods are commonly used in research reports. The type of data or the emphasis the researcher wishes to put on a given set of data determines which method to use.

Tables

A statistical table is a method of presenting and arranging data that have been broken down by one or more systems of classification. Analytical tables are designed to aid in a formal analysis of interrelationships between variables. A reference table is designed to be a repository of statistical data. The distinction between these two types of data is their intended use and not their construction. Table 11.1 is an example of an analytical table and Table 11.2 is an example of a reference table.

Table 11.1 was prepared to analyze differences in preferences based on the age of the respondents—an analytical table. Table 11.2 was prepared to report to the reader the number of respondents of each sex that were interviewed—a reference table.

Care should be taken in preparing tables to include proper headings, notes about discrepancies (percentages that add to more than one hundred, for example), and sources of data. This helps the reader interpret the data contained in the tables and avoids obvious questions such as, "Why don't the figures add to 100 percent?"

Graphs

Many types of graphs can aid in presenting data. Three of the most commonly used are bar charts, pie charts, and line charts. These charts add a visual magnitude to the presentation of the data. Graphics software packages offer a wide variety of options and are easy to use in creating a report with more visual impact.

TABLE 11.1. Preferences for Motel-Related Restaurants by Age of Traveler

	Prefer Motel Restaurants		Prefer Non-Motel Restaurants		Totals by Age
	Number	Percent	Number	Percent	
Under 25	7	5.5	130	45.3	137
25-34	13	10.3	62	21.6	75
35-44	29	23.0	38	13.2	67
45-54	33	26.2	35	12.2	68
Over 55	44	34.9	22	7.7	66
Total	126	*99.9	287	100.0	413

Source: Survey Data

Notes: Preference was defined as where they would eat if they were traveling and staying at a motel with a restaurant.
*Does not add up to 100 percent due to rounding.

TABLE 11.2. Sex of Travelers

	Number	Percent
Male	294	71.1
Female	119	28.9
Total	413	100.0

Source: Survey Data

A bar chart is easily constructed and can be readily interpreted even by those not familiar with charts. They are especially useful in showing differences between groups as shown in Figure 11.1. From this chart it is easy to see the differences in the preferences for motel and non–motel-related restaurants by age group.

A pie chart is a useful graph in marketing studies especially when showing market share or market segments. Figure 11.2 presents a sample pie chart. Adding color to highlight certain sections increases visual impact to pie charts. This also permits identifying different shares held by different competitors.

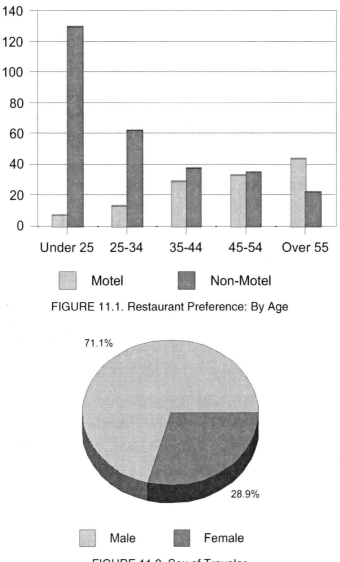

FIGURE 11.1. Restaurant Preference: By Age

FIGURE 11.2. Sex of Traveler

Figures 11.3 and 11.4 are line charts that are especially useful in showing trends in data and comparing trends for different products, customers, and market areas.

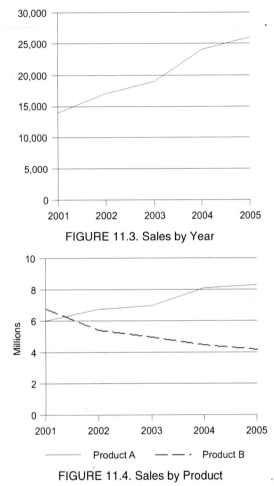

FIGURE 11.3. Sales by Year

FIGURE 11.4. Sales by Product

SUMMARY

This chapter has presented a brief overview of the steps involved in preparing a research report. (See Appendix E for an example of what an actual report contains.) The research report is not only a communication tool, but it is also a source document for future reference. The preparation of the report provides the researcher with the major vehicle to communicate findings to management and to display the results of the work that went into completing the project.

WORKSHEET

1. What is the nature of the audience who will read the report? Do they have a good background in research methodology and statistics?

   _____

   _____

   _____

2. Will the report be read by a variety of people in different levels of the organization?

   _____

   _____

   _____

3. Will you also make an oral presentation?

   _____

   _____

   _____

4. Do you want to provide detailed data analysis in an appendix (or has this been requested by the audience)?

   _____

   _____

   _____

5. Prepare a topical outline of the body of your report including major headings and subheadings.

   Major A. _____

         1. _____

2. _____

3. _____

Major B.   _____

    1. _____

    2. _____

    3. _____

Major C.   _____

    1. _____

    2. _____

    3. _____

6. Now decide what data need to be shown in tables and charts and prepare these.

Data Used: _____

Table Needed: _____

Chart Needed: _____

Data Used: _____

Table Needed: _____

Chart Needed: _____

Data Used: _____

Table Needed: _____

Chart Needed: _____

7. Use the previous outline tables and charts to prepare the body of the report, then prepare the following:

   A. Title Page

   B. Executive Summary

   C. Table of Contents

8. Types of appendixes needed:

   A. Questionnaire(s) _____

   B. Data analysis _____

   C. Background information _____

   D. Other related information _____

9. Oral presentation needs:

   A. Computer presentation slides or overhead transparencies _____

      1. Number_____

      2. Type _____

      3. Color _____

      4. Data/topics of slides

         a._____

         b._____

         c._____

   B. Videotape segments _____

      1. Topic _____

      2. Session _____ _____

    3. Length _____._____

    4. Conclusion to be drawn _____

10. Copying/binding

    A. Number of copies needed (including your own) _____

    B. Type of binding _____

    C. Colors used in binding _____

    D. Imprints/logo on covers _____

SPECIAL TOPICS
IN MARKETING RESEARCH

Chapter 12

Industrial and International
Market Research

Industrial and international represent areas of special applications of the marketing research techniques that have been discussed thus far. The overall process is the same in terms of steps involved in a research project, but the problems and issues are unique to these areas that need further elaboration.

INDUSTRIAL MARKET RESEARCH

How Industrial Marketing Differs

A number of key factors differentiate industrial marketing from consumer marketing. These differences in turn, reflect on how market research is approached, designed, and executed.

Industrial, commercial, and business-to-business strategies have more of a focus on market definition and the dynamics impacting the marketplace. Evaluating the various dimensions of the marketing mix will certainly be commonplace in assisting the industrial marketer and strategic planner in their decision process. However, the evolving nature and impact of technological innovation has created incredible flux in the very assumptions driving the particular market. Keeping up with the changing assumptions, having a grasp on not only emerging opportunities, but also a sense of the timing associated with the opportunity, has become essential to survival in markets that are becoming more globally driven than ever before. Although there are certainly exceptions, research done in the industrial arena is more typically referred to as *market* research, and research in the consumer realm is usually *marketing* research.

Within industrial markets the marketing concept has a focus on customer needs, but with a twist not always apparent in the consumer arena. Identification of customer needs also requires an understanding of the economics of the customer operation, the structure of the industry in which the customer operates, and how the customer competes.

The product/service design package is quite often more important than the product itself. Custom designs, along with packages that may include turnkey startup or even operations, are not uncommon. Although standardized widgets are available in the industrial sector, much of the purchasing includes customized packages including various types of products, services, and financing arrangements, as well as much by way of equipment engineered and designed specifically for a particular situation and need. Technical product complexity quite often reflects requirements that do not fit in clearly defined standardized products and models. In other words, different companies may offer totally different designs with different features and attributes.

Market segmentation in the industrial sector is also quite different and typically more definitive. Whereas the consumer sector places much emphasis on demographic differentiation, the industrial segments are driven by type of product usage requirements and type of industrial function that is served. Industrial segments may follow geographic lines, end-use criteria, buyer firm typologies or, as has been noted, product-usage criteria.

The universe for an industrial market sample or segment may be much, much smaller, as well. For example, markets for offshore drilling rigs will focus on a limited number of offshore drilling contractors. Other applications might have a much larger target market, but with the requirement to understand the specific needs of each segment. Bar stock steel, for example, comes in various shapes, lengths, and quality yields. Manufacturers of drill pipe will have certain requirements, and construction fabricators will have totally different specifications for their bar stock.

The areas of industrial purchasing and marketing are quite often not clearly defined. For some types of buying where products are reasonably standardized, such as drill pipe, purchases can be made by purchasing agents, engineers, or field forepersons depending on the particular company, its size, and the way it is organized. Purchases of larger forms of equipment and systems packages may involve committees formed to examine and evaluate procurement alternatives. For still other types of large major equipment purchases, negotiated contracts may also involve senior levels of management, including the chief executive officer (CEO).

Marketing in the industrial sector parallels the patterns for purchasing. Depending on the size and complexity of the product, service or equipment involved, the first level in developing a research project may involve approaching the sales force or an engineering sales force. However, for larger and more complex types of equipment and contracts, the interaction of sales, engineering, and quite often field and/or operational decision makers can be expected in the decision process. In many instances decision input will include senior management levels when negotiations get to very serious levels. Understanding these dynamics therefore becomes critical in approaching the design of an industrial market research project.

Overview

Industrial market research begins with its primary purpose as serving the strategic-planning function. Consumer research, on the other hand, usually has its primary purpose associated with advertising and marketing. Although there are indeed exceptions, and industrial research is certainly used for marketing and advertising purposes, the factor that usually initiates an industrial study is the senior decision process and strategic corporate planning.

As previously indicated, the primary purpose of the research function is the reduction of error in decision making, although the reasons for conducting industrial market research generally fit in one or more of three major categories.

- To capitalize on an opportunity, or to clarify the extent to which the opportunity exists.
- To avoid mistakes or errors in situations where an opportunity is assumed to exist, and indeed may or may not exist.
- To monitor corporate and/or marketing strategy, thereby providing the essential information to adjust strategy accordingly to maintain or further develop the planning objectives set by the firm.

Before a research project is initiated certain key questions should be outlined. If these questions cannot be adequately answered before starting the research, the research may not be worth doing. These questions are designed to initiate the conceptualization process needed to develop a viable research project. For more definitive questions as they may be incorporated in the strategic planning process, be sure to examine Chapter 1.

- Why is the information needed?
- Specifically, what information is needed?
- What resources will be required to obtain it?
- What will be accomplished by the research project?
- When can the results of the research be obtained?
- What conditions must be met?
- What action will be taken as a result of completing the project?

Once these questions are addressed, more definitive focus may be needed to assist in developing the parameters being sought by the results. Understanding the focus will also help to determine what type of methodology will best serve in addressing the issues of focus. Examples of some key points that will assist in this process are as follows:

- Identify the alternatives (through expert opinion interviews).
- Evaluate the expectations (through surveys, panels, group discussions).
- Identify the changes (surveys and tracking studies).
- Determine the extent (surveys).
- Evaluate the effects (forecasting studies, expert opinion interviews).
- Identify the customer/market (surveys, market investigations).
- Evaluate performance (satisfaction surveys, competitive evaluations).

Determining the value of the research is another step that should be made prior to the project. In many cases this becomes a matter of common sense in evaluating the cost of the research project against the risk and potential associated with the corporate decisions being considered. For example, the extension of a particular equipment line that would involve a $100,000 piece of machinery and $20,000 in initial advertising should not justify a $50,000 expenditure in market research. On the other hand, a potential $50 million acquisition should not be cutting corners with a $20,000 survey, when a study of that size will only provide preliminary information. Other questions that perhaps should be addressed in determining whether or how the research is to be used include:

- How will the information be used?
- What cash flow and profit contributions are at risk?
- What alternatives will be determined from the results?
- What will the impact be on the long-term corporate objectives?
- Are there barriers that may inhibit the achievement of the goals?

APPROACHING THE INDUSTRIAL MARKET RESEARCH PROJECT

Each industrial market research project is different and unique, so explaining a series of steps that outline a typical format may be helpful.

Definitive Problem Statement

The first step involves developing a definitive problem statement, followed by specific information objectives. A problem statement may be as simple as, "Company XYZ is conducting the planning to determine the market potential and corporate viability of penetrating the ABC market sector with a new industrial widget design." Specific objectives may include determining market size and market share of key competitors; evaluating satisfaction of widget users with current designs and competitors; determining demand for the features represented by the new design; identifying competitor strategies; evaluating market conditions and dynamics that impact the timing of a new widget supplier; and if deemed feasible, determine a strategy that would provide the most likely market acceptance and earliest return on investment.

Proposal Preparation

Whether the study is being attempted in-house or being conducted by an industrial market research consulting firm, a definitive, written proposal is necessary to ensure a clear understanding of exactly what is being done, who will be the key players conducting the work, how it is being done, what time frames will be involved, and what kind of budget can be expected.

Planning Review

Once the proposal is accepted, it is time to sit down and develop the details associated with the approach outlined. This may involve refinements in the proposal, so all key players should be involved. This is also an opportunity to gain insight and feedback from as many functional perspectives in the firm (engineering, operations, management, sales, etc.) as possible. These perspectives represent both insights into the marketplace, as well as assumptions that can be evaluated from the market's perspective in the conduct of the actual information gathering. Once the planning review is completed, current and upcoming dynamics of the industry become the focus. The dynamics of the industry are given focus at this point, because they will provide the overall context or framework to use in considering answers to the specific research questions of interest.

The Dynamics and Tempo of an Industry

Understanding the dynamics impacting a particular sector of industry, its economics, whether or not it is currently a growth sector or in a decline, as well as the factors that may be operating to create change, are essential elements of information to those involved in making strategic decisions for their respective operations in the industrial sector. It may be that obtaining this knowledge is itself an objective of the research. However, in more cases than not, clients will have a reasonable appreciation for the state of their industry and will expect the market research study to reflect a design that incorporates this understanding. Such an understanding will reflect where the focus is placed in the study.

For example, in the area of environmental site remediation, a great deal of opportunity occurs for contractors, engineering firms, and equipment suppliers in developing in the cleanup of Superfund sites. The dynamics of this very interesting market arena are being defined. Environmental compliance and site cleanup will be a priority for military and other governmental installations. Environmental business within governmental sectors, therefore, is setting the pace for what can be expected to develop in the private sector in the days ahead, not to speak of what may follow in the area of overseas expansion of these market opportunities. Such an understanding would make a large difference in how this market might be examined on behalf of a firm that was evaluating the risks in entering this market.

Background Information

The first step in understanding the dynamics of a particular marketplace usually entails reviewing background information, a literature and database search, evaluation of technical and other sources of industry data, and a review of previous research efforts. Trade journals, association and government data, technical society and trade group information are important possible sources of current information. Many government agencies have current information that is available simply for the asking. Many industry sectors have trade journals that regularly publish accurate market data. Multiclient studies are a good place to start in looking at specific industry sectors. One of the best directories of multiclient studies is the *International Directory of Published Market Research,* which is compiled each year by the British Overseas Trade Board and covers multiclient studies from around the world. Data such as this can be used to extrapolate, combine, and project information gathered from surveys and other types of primary market information investigations. This data will further assist in developing an understanding for the structure of the industry under study. This should also be the phase in which key individual and company respondents are identified. There is no point in reinventing the wheel. Researchers must have access to all available secondary information at the start of the study. See the Web sites identified in Chapter 5 and Appendix B for other sources of background information for industrial markets.

Exploratory Studies

Quite often it will be necessary to conduct a preliminary examination of a market sector for the simple purpose of identifying the appropriate issues that need to be addressed in detail in the comprehensive study. If time and budget allow, the best way to conduct exploratory studies is by open-ended interviews with key decision makers. Using a discussion guide rather than a structured questionnaire, respondents are selected based on their perspective of a particular dimension of the marketplace. Some respondents may reflect a broad, industry-level perspective, others may reflect an engineering, operations, or field perspective. This input may reflect a consensus of knowledgeable industry opinion (often referred to as Delphi technique), and as such represents judgment quota samples of key experts.

On the other hand, exploratory research may be preliminary in nature with its purpose providing some topline survey input to further refine a major market research thrust. Some exploratory research may be all that the research value equation supports. In other words, the risk is not all that high, but some indicators are needed to help guide the decision making. Exploratory research may likewise serve to identify key selection attributes that then will be quantitatively measured in the full-scale survey study.

The Sample

In industrial studies the sample more than likely will be stratified quota samples. Quotas may involve certain types of companies, as well as certain types of job functions, such as a Vice President of Engineering and an Operations Manager. Since different titles may involve different responsibilities in different firms, respondents are further qualified on the questionnaire by the functional responsibilities they may have. For example, it may be that the input being sought is from the person responsible for the major machinery purchases in a manufacturing plant. This responsibility may involve input from engineering, but a final decision from a plant manager. Input from both levels may be sought because an understanding of the difference in their perspectives and what each deems important may be significant.

In most instances, respondents are qualified at the time an appointment is made or at the beginning of the survey if the survey is being conducted by telephone. Industry directories typically are the place to start. If the industry sector does not have a directory, then the Thomas Register is another possibility. Industrial samples are now being compiled by sampling firms from yellow page listings. In some cases, a list of firms will be compiled and the appropriate person will have to be identified by asking for the department and then inquiring of the department receptionist.

Preparation of the Primary Data-Collection Instrument

Whether this involves mail questionnaires, interview discussion guides for telephone or personal interviews, or topic outlines for group discussions, this is the point where specific questions related to the study objectives are formulated. These in turn should be tested and further refined before doing what is typically referred to as the fieldwork and basic data collection.

Market Feedback/Data Collection

At this point all the conventional techniques used in consumer market research can be used. However, personal interviews and senior level meeting/interviews conducted by consultant level investigators are used with much greater frequency for industrial studies than in consumer studies. When the sample can be clearly defined and identified, well-designed structured questionnaires administered by interviewers who are fluent in the technical terms involved work quite well. Focus groups with purchasing managers, office managers, and data-processing managers have been conducted by authors of this book with excellent results.

An industrial panel is another technique that represents significant promise. Industrial panels are used in similar fashion to consumer panels. The key is to ensure they are being set up by someone with an understanding of the market involved and the uniqueness associated with selecting certain types of industrial decision makers such as engineers, purchasing agents, operation managers, and so forth. Some trade journals use preselected panels of executives to gain insight for articles related to industry trends they periodically publish.

During the data collection, take a realistic look at all pertinent parts of the industry being studied. This may include customers, noncustomers, prospects, distributors, dealers, agents, service organizations, suppliers, and other participants in the chain of distribution from raw materials to finished goods purchased by industrial users. Researchers may even talk with government agencies that are involved in regulatory and control aspects of an industry. Usually, a comprehensive study will also involve cooperation with trade associations and trade groups.

The accumulation of information from field data then becomes something akin to a giant jigsaw puzzle. However, when all the bits and pieces start fitting together, the overall picture begins to take shape. When this takes place the alternatives and answers to the specific management questions being addressed by the company conducting the study start coming into a realistic focus.

Data Assimilation and Analysis

Sometimes it is appropriate to use the computer for analysis, but oftentimes it is not. For example, certain industrial market sectors may only require a sample size of between 30 to 40. If a larger database is used and the data-gathering instrument is adequately structured, then conventional forms of computerized statistical analysis may be used. Smaller samples may provide indicators from which extrapolations from published industry data are made. Smaller samples that follow structured questionnaires certainly can always utilize frequency and correlation analyses, as well as analyses used to measure response to specific equipment benefits. Sample populations of 100 and larger can start employing the various multivariate techniques available. Projection techniques can assist in identifying market directions as well as emerging changes and trends.

Market size and share are important elements of information sought in the industrial study. Both can be presented in units, dollars, or both. In many industrial markets, published data do not include market size and market share estimates. These estimates must therefore be extrapolated from a combination of known industry data (e.g., drilling activity or production activity in the oil industry), survey results, and good judgment. This type of judgment usually requires a definitive understanding of the dynamics involved in the industry being studied.

The Report

Many formats may be considered acceptable. Most industrial market studies are designed not only to answer specific management questions, but also to serve as a reference volume after being presented and discussed. A typical report prepared for senior management, therefore, should consist of an introduction, executive findings, and a conclusions section. Depending on the focus of the study, a section on background market data normally would be included. The analysis may consist of a detailed discussion from survey results or the consultant's market and background investigation. Likewise, if there are survey data, a section that outlines and presents this data should be a part of the study.

The introduction should include a background and problem statement, along with the specific study objectives. The methodology chosen for the study should then be explained. If a perspective relative to the results needs greater explanation, then it should be highlighted in the introduction. How the sample was derived normally is explained in this section, as well as providing details associated with decision levels interviewed. If not too long, a list of firms interviewed is also included in this section. In that event, the list should be included in the appendix. It should be noted that confidentiality and anonymity of the individual interview is a normal and courteous expectation of those who have given their time to participate as respondents. Knowing which companies participated should be sufficient. The introduction serves also to provide a brief outline of the volume(s) and to explain how it might best be used.

This section might follow a topical progression based on an outline of the management questions. The conclusions section answers the question: "What does the key point made in the findings mean to the company?" or may include the recommendations and steps to be followed to best address the objectives being considered by the company.

The written analysis should logically follow clearly outlined topics. In many cases, this may involve individual chapters related to specific topics being addressed. The written interpretation of survey results should attempt to use summary graphics wherever possible. Market and survey data should intersperse graphics with the "numbers" wherever possible to highlight, illustrate, and add to the readability of the report.

In studies that involve small samples of select industry experts, a section may be included that provides highlights from each interview. This can be done by a summary of the discussion and the significant comments made. It may also provide verbatim comments, if good notes were taken. To maintain accuracy, such summaries should be written up shortly after the interviews. In cases such as these, the job responsibilities of the persons interviewed and the type of firm they represent may provide a good context of their perspective, without betraying the confidentiality and anonymity that should be associated with the interview.

INTERNATIONAL MARKET RESEARCH

Introduction

The impact and response to change has been a major topic in business circles for the last two decades. Fundamental economic, technological, political, and competitive change have all contributed to an evolution of the basic assumptions comprising what heretofore has been considered the natural order and structure of business. The rise of global markets, the emergence of instantaneous worldwide media and communication systems, the entrance of third-world producers into the area of world trade, high levels of saturation for certain product lines, increased competition, as well as the impact of the role of public opinion internationally have all contributed to the requirement of new responses to "business as usual."

The results of a recent study estimated that approximately 95 percent of the world's population and two-thirds of its total purchasing power are located outside the United States. In recent years, foreign markets have been growing faster than the U.S. domestic market. In real terms, the rate of growth for world trade has exceeded the rate of growth of the U.S. economy. Thus, the shrinking of worldwide markets, the capabilities represented by international faxes, e-mail, teleconferencing, and travel, have resulted in more and more businesses of all sizes becoming involved in both export and foreign operations.

One of the vital keys to the success of those entering the international marketplace has been the correct identification and evaluation of the markets to compete in. As a result, international market research has begun to play an increasingly significant role in providing essential market information for those entering, expanding, and operating the arena of overseas business.

Evaluating overseas markets, therefore, is becoming a task not only for the highly visible multinational firm already operating in or considering expanding into a particular overseas market, but also for the entrepreneurial firm with a niche product or equipment line seeking additional opportunity. International market evaluations may incorporate

1. the identification of markets with the maximum potential and demand, as well as the optimum conditions for the company's products, services, or equipment;
2. an identification and evaluation of competition, by way of companies, products/services/equipment and competitive strategies existing in the market or markets being considered;
3. ascertaining any unique dimensions that may exist in the market, by way of needs, distribution, culture, and so forth that might require modifications to the product/services/equipment;
4. determining the most realistic and incisive market entry strategy for the target market; and
5. determining the most efficient means to develop and sustain profitable operations in the market.[1]

International market research does not require unusual talents to conduct. It involves evaluating some of the same basic considerations and subtleties that might apply to good, prudent domestic market research. But it also will involve several dimensions and differences, such as culture, language, consumer appeal, individual purchasing power, and unique distribution and purchase criteria that need to be incorporated into the planning of the research being conducted.

New parameters, environments, and factors will enter international market research that are not normally a consideration in domestic research. Differences in exchange rate, duties, as well as modes of transporting and merchandising products need to be considered. The culture, the legal system, as well as the political climate of a target region can bear significantly on not only how products are marketed, but how the research is able to be conducted. Many markets will prove to be multicultural and multilingual. Coordination therefore becomes more complex and at times can be difficult. Simultaneously, not only may different forms of competition exist, but different rules may apply for different types of competition.[2]

Background Information

Prior to initiating any form of primary research in the target market, a background investigation should be conducted. Primary data may be available from numerous domestic sources without having to collect it abroad. Interviews concerning buying behavior from a particular nation can be conducted in a preliminary ad hoc manner with foreign students, local ethnic community members, embassy personnel, or domestic experts on a market. Such sources should only be considered preliminary, however. For example, they may not represent the target group of "typical consumers," if they are reflecting an elite class that serve in a nation's embassy.[3] However, such information can serve as good background information when defining the parameters of a particular research project.

A great deal of published market information that is readily available. Because the U.S. Government actively supports the role of U.S. businesses expanding overseas, there is an abundance of published market information available as good background data from government agencies. The U.S. Department of Commerce, the Small Business Administration, the Export-Import Bank of the United States, The Overseas Private Investment Corporation, The Agency for International Development, and others have information services and publications of market data that will provide an excellent basis from which to begin. This information is compiled from a variety of sources, some excellent and some not as complete or accurate as others. Public libraries also will typically have published market data on numerous nations around the world.

Generally, the consulates and embassies of the nations of interest can be a good source of background information regarding their countries. They also might prove to have good contacts when seeking information that may be available from published government statistics, banks, and universities within their nation, or to assist with contacts to enable the hiring of in-country nationals who are professionals in conducting fieldwork.

The U.S. Chamber of Commerce serves as a liaison with the American Chambers of Commerce located in most developed and some developing countries. These overseas American Chambers are nonprofit associations whose members are American companies and individual businesspeople in that nation. The Chambers serve to represent the interests of present and potential American business interests in their nations. They provide many complementary services that normally include good insights and market information relative to their nation, as well as contacts that could prove quite valuable.

Most international banks retain specialists who are knowledgeable about specific foreign markets, who usually are available to offer useful advice on current developments, regulations, and trends. Airlines and shipping firms quite often publish their own materials on markets they serve that can be valuable sources of information. Numerous international accounting firms with offices overseas have in-depth country information for the locations they serve. A growing number of online databases include market and economic data, opportunities and contacts, and forecasts and industry statistics. Two publications provide comprehensive listings of these databases:

> *Directory of Online Databases*
> Cuadra Associates, Inc.
> 11835 West Olympic Boulevard
> Suite 855
> Los Angeles, CA 90064
>
> *Omni Online Database Directory*
> Collier Books
> 866 Third Ave.
> New York, NY 10022

Levels of Difficulty and Differences in Purposes of the Research

Primary international market research can be a relatively simple or a very sophisticated process depending upon the research purpose and client. For example, the numerous industrial operations functioning overseas with U.S.-based purchasing and engineering departments can be an excellent source of market feedback and insight. Although this might provide sufficient data to identify basic market trends, most industrial and consumer-type international market research will require in-country feedback. The purposes for international market research range from multinational firms already established in a particular area wanting to improve their market penetration; to those wanting to further expand their overseas operations into new overseas markets; to those wanting to test demand for new product or equipment lines in an existing market area; to those considering a joint venture with a national group to establish a factory in a new area; to those operations making their first move into the international realm, who need to identify the market demand and market strategy needed to maximize the potential and profitability of their venture. Whether the target market is an industrial or commercial market or whether it is a consumer market will likewise make a major difference in the complexity and approach to the research. The differences in need and type of information sought will establish the differences in approach, methodology, and budget required for the research.

Approach, Methodology, and Budget

Approach, methodology, and budget are often interrelated. Budget limitations may determine the approach and methodology used for an overseas research assignment. Ideally, the value of the research being conducted will be determined by the risk involved in the market venture.

If the risk is at the lower end of the scale, then it may be that topline results gained from published data and a short pilot survey will suffice. On the other hand, when major risks are being considered, comprehensive insights will be required. When this is the case, the approach and methodology will dictate a much higher budget. The approach in this case may require in-country personal interviews if it is an industrial study. Or if it is a consumer operation, it may require the hiring of a firm or professionals from that nation to conduct interviews in person or by phone, in a developed nation. The use of mail surveys has certain good overseas research applications that can serve both high- and low-risk ventures with budget requirements lower than that normally associated with telephone interviews from the United States, in-country telephone interviews, or personal interviews.

Cultural Sensitivity

The need to carefully approach and research new markets overseas cannot be too strongly emphasized. One of the most common causes of difficulty for overseas business operations, not to mention international market research, is the failure to do the necessary preparatory work before charging ahead. At least in part, this relates to a typically Western attitude that views the world through its own perspective, and assumes those within the host nation will think and react the same way. A colorful example of this type of Western attitude or bias is illustrated in the story of an American businessman in London. He was stopped by the local police for some minor traffic infraction. When the bobby recognized his American accent, he asked the businessman if he were a foreigner. The indignant American replied, "Hell no. I'm a Texan."

Overseas business decisions, and the approach to marketplace must reflect the perspective of those representing the decision makers and culture of the target nation. Overseas customers and decision makers usually can be counted on to have minor to major differences in their way of eating, drinking, clothing themselves, sleeping, acting, and thinking than we do in the United States. These differences must be recognized, understood, respected, and incorporated into the project planning of the research, as well as in the results.

Other Differences in International Market Research

Although it is difficult to generalize about differences that will be found from various areas of the world, be alert to them. Some published data available from host nations may be excellent, but other sources of government-sponsored information may be incomplete, confusing, and inaccurate. Market research may be viewed suspiciously in some areas. In other areas, the time required to conduct the fieldwork may represent a multiple of what it would take domestically, because of either distances, the lack of phones, or the lack of available or efficient internal transportation systems. All of which concludes with the need to be able to have the latitude and associated experience and judgment to modify work methods or compile when necessary a realistic picture of the market being evaluated.

SURVEY DATA-GATHERING METHODOLOGY DECISIONS

Consumer surveys should be handled through professional field service companies that specialize in the particular language and nation. In many, if not most of these instances, these requirements will be handled by firms either within or in close proximity to the nation where the market is located. The costs for these services typically will not be inexpensive.

Industrial and commercial market research, although considered more complex for domestic research, may prove more straightforward than consumer research when conducted internationally. Executives, managers, and government officials can be identified through directories and by referrals. In many instances, these individuals may be multilingual. Because of this, international, industrial, and commercial market research data gathering reflects more flexibility than consumer studies. Personal interviews with senior managers and executives can be conducted by the consultant from the United States.

Where language may represent a slight problem, a local assistant may be hired to accompany the consultant on the interviews. If good contacts are available and personal interviews to be conducted by local interviewers are sought, many local international banks, accounting firms, legal firms, and universities are willing to assist in contracting professionals to assist. This may be an advantage where the interviews are conducted in the language of the nation and then are required to be translated back into English. When this is the case, great care needs to be taken to ensure excellence in the language capabilities of the interviewers and in the accuracy of the questionnaire or discussion guide translation. U.S.-based market research operations experienced in international research will often have "associates" to carry on their interviews within the nations where they conduct international work.

TYPES OF INTERVIEWS

If costs are not an issue, then personal interviews for industrial or commercial studies are the most preferred, with telephone interviews sometimes an expedient alternative. Personal interviews potentially yield much more by way of depth of information than interviews conducted by phone. However, when the distance in locations of target respondents is such that only one or two respondents are available in each city to be visited, then telephone interviews can be scheduled.

Telephone Interviews from the United States

Each alternative assumes good directories are available. The first involves telephone interviews from the United States directly to the internationally based target respondents. When this approach is used, the effectiveness of the response can be improved by first sending out personal letters on company stationary asking for their cooperation. These letters should explain what is being researched, why it is important, why the researcher would like to interview the respondent or a key member of his or her staff, approximate time of the call, as well as an offer to send the respondent a "summary of the results." The summary of the results should simply be straightforward market information that would not prejudice the company for whom the research is being conducted if it fell into the hands of a competitor. If the language is a potential issue, bilingual consultants or interviewers should be used to make the calls.

Mail Surveys

Another cost-conscious alternative to conducting international, industrial, or commercial market research is mail surveys. The same advantages and limitations of domestic mail surveys apply for those being done internationally. International mail surveys will involve a few more sensitivities to be aware of than domestic surveys. The key to the value of the results of international mail surveys rests with the availability of directories and mailing lists for the target respondents. Unless information is available to the contrary, the problem of language may require that bilingual questionnaires be sent out. International mail surveys will also take more time. Having made these points, however, it should be understood that international mail surveys are used by the United Nations, by industrial and business firms with overseas markets, by publications with a substantial number of overseas subscribers, and by institutions and organizations interested in market and opinion feedback from other parts of the world.

International Mailing Lists

Probably the greatest limitation to international mail surveys is the difficulty in obtaining up-to-date mailing lists for a segment of industry or government. Certain industries have excelled in the publication of complete, current directories, but others are lacking. Subscriber lists to international publications can serve as a good "list" source. Assuming the publication's readership accurately targets the group of respondents sought, it can generally be concluded that the list will be up-to-date, reflect a socioeconomic level that is above the norm, and result in a likelihood of a good response. Information regarding directories can usually be obtained from industry trade associations and consulates of the target countries. International customer lists may be available for certain industry segments. Likewise, membership lists of international trade associations sometimes can be counted on for good reliability. Published lists of government officials are available from certain countries. International organizations ranging from the United Nations to the Organization of American States (OAS) to the U.S. Department of Commerce will typically have informative lists available. Then the lists of attendees of international conferences and conventions may prove to have value.

Insights on Language and Custom for Mail Surveys

Sampling procedures for international mail surveys differ little from that of domestic mail surveys. However, it is an advantage to have someone involved in the work who understands the language of the country involved. Without the knowledge of the language, some scripts would be impossible to discern between the name of the person and the name of the company. In some countries the last name is written first. In Spanish, the last name is usually in the middle. For example, Sr. Felipe Moroles Garcia should be addressed in the salutation as "Estimado Sr. Moroles" rather than "Sr. Garcia." Some titles require certain salutations in that language.

In most international surveys, some familiarity with the customs and language of the country involved will be required. Common mistakes made involve assuming Spanish to be the language of the Philippines and Brazil. Such mistakes will adversely affect the response rate. Likewise, some Latin Americans resent Americans assuming that we are the only "United States" and ignoring the Estados Unidos de Mexicanos and Estados Unidos do Brasil. Reply envelopes also can involve local subtleties. Brazilian airmail envelopes have green and yellow borders and some Brazilians do not react favorably to the standard international red and blue borders. Nations such as China use an entirely different form of script. When possible it is helpful to address the letter in that script and simply put the name of the country in English beneath it so it can be properly routed by U.S. postal workers. Although most regional post offices in countries such as China have workers who understand English, being able to address the envelope in their own language or in both will simply speed up the process of getting the mailing to the respondent.

Postage and Stationery

Care should be taken to have international airmail stamps and airmail stamped on the envelope. Receipt of quality company stationery carries a certain level of prestige. Stamped reply envelopes with the appropriate postage from that nation can add to the survey being well-received. If advance notice is given, these stamps can be ordered from local postal centers or from stamp dealers, who can determine the correct postage for the weight of the return questionnaire. It should also be noted that lightweight paper, as well as the company letterhead, can be used for the questionnaire without sacrificing quality. This can serve to minimize postage costs.

Response Rate and Language

Follow-up mailings, reminders, and incentives can also be used for international mail surveys. In some cases the prestige of the sponsor may take the place of an incentive (i.e., a survey being conducted for a well-known publication). Incentives can range from pens to maps to books or money. However, postal and custom regulations of the individual country should be checked to ensure the premium is admissible and not subject to duty.

The language of the survey is always an important consideration. Some areas in Europe can be counted on to have a high ratio of those who speak fluent English. When respondents come from an English-language publication subscription list, this can be assumed. Some international surveys are sent out in two or more languages where appropriate. In cases where it is not deemed necessary to include English in the mailing, or where a very low ratio of target respondents are expected to be fluent in English, it is advisable not to.

Ideally, the person used to translate the questionnaire and accompanying letter should be a bilingual native of the country surveyed. If not, the person should at least be fluent enough with the language to know the idioms of the target nation. In similar fashion, a survey that targets another English-speaking area of the world should carefully review both the cover letter and the questionnaire for expressions and words that may be ambiguous to non-Americans. Examples are "apartment" versus "flat," or the difference between "kilometers" and "miles." Questions involving monetary responses should be reflected in the monetary units of the nation being surveyed (i.e., rupees, yen, Euro, etc.).[4]

Hybrid Methodologies

A number of effective approaches use more than one methodology in obtaining the information sought in international industrial market research studies. For example, a short mail survey may be sent out and then followed up by a more extensive phone interview. On the other hand, mail surveys may be sent to industrial respondents who were not able to be reached in person or by phone. Reasons for not reaching respondents include schedule conflicts, a language barrier, an inability to contact them by phone, or simply being unable to get to their particular locale while the fieldwork was being conducted.

Other Considerations Involving Cultural Distance

Conducting research overseas involves different levels of cultural distance. Three primary levels of cultural distance should be kept in mind. The first involves different nations that share a very similar culture to our own where English is normally used. The second level involves crossing a cultural frontier, where significant cultural and language differences are present. The third also involves a very different language, but in addition involves cultural patterns that are totally distinct from our own. Recognize the level of cultural distance involved in the target nation. As Westerners, we often note how much international businesspeople or international students we interchange with in the United States are like us, when in fact they are more sensitive to the cultural differences and have adapted for our sake. To maximize the potential of any research being done internationally, cultural distinctions within the nation being targeted should be recognized, respected, and assimilated into the planning of the research project.

THE IMPORTANCE OF RELEVANT MARKET INFORMATION

With the trends toward globalization of an increasing number of markets and the consequent increase in global competition, the importance of good market data and market intelligence cannot be underestimated.

More and more companies are entering the international arena with well-thought-out and carefully developed plans. In most instances, these plans are based on current, pertinent information related to the target market. The assumptions driving global markets are changing and the rates of change are increasing. More subtle assumptions impacting specific markets such as procurement procedures, the use of national representatives, organizational decision input structures, pricing versus product attribute benefits, distribution systems, and so forth, are also evolving in both the fast-paced international market centers, as well as in nations that are considered new entrées to global business. The normal order of conducting business internationally is indeed changing. Relevant market research is becoming a requisite means to stay abreast of the trends, as well as to acquire accurate readings on the very pulse of the dynamics of international markets.

NOTES

1. Czinkota, Michael R. and Ilkka A. Ronkainen. 1988. *International Marketing.* Chicago, IL: The Dryden Press, pp. 181-203 and 391-417.

2. Ibid., pp. 391-417.

3. Erdos, Paul. 1970. *Professional Mail Surveys.* New York: McGraw-Hill, pp. 237-241.

4. Nelson, Carl. 1990. *Global Success.* Blue Ridge Summit, PA: Liberty Hall Press, pp. 97, 142-144.

Chapter 13

Mail Surveys

Mail surveys are an important component of the data-collection process. The increase in unlisted telephone numbers and the large proportion of households with caller ID have reduced the effectiveness of telephone interviewing. A well-planned, carefully organized mail survey can yield excellent insights and information. Misapplied mail surveys can result in faulty samples and misleading results.

Abuses in the use of telemarketing techniques have increased negative consumer reaction to any type of phone intrusion. Privacy laws are becoming stricter and can be expected to increase. Hopefully, the impact on telephone survey interviews will be minimal. However, numerous applications are appropriate for mail surveys. Understanding the advantages and limitations of mail surveys, as well as the techniques necessary to administer them effectively, is becoming an increasingly important part of the capabilities of today's well-rounded researcher.

Generally, costs to conduct a mail survey are comparatively cheaper than telephone interviews and significantly less than personal interviews. Specific applications of mail surveys offer a distinct advantage. When the sample includes a special group of respondents with several common denominators, the results from a mail survey can provide essential decision-making information. An example might be users of a unique product line, such as fishing equipment or a particular line of automobiles. Likewise, mail surveys serve very well when the sample includes a group of people who are in some way tied to the survey client. This might include different segments, such as new customers, regular customers, one-time customers, and so forth. If you already have a well-developed *mailing list* that consists of the type of people you want to survey, then it will most likely yield acceptable results.

The validity of the sample is the point called into question regarding mail surveys. Is the sample a dedicated sample? In other words, is the sample selected on the basis of being "our customer," or having attended a particular event during a specified time frame? Understanding the motivation for taking a few minutes to complete and return the mail survey is important. Will completion of the survey result in improved service that the respondent uses frequently or even occasionally? Or is there an incentive involved in participating in the survey ... a free ticket, a discount, a premium or gift? Will it help decision makers better understand what consumers expect from the product, services, or equipment provided?

Enhancing the motivation of a dedicated respondent is also important. Generally this involves a cover letter or a short letter that can be written into the beginning of the questionnaire itself. Such a letter should briefly tell the respondent what the questionnaire is trying to achieve (i.e., improve services); how important his or her input will be (your opinion does count!); how easy it will be to fill out (it will only take a few minutes of your time ... or five minutes ... or ten minutes); and how easy it will be to return it (slip it in the enclosed prepaid envelope).

ADVANTAGES AND LIMITATIONS

The major difference between mail surveys and telephone or personal interview surveys is that no interviewer is present to explain the purpose, solicit cooperation, ask the questions, record the answers, and in general to troubleshoot any problems that may arise. This places a great deal of importance on the construction of the questionnaire and the accompanying cover letter.

Mail surveys are not suited for unstructured interviews involving any type of improvising or flexibility required on the part of the interviewer. Mail surveys can reach almost any type of group that can be defined by a mailing list. Samples that are comprised of hard-to-reach respondents will cost appreciably more when done by telephone interviews. Quite often such samples can be reached effectively by a mail survey simply because specific definition mailing lists are more available than similar sample phone lists.

Mail surveys yield more accurate results among those completing the surveys. Because the mail questionnaire is filled out at the respondent's discretion, replies are likely to be more thoughtful. Mail surveys are found to have a distinct advantage when asking about sensitive or potentially embarrassing topics, or when numerous questions related to finances are involved, because of the respondent's higher confidence in the anonymity of a survey that is sent back in with no return address.[1]

The primary advantages of mail surveys over surveys using other means of data gathering include

- Wider distribution potential.
- Less distribution bias in connection with the neighborhood, type of family, and the individual.
- No interviewer bias.
- Higher probability of truthful and thoughtful replies.
- Centralized control.
- Potential for greater cost-saving, resulting in more flexibility for the cost.

On the other hand, the use of mail surveys can have limitations. These limitations may include

- No mailing list available for the sample needed.
- Available mailing list is incomplete or biased.
- The subject matter requires a trained interviewer.
- The questionnaire cannot be structured.
- The questionnaire is too long or too difficult.
- The information required is too confidential.
- The available budget is inadequate.
- Not enough time is available to wait for returns.[2]

Whereas the greatest advantages of the mail survey are cost, simplicity of control, and ability to reach specific or dedicated target groups, the greatest weaknesses are response rates and control of the sample. Although acceptable response rates are very achievable, being able to forecast the response rate is quite difficult. Factors that usually serve to influence the rate of response include

- The perceived amount of work or time required to complete the survey, which can relate to the length of the questionnaire and the apparent ease with which it can be completed.

- The basic interest the respondent has in the topic.
- The specific characteristics of the sample.
- The credibility of the sponsoring organization.
- The level of motivation achieved through the cover letter and with any incentives offered.[3]

Nonresponse is a problem because those who respond are likely to differ substantially from those who do not. Improving response rate is one way of dealing with this limitation. Techniques to improve the response rate will be discussed later in this chapter. Creating quota samples and subsamples to compensate for lower response rates that may be anticipated from subgroups known to have lower response rates is a means of dealing with the nonresponse problem by controlling the sample.

DESIGN

Designing a mail survey follows steps similar to that of surveys using other data-collection methods.

- Define the problem and research objectives.
- Conduct a background investigation into existing research on similar topics.
- Determine the parameters of the population to be studied.
- Evaluate the reliability sought versus the budget required.
- Determine the target sample and sampling methodology.
- Develop the research designs required for the results needed.
- Decide on the survey sponsor (i.e., independent research company or the company actually sponsoring the survey).
- Design the questionnaire and cover letter.
- Outline the mailing strategy and schedule required for analysis.

MAILING LISTS AND SAMPLING

A mailing list is required in order to conduct a mail survey. Many different types of mailing lists are available. These include product warranty lists; subscriber (publications, cable TV, newsletters, etc.) lists; records published by federal, state, and municipal governments (homeowners, auto registration, etc.); lists of association members; customer and prospective client lists; a wide variety of lists from various directories; specific lists that can be purchased from list brokers; voter registration lists; lists of key personnel from specific types of institutions; and so forth.

For mail surveys, check the sample and composition of the list from which the sample is being drawn against some known distribution of the universe. A stratified sample selection combined with an analysis that compares key differences in the subgroups evaluated in the survey may be the best way to approach a particular list. For example, conducting a satisfaction survey of cable TV subscribers might require three lists to target: long-term subscribers, new subscribers, and lapsed subscribers.

Creating a sample depends on how large the list is and the estimate of the interest level in the dedicated list. A customer who last used a particular service over a year ago might be somewhat less inclined to ascribe a priority to participating in a survey than one who has used a service four times in the last two months. Without incentives, dedicated lists can result in 25 to 30 percent or higher response rates. Lower levels typically fall in the 5 to 8 percent response rate range. It is usually not wise to overestimate.

In a recent image survey conducted for a nonprofit institution, a comparison was made between core donors, lapsed donors, and new donors. The core donor response rate was significant, while that of lapsed donors and new donors was about one-third of the long-time core donors. The only incentive given was a cover letter that explained how participation in the survey would help improve the effectiveness of the services the organization provided, as well as how they would communicate with their donor public in the future. The client chose not to offer a premium or incentive, which certainly would have increased the response rate. Part of the reason was to maintain consistency with the organization's frugal policy and image. Part of the reason was to maintain anonymity of the respondent.

Small, inexpensive premiums can be included with the survey as an incentive. However, the costs of incentives do not have to become very high before the cost advantage, as well as the simplicity advantage, of conducting a mail survey instead of a telephone survey is negated. By using this particular study as an example (very similar estimates were made prior to this study), the desired sample size for each subsegment (core donors, lapsed donors, new donors) was determined and then the mailing level to each subsegment determined based on those ratios.

Sampling for mail surveys should follow two basic rules: (1) an acceptable selection *procedure* should be used; and (2) when using a simple random sampling method, every unit or subunit targeted in the universe or list should have an equal chance of being selected.

A commonly used procedure for selecting the samples from a list for mail surveys is known as *systematic sample selection*. This typically involves selecting every *n*th name on the list. For example, if the list contains 7,000 names and a mailing of 1,000 is being planned, then every seventh name on the list would be selected. One thing to avoid with lists, however, is starting with the first name and then going to every *n*th name. Statistically this negates the rules of random selection from the list. In this case, a role of the dice could produce a number under seven that would represent equal chance in being selected. Computer-generated random numbers are also available on many programs to initiate the selection process. Obviously, such an approach is inappropriate when using a stratified sample.

QUESTIONNAIRE DESIGN

Several important considerations are involved in the construction of a mail questionnaire. The questionnaire should appear brief and easy to complete. The reader must be made to feel that he or she is participating in an important and interesting project. Questions need to be designed so as not to bias the answers in any way.

Simplicity is a desirable design objective. This involves several dimensions of the mail questionnaire. The format. The readability. The ease of answering questions. The ease of returning the survey. The format should be well laid out and easy to follow. Instructions should be very clear. Questions should be easy to understand without being lengthy. Ideally, the responses to questions should be closed-ended whenever possible. This means possible answers should be well thought out, clear, precise, and made easy to answer by checking a box or circling a number. Some questions might simply need to be asked in an open-ended format, but these should be kept to a minimum.

A good questionnaire always maintains the interest of the respondent. It requires mixing more "interesting" questions throughout and interspersing more sensitive questions throughout the last third of the questionnaire. Once again, the positioning of the questions and keeping the respondent interested is very important and will involve pretesting and refining the questionnaire. The questionnaire should begin with good, clear general instructions and a couple of answered example questions.

The length of the questionnaire in most instances should not exceed six pages. A four-page 8½" × 11" format can be printed on 11" × 17" paper and then folded in the middle to create a questionnaire that is easy to handle and will not result in any lost pages. A six-page format would follow the same first step (11" × 17" folded) as the four-page, but would also have an additional 8½" × 11" page inserted in the middle of the folded 11" × 17". This is not to say an eight-page format would not work. It all depends on who the respondent sample is in relationship to the client conducting the survey and how well the motivating factor of taking the time to fill out the questionnaire is communicated. At some point, the length of the questionnaire begins to strongly affect the level of response rate.

The layout of the questionnaire should be professionally done without looking "slick." This should involve a neat, printed page that is easy to read and appears easy to fill out. The questionnaire should not appear overcrowded. Directions should be made very clear. They should appear in capital letters, parentheses, or even involve a different color. For example, making it very clear whether one or multiple answers are sought in an answer is very important.

The listing of possible replies to a question should be formatted in an orderly fashion that leaves no chance of missing possible answers. For that reason, questions should not be broken up between pages.

When different subgroups of a sample are targeted, questionnaires can be printed in different colors so these groups can be easily identified when they are returned.

An addressed envelope displaying a business reply permit or stamp will have a very positive impact on the response rate. The business reply envelope is generally preferred because, although the amount for the postage is slightly higher than first class postage, you are only paying for the surveys that are being returned.

INCENTIVES

Using incentives will usually increase the response rate, which in turn will enhance the reliability of the survey. Incentives must serve to (1) be effective in increasing the response rate; (2) increase the response rate without biasing the distribution of the returns in any way; (3) reflect a cost that fits in the budget; and (4) should be small and light enough to be mailed easily and inexpensively. Incentives can either be mailed out with the questionnaire or promised as a gift to those answering and returning the questionnaire. Incentives can range from a coin, to a dollar bill, to pens, to small books, and so forth. Money, in most cases, seems to be the most effective and least-biasing incentive, the easiest to mail, and the most useful to all recipients. Money simply is a good attention-getter, especially if it is "new," and neatly and attractively presented.

THE ACCOMPANYING LETTER

The letter can be a part of the questionnaire or a separate cover letter. The letter provides a very important inducement for the respondent to take the time to fill out and return the questionnaire. The accompanying letter should include the following elements:

- Asking of a favor ("Will you help us out?").
- Purpose and importance of the research project.
- Importance of the role the recipient has in the results.
- How the respondent may benefit from the research.
- Completing the questionnaire will take only a short time.
- Ease of answering the questionnaire.
- A stamped or business reply envelope is enclosed.
- Answers are anonymous and confidential.
- How the respondent was selected.
- Urge respondent to fill it out very soon.
- Importance and appreciation of sender and sender's organization.
- Description and purpose of incentive.
- Offer of "summary" of results.
- Style, format, appearance, and brevity.[4]

Not all of these elements are always needed nor can they always be used. Brevity is essential to the cover letter. Exhibit 13.1 is an example of a good cover letter.

MAILING PROCEDURES

The first thing the respondent sees will be the outside envelope. The impression should be given that it contains personal communications that ought to be read. Good-quality paper should be used in the envelope, it should be personally typed, and sent first class. Every appearance of "junk" mail or mass production (such as the use of mailing labels) should be avoided. Dignitaries, clergymen, physicians, persons with doctorates, and so forth, should be addressed appropriately. Full names rather than initials should be used whenever possible.

Follow-up mailings will always increase the response rate, even when the initial mailing produces a high rate of return. Most mail survey samples consist of three primary groups of persons:

- The cooperative group who can always be counted on to help.
- The middle-ground folks, whose interest or schedule makes their return a toss-up.
- Those who typically just do not like to be bothered.

Follow-up mailings are aimed primarily at the second group. The second mailing is a simple nudge and reminder that typically will increase the returns. In most instances, about 90 percent of the returns will be back within two-and-a-half weeks from the time they were initially mailed.

A reminder postcard that is sent out a few days after the first mailing is an effective reminder and incentive to complete the survey. An additional postcard can also be sent out after a couple of weeks.

If respondents are identified or can be deduced from the returns, a second mailing to only nonrespondents will also increase the returns. A second incentive is not necessary, although sending a second questionnaire can prove helpful.

EXHIBIT 13.1. Sample Cover Letter

MAIL SURVEYS INC.
5128 Questionnaire Drive, Suite 730
Response, Colorado 80239

(Date)

Dear Mr. Jones:

Will you help us out?

Filling out the enclosed survey will only take a few minutes of your time and your participation will be very important to the results.

This survey is being conducted nationally among a select list of executives from corporations involved in providing equipment and services to military installations.

The purpose of the research is to make doing business with the federal government easier. Your name and the name of your company were acquired from a random selection of names from a list of military installation suppliers.

All answers are strictly confidential and will be used in combination with the responses from other executives from firms doing business with the Department of Defense to determine ways we can make the procurement process more efficient.

After completing your questionnaire, if you are interested in receiving a summary of the findings, just fill in your name and address on the enclosed card and send it back to us under separate cover. We will be glad to send you this special report when it is completed.

Again, please return the completed questionnaire in the enclosed business reply envelope, if at all possible within the next three days. Thank-you very much for your assistance.

Sincerely,

John B. Smyth, Director

NOTES

1. Wiseman, Frederick. 1972. "Methodological Bias in Public Opinion Surveys," *Public Opinion Quarterly,* spring, pp. 106-108.

2. Erdos, Paul. 1970. *Professional Mail Surveys.* New York: McGraw-Hill, pp. 5-6.

3. Aaker, David and George S. Day. 1980. *Marketing Research: Private and Public Sector Decisions.* New York: John Wiley & Sons, pp. 135-136.

4. Erdos, *Professional Mail Surveys,* pp. 102-103.

Chapter 14

Concept/Product Testing

When all is said and done, a product must be accepted by the consumer in order to be successful. Technology is a wonderful thing, but regardless of how technically advanced or well designed a product is, it must pass the test of consumer trial and repeat purchase. The successful product, then, is the one that has created enough interest for trial and has met needs sufficiently well to become a satisfactory alternative in the marketplace. In order to improve the chances of a product achieving acceptance in the marketplace, a systematic approach to product testing is prudent.

Product testing has several stages. In this chapter we will discuss the following:

- Concept testing
- Developmental testing
- Fit of product/concept
- Testing Techniques

We will then address the testing procedures (i.e., location and methods) that can be used to perform these product tests.

CONCEPT TESTING

Concept testing begins with the generation and screening of ideas. Ideas are generated that will mesh with the existing product lines and will compliment the overall goals of the organization. Once the ideas are developed, screening provides a preliminary evaluation of new products with the objective to identify the most promising ones and eliminate the poorer ideas as quickly and inexpensively as possible. The basic methods of idea generation are:

- Brainstorming
- Focus groups
- Synectics
- Problem detection

Brainstorming dates back to the late 1930s and is popular with many groups for its dynamic, creative atmosphere. Although the format may vary, the groups are normally small working sessions where the objective is to create as many ideas as possible quickly and in a noncritical manner. This approach can produce many ideas in a short period of time, with no guarantee that the ideas will be something that can be commercialized.

Focus groups are used frequently to refine concepts and are sometimes used for idea generation. These groups are sometimes referred to as "ideation" sessions. See Chapter 5 for an extended discussion of how to get the most out of a focus group.

Synectics combines basic problem-solving procedures and group dynamics. Although similar to brainstorming, there are significant differences. Composed of specialists from different disciplines, the group is focused on a structured problem statement and procedure with the goal of combining the best of rational discussion and unbridled creativity.

Problem detection can lead to new product ideas. Problem detection can come from a wide variety of sources. Customer complaints, consumer surveys, R&D, competitive responses, and a myriad of other sources can provide insight into problems and potential solutions to problems. These solutions often lead to new product ideas.

Once ideas are generated, they must be screened and evaluated further. The purpose for screening is to eliminate deficient and/or infeasible ideas due to the high cost and risk associated with developing products. An example of the evaluation process used by a major manufacturer of consumer products is described by Patrick McGuire in his book, *Evaluating New Product Proposals*.[1] That process is summarized below:

1. *Judgmental screening.* All ideas generated must pass through a judgmental screening. Only a few of the several hundred ideas submitted are selected for continuation in the process.

2. *Preliminary consumer reaction tests.* The surviving ideas are submitted to a small sample of consumers to determine their degree of interest. The idea is expressed in a short thirty- to forty-word paragraph concept description and given to the consumers for their reaction.

3. *Preliminary marketing criteria evaluation.* Each idea meeting a basic criterion is evaluated according to salient considerations outlined by management. The remaining ideas must attain a hurdle level rating of criteria such as expected sales volume, product uniqueness, stage of product life cycle, degree of competition, and inherent consumer appeal.

4. *Preliminary feasibility evaluation.* At this stage of the process, the new ideas are assessed by research and development as to their feasibility in manufacturing. Patents are investigated and broad estimates are made of required development time and capital expenditures that might be required.

5. *Preliminary concept test.* As a follow-up to the second step, alternative presentations of the concept are made to focus groups in order to develop a promotional or positioning stance for the product.

6. *Final concept test.* This part of the process presents the concept to consumers in order to identify the characteristics of consumers to whom the product appeals. The information for this phase of the process is normally collected in central location or mall intercept facilities from a relatively large, broad-based sample.

7. *Final marketing potential and feasibility evaluation.* In this phase of the process, a thorough business analysis is accomplished. Refined estimates of price structure, profitability, capital outlays, and return on investment are included. Products that clear this hurdle are passed on to the R&D department to be prepared for further market tests and commercialization.

DEVELOPMENTAL TESTING

A significant amount of research is normally conducted before a product actually goes to product testing. The purpose of this research is to develop ideas and to refine the product to produce the best possible alternatives for ultimate evaluation by consumers. Although this might vary from company to company, this research is usually conducted by the R&D department. Sensory evaluation takes place using small panels of people to test for discrimination and to determine descriptive aspects of the product. Both trained and untrained panel members are used in this developmental testing process. Quite often these panel members are company employees. Because of the controlled nature of the environment, smaller sample sizes are utilized.

The steps that new products normally go through for developmental guidance are:

- *Benchtop analysis*—This consists of evaluations of the product developers while the products are still in the prototype development stage.
- *Expert panels*—In this phase of evaluation, 10 to 20 people who are known discriminators. These panels are used for sensitive tests of discrimination and descriptive analysis.
- *Untrained panels*—These panels consist of 50 to 60 people who are not trained or expert panelists. These panels are used as a prelude to consumer product testing.

FIT OF PRODUCT/CONCEPT

The way a product is positioned makes certain promises and creates specific expectations about how the product will perform. A product should perform in some congruence with its imbued characteristics. In fact, even a good performing product may fail to achieve adequate repeat purchase if expectations are set beyond the product's ability to deliver. A product may achieve a high degree of trial purchase but if its actual performance is not in an acceptable range with product expectations, repeat purchase will suffer. It has been said that Madison Avenue can sell anything to the public. This is doubtful for even the initial trial purchase of a product, but unless a product delivers what is promised, no amount of promotion will induce repeat purchase on a large scale. The process of evaluating and refining the product concept is called product testing for fit to position. This will determine whether the expectations created by the concept are met or not. If not, guidance is given for further optimization of the product.

The purpose of testing the fit of the product and concept is to ensure that the desirable expectations of the concept converge with the performance of the product. If the product is far superior to the concept depicted, trial purchase will suffer. On the other hand, if the product is not as good as expected, consumers may be dissatisfied and not become repeat purchasers.

Product Improvements

In today's competitive world, companies have high interest in doing everything they can to maintain or improve their market share positions. A primary way to accomplish this is to improve their existing products to make them more appealing and better performers in the eyes of consumers. In fact, manufacturers may need to be constantly improving their products just to keep up with competitors who are improving theirs. Improvements of a product by a competitor can have an immediate and substantial loss of share if not countered by comparable improvement of your product.

Product improvement tests are designed to determine if the product changes being contemplated are seen by consumers as actual improvements in the product. The test product is compared with current products that serve as benchmarks. Competitive products may also serve as benchmarks to provide data on the relative appeal of the new product under consideration.

Ideally, a consumer should not only be able to discriminate between products, but prefer the new product. A product improvement test seeks to answer these questions:

- Is the new product perceived as "better than" the current product or a primary competitive product?
- How much better is it? Is it worth the investment required to improve it?
- Why is it better?
- When alternative formulations of the new product are being considered, which test alternative is "best?"
- How does the improved product compare to competitive products?

Specific methodologies for testing products in the product improvement context will be discussed later in the chapter.

Cost Reduction (Profit Improvement)

Although products may be changed and become "new and improved" in order to increase and/or protect market share, an established product also may go through a change in formulation, processing, or ingredient quality in an attempt to reduce the cost of producing the product without introducing a noticeable change among consumers.

Product testing for *product improvement* is focused on determining if customers can distinguish a difference and perceive it as a valued improvement, and product testing for *cost reduction* is essentially just the opposite. Cost-reduction product tests are designed to determine if consumers can discriminate between the new product and current and/or competitive products. In other words, the tests are done to see if consumers believe the new product or formulation is just "as good as" the current product.

Before the consumer-testing stage, the newly reformulated products go through some of the developmental testing procedures already mentioned. This is done with R&D sensory testing panels. This approach narrows down the possible alternatives and provides input to further product development.

Unlike product improvement tests, the ideal outcome for product cost-reduction tests is that consumers *cannot* discriminate between products or may in fact prefer the new one. When this occurs, the change in product can be made with relative confidence that consumers perceive the product at least "as good as" the current product. In this situation, the product can be changed with relative low risk to the franchise. However, risk to the franchise exists if observed differences between the products are substantial. In this case, a decision would have to be made weighing the potential risk of lost sales relative to the benefits of cost savings.

Cost reductions are generally considered in the following situations:

> *Increased cost of raw materials.* If the cost of the raw materials required for production increases causing production costs to exceed acceptable levels, management must decide whether to substitute raw materials and/or reformulate, accept a lower margin on the product, or increase prices. Rather than tamper with margins or prices, often management will direct R&D to experi-

ment with lower-quality ingredients or develop alternative formulations that allow the product to be produced at a lower cost.

Competitors offer lower price products. A strong competitor offering a lower-cost product could result in erosion of the company franchise, or could limit development of market share by lowering trial purchase. The need to reduce the costs of production may be imposed by competitive response. If their current or new products are gaining share due to a price advantage, management may have to change the product price structure to remain competitive.

In both of these cases, the cost-reduction product test will determine if there is risk in making the change (Can consumers discriminate?), and how great is the risk (What percent can discriminate and how different are the products?).

Sampling issues come into play when designing *product improvement* and *profit improvement* studies. These will be discussed later; however, the essential difference is that profit-improvement ("as good as") studies require larger sample sizes because of the importance of ensuring that parity is not declared on insufficient evidence.

Acceptance of New and Established Products versus Competition

As mentioned previously, the competitive environment is dynamic, not static. Manufacturers are constantly introducing new products and, over time, the nature of specific product categories can change dramatically. Consequently, product testing for acceptance of new and established products relative to each other and relative to competition is useful on a periodic basis to provide an assessment of product performance and insight into strategic product planning.

The purpose of acceptance product testing is to determine the satisfaction or dissatisfaction with products available. This assessment of relative performance provides direction for further product refinement or development. The acceptance product test essentially provides information about the relative appeal, acceptance, strengths and weaknesses, and performance attributes of products, both the company's and those of key competitors. Common situations when acceptance testing is required include

- *Introduction of a new product in an old category.* In this instance, the objective is to determine performance strengths and weaknesses of the company's product relative to those it will be directly competing with.
- *Introduction of a new product in a new category.* In a brand new category, no benchmarks exist so comparisons cannot be made to existing products. Consequently, monadic ratings or evaluations are made of several test products to select the alternative with the greatest probability of success.
- *Revision of an existing product in a new category.* Tests may be done comparing the new revision with current, as well as competitive products.
- *Existing products in an old category.* The test in this situation helps assess the strengths and weaknesses of the company product. If weaknesses exist, corrective action and optimization can be initiated. In addition, the results can provide information that will assist in anticipating competitive reaction.

Acceptance product testing helps answer such questions as:

- Which product is preferred?
- How do products differ from one another?
- On what specific performance dimensions do they differ?
- What steps should be taken to improve the product?
- What elements of the product are just right and what elements should be changed?

TESTING TECHNIQUES

We have just discussed a variety of situations in which products should be tested. A product test can be accomplished in many ways, however not all techniques are applicable in every situation. A primary goal of good research is to match the study objectives to the most appropriate research design or technique in order to provide the best possible solution or answer to the research question. Some of the generally accepted product-testing techniques that will be briefly discussed in this chapter include

- Monadic testing
- Paired comparisons, both sequential monadic and side by side

- Balanced incomplete block design
- Discrimination testing, both repeat pairs and triangle tests

Monadic Testing

Monadic simply means a unit or one entity. Monadic tests involve placing only one product with a respondent for evaluation. Typically a respondent is given one product to taste or use either at a central location or in the home. The test closely represents the conditions in which a typical consumer would use the product. After using the product, the respondent answers a series of questions about it. The evaluations are based on the respondent's personal experience with that product and recollection of similar products rather than comparisons with another specific test product. In multiple tests, a different independent group of respondents would try each product being tested. Monadic tests may not detect minor product differences because direct comparison with another product is not made.

Monadic testing is most appropriate when:

- The study objective is to check the acceptability of one product rather than choosing among alternatives.
- The nature of the product makes direct comparison infeasible such as infrequent or very long usage.
- Timing is critical and results are needed immediately.
- Respondent wear out is a major concern.
- A product is so unique that no other products can be compared to it.

The basic advantages of monadic tests include

- More "real world" than direct comparison. Consumers usually try one product at a time and evaluate it in terms of recollection and personal impressions of their current brand.
- Establishes an independent, standard set of evaluation scores that can be compared to scores of other monadically tested products.
- Is unbiased. The monadic method eliminates the danger of order bias and respondent wear out.
- Is quick to execute.
- Is simple, straightforward, and easy to understand.

The monadic approach is not without some disadvantages:

- Requires relatively large sample sizes. This is particularly true when many products need to be tested, since an adequate separate sample is required for each product being tested.
- Is relatively more expensive. Since each respondent evaluates only one product, the large sample sizes translate into higher costs. Since a large portion of research costs are taken in just recruiting participants, using a respondent to test only one alternative is more costly than using one consumer to test several products. This is especially true in low-incidence categories such as expensive imported scotch drinkers.
- No benchmark exists. Products are evaluated based on respondent experience and perception, but no benchmark exists for comparative purposes.

Paired Comparisons

In this type of product test, consumers test two or more products. This can be done sequentially, one after the other, or side by side, with both products being used simultaneously.

The *sequential monadic* approach contains virtues of both the monadic and paired comparison techniques. In this method, consumers test two or more products in a staggered sequence, one at a time. Evaluations can be made at a central location or after in-home use, however usage of the first product is completed before usage of the subsequent product(s) begins. Order bias must be controlled carefully to avoid primacy and recency effects. This is done by rotating comparably first-position evaluations. As a result, the sequential monadic design yields both monadic (first position) and paired comparison information.

For most in-home use tests, consumers receive both products at the same time and they are clearly marked which one is to be used first and which one second. The callback interview will contain a double-check to determine the order in which the products were actually used. In some cases, the first product may be removed before use of the second product begins. This is done by picking the product up or having the respondent mail it. In other situations, respondents use and evaluate the first product before they realize they will be using additional product(s).

Appropriate uses for the sequential monadic method include

- When decisions are being made between test alternatives.
- When evaluations versus competitive products are required.
- When smaller sample sizes are necessary due to cost concerns or product availability.
- If the same consumer must evaluate several alternatives, as in: cost reductions, product improvements, and deciding among new product alternatives.
- If incidence of respondent qualification or usage is very low.
- Wear out is not considered a major factor.

Sequential monadic methods have a number of attractive advantages:

- Cost efficiencies. A major share of the cost of fieldwork is in locating and recruiting the respondent. This type of test takes advantage of the screening already completed and utilizes the respondent to provide information on more than one product. Having each respondent use a second product adds much less to the total costs of the study than doubling sample size.
- Smaller sample sizes. Consumers use both products and sample error is minimized.
- Monadic ratings can still be obtained by looking at each product when evaluated in the first position.
- Position bias and wear out effects, if they exist, can be minimized via appropriation and quantified by looking at ratings of products in first and second position.
- Results are clear-cut and easy to report and understand.

The following are some limitations or disadvantages to the sequential monadic approach:

- May be difficult to administer if many products are tested in pairs versus all other products.
- Order effects may be strong if no major differences in products are found. In other words, if some are very good and some are very poor.

- Wear out could bias results. For example, it may be difficult for one person to taste test a large number of highly seasoned products.
- Less real world. Generally, consumers do not actually use products sequentially and evaluate them in this manner.
- Because direct comparisons are being made, differences may be highlighted that would not occur in the real world.

Another commonly used paired comparison method is the *side-by-side* approach. As with the sequential monadic method, the side-by-side technique allows consumers to test two or more products; however, the usage periods are not separate—they overlap. In this method, both products are used and evaluated simultaneously, allowing for head-to-head comparisons. Evaluations can be made at a central location or in-home.

Not all products can truly be tested side by side. Most consumers do not use one product to clean half of the bathtub and another to clean the other half. Side-by-side product testing generally involves consumers using two or more products over the same time period, even though one may be tried before the other. The most frequent use of side-by-side tests is in a central location taste test.

Side-by-side paired comparisons are applicable in many situations where sequential monadic testing also applies, such as:

- Decisions being made between test alternatives.
- When smaller sample sizes are dictated because of cost constraints or product availability.
- When the same consumer must evaluate several alternatives.
- Incidence of qualification or usage is low.
- Wear out is not a major factor.

The technique is particularly applicable for taste tests and when differences between test alternatives are very minor.

Specific advantages of a side-by-side approach include

- Differences between products are highlighted so this is a very strict, conservative test.
- Effects of some unknown intervening variables are minimized, since both products are used in the same period of time and space by the same respondent.

- Cost-effectiveness. More mileage is achieved from each respondent since he or she tests more than one product.
- Smaller sample sizes may be used because sample error is minimized since consumers use both products.
- Results are clear-cut and usually easy to report and understand.

Disadvantages include

- Differences may be noticed and reported that otherwise may be unnoticed.
- Monadic ratings cannot be obtained by looking at products in the first position.
- Position bias and wear out cannot be measured, since usage overlaps and product-usage positions are not clearly assigned.
- It gets unwieldy if many products are tested in pairs versus all other products.
- Less real world than the monadic approach, since few consumers use products side by side and evaluate them in this manner.

Balanced Incomplete Block Design

The balanced incomplete block (BIB) test design is suitable for taste testing and other situations where a respondent cannot test all products due to physical or other restrictions. The purpose of this technique is to efficiently test a large number of products. The design specifies the order products are to be used in as well as product pairings that each individual respondent should test. The effect of each product on another is controlled for by the design. This is done by "balancing" the positioning of the limited number of products each respondent evaluates and ensuring that each test product is evaluated an equal number of times as well as against other products a comparable number of times.

The most common uses of the BIB technique include central location or in-home product tests in which a large number of products must be evaluated. The basic advantages of the technique include

- Is a good experimental design that controls for the order of product usage and pairings of product evaluation.
- Statistically efficient.

- Controls order and positional bias.
- Flexible and can incorporate almost any number of products into a test such as 3 of 7, 4 of 11, 3 of 19, 6 of 11, etc.
- Makes efficient use of sample size by eliminating need for sufficient number of direct pairings to read. For example, a 2/5 with 120 evaluations of each using BIB requires a sample size of 300 (120 × 5/2). If 120 evaluations of each pair were collected, a sample of 480 would be required. Conversely, the sample of 480, if used in a BIB context, would yield 192 evaluations compared to 120.

Some of the disadvantages of the approach are:

- Although the design will yield more evaluations per a given sample size, it does not yield many direct comparisons on each specific product on a "paired-comparison" basis.
- It may be difficult to execute and may have control problems both at central locations and particularly in an in-home venue.
- The proper use of the method requires the utilization of "blocks" of treatments, and one complete rotation may involve very large sample sizes. Since the design cannot be cut at an arbitrary point without disturbing the "balance" of the design, special care must be taken to establish the exact sample size.

Discrimination Testing

The basic purpose of discrimination testing is to determine if there are differences between specific products. The two most commonly used methods of discrimination testing are repeat pairs and triangular testing.

Repeat pairs testing is designed to measure genuinely perceivable differences between two similar products and to determine which of the two is preferred. The technique measures whether consumers can truly differentiate between two products and when distinguished, which is preferred. The technique is relatively straightforward. Respondents are screened to meet certain qualifications and are then asked to come to a central location. They are given two coded products side by side and asked their preference between them. Then they are given another pair of differently coded products (actually they are the same products) and asked which of this pair they prefer. The test is based on the assumption that if a respondent truly prefers one product over the other he or she should be able to pick that preferred product twice in a row.

Since product preparation may be required, and multiple products coded and served, the prescreened central location is the most common method of fielding a repeat pairs test. Other personal interviewing methods may be used when product preparation is simple or no preparation is required. Door-to-door placement is more costly, since multiple visits are required. In-home testing using this technique may be cumbersome if many products are being tested. For some products mail could be used, but this would require multiple mailings and would be difficult to administer. This type of research cannot be done over the telephone except for the callback portion of an in-home product test.

If the products cannot not be distinguished from one another, in other words if no "true preferences" between products are made, and choices are random, it would be expected the preference would be evenly distributed between the two products. The results would look similar to the following:

First Pair Preference	Second Pair Preference	Percent of Respondents
A	B	25
A	A	25
B	A	25
B	B	25
		100

True preference for each product is measured by the extent to which the proportion of consumers expressing consistent preferences exceeds the number that would be expected to randomly make that choice. Based on the "true preference" assumption, the extent to which the proportion of consumers who express consistent preferences for product A is compared to the proportion of consumers who express consistent preferences for product B.

Repeat pairs testing is especially applicable whenever a researcher wishes to determine consumer preferences between alternatives, such as in:

- Cost reductions, where the ideal outcome is that consumers cannot discriminate between products.
- Product improvements, where the anticipated outcome is that consumers will prefer the improved product.
- Formulation changes, where the desire is to determine which, if any, product is best.

The advantages of the repeat pair test are:

- Is a clean way to measure "true preference" between two similar products.
- Avoids the dilemma of fifty/fifty preference split where it is unclear whether the market is truly bimodal or consumer's preferences are just random.
- Minimizes risk in cost-reduction situations by measuring "true preferences."
- A very logical approach to measuring preference.
- More realistic than triangle testing. People are asked to express "preference" not to just "look for the different product."

The disadvantages of this approach include

- Does not handle large numbers of products well, since the test always has to be conducted in pairs.
- May be difficult for in-home testing of many products, particularly if preparation by the homemaker is desired.
- Is not suitable for products that wear out quickly.
- Some people consider it unconventional, which may make it difficult to understand and promote among product managers.
- Can be costly for certain types of studies.

Triangle discrimination testing is designed to measure whether genuinely perceivable differences exist between two products. Unlike repeat pairs, it is *not* a preference measure. The specific purpose of this technique is to measure whether consumers can truly tell the difference between two products. Triangle tests are often used internally with expert panels. The assumption at this level of testing is made that if experts cannot discriminate, consumers will not be able to either.

On the consumer-testing level, respondents are screened for qualifications and are asked to come to a central location. They are then given three coded products and asked to report which one is different. Two of the products are the same, and the other is indeed different. This test is based on the assumption that if the difference between the products is actually perceivable, consumers will be able to pick out the different product.

Fieldwork for this type of study is usually conducted at a central location, either prerecruited by telephone or intercepted. Other methods such as door-to-door and mail are possible, but each presents special administration problems. Specific procedures for executing this triangle discrimination test, as well as other techniques, will be discussed later in this chapter.

If product differences cannot be perceived by consumers, an expected one-third should choose the "different" product by random choice. True discrimination is defined as the extent to which the proportion of consumers correctly identifying the different product exceeds the 33 percent that is expected to result from random selection.

Common uses of triangle discrimination testing focus on the issue of determining difference, not preference. Situations where the procedure is appropriate include

- Lab tests among expert panels to determine if differences are perceivable. If they are, then further tests with consumers may be contemplated.
- Cost reductions, where the primary concern is whether or not respondents can discriminate. If they cannot, then preference is immaterial.
- Formulation changes, where minor changes are made and the test is conducted as a check that these changes have no noticeable effects on the altered product. The assumption is that a minor change that is not distinguishable will not risk the franchise.

The specific advantages of triangle testing include

- Risk minimization, in cost reduction and reformulations by measuring true discrimination.
- Straightforward and clear way to look for real differences.
- Logical approach to product differentiation.

- Easy to report measure in clear-cut terms.
- Relatively cost-effective.
- Small sample sizes may be used since sample error is minimal.

Although possessing specific strengths, the technique has limitations such as:

- Does not handle a large number of products well, since only two alternatives are compared by a consumer in one testing cycle.
- Can be difficult to administer and even become unwieldy for in-home testing when the product preparation is complex or preparation by the consumer is important.
- Some products are not suitable, such as highly seasoned items that wear out the consumer.
- Considered by some as being "unconventional" and not as readily acceptable as some other techniques.
- Results may not be easy to interpret since either alternative may or may not be acceptable.
- Accentuates differences because consumers may be able to discriminate product differences with this test design that would go unnoticed in the "real world."
- Technique is more "researchy" and less "real world."
- No way to measure order or wear-out.

TESTING PROCEDURES

Most of the testing techniques (concept tests, developmental testing, etc.) can be executed in different venues and procedures. The discussion that follows identifies the most commonly used procedures to accomplish product testing.

Central Location Test (CLT)

Central location product evaluations are used when preparation is not an issue but finished product evaluations are the key measures. Respondents are recruited for CLT work in two primary ways.

- Consumers can be prerecruited, usually by telephone. This allows for more sample control since random-digit telephone interviewing procedures can be utilized. This also allows for utilization of CATI procedures.

- Consumers may be intercepted in an appropriate venue such as a shopping mall. The convenience samples generated by this procedure may or may not be representative. However, if strict screening criteria are used and/or quotas established for key population parameters, the resulting convenience samples can be quite representative.

Whether prerecruited by phone or intercepted, consumers are screened for qualifications to participate in the study. Qualifications for testing products such as food usually include the following criteria:

- *Primary shopper* must be the person who is primarily responsible for buying decisions.
- *Age* generally includes those in the 18 to 65 inclusive range unless the target market requires a more narrow age range.
- *Communication* ability required (i.e., may not have difficulties due to illness, disability, unfamiliarity with English, illiteracy, etc.).
- *Security* check usually includes prohibiting respondent or any member of his or her immediate household working for an advertising agency, market research company or manufacturer, wholesaler or retailer of the product being tested.
- *Past participation* in a marketing research study on a product in the same category in the past three months disqualifies an individual from participation.
- *Category usage* will be based on specific client requirements. If the product is a new, unique product, and/or no similar products are currently on the market, the sample should be drawn from the general population without screening for specific category usage. In cases such as these, defining the category may be difficult. If the product is an existing one or a line extension and it is fairly well-defined, respondents should be further qualified as having used the product in an appropriated time period, usually the past three months. If the product is similar to existing products but is deemed to be appealing to current noncategory users, the opinions of both category users and nonusers should be solicited. This is usually accomplished by obtaining a representa-

tive sample of appropriate shoppers and then screen for additional category users, up to a minimum number considered enough for a "readable" subsample size. This "over-quota" of category users will allow for comparison of the reactions of both current category users and nonusers.

Those who qualify by meeting the predetermined qualifications are asked to participate in the study. Those who agree see the concept, answer questions about it, and then are given products prepared by company personnel, trained technicians, or home economists. On occasion, consumers may prepare the product at the central location themselves, if preparation is very easy.

Since the objectives may vary depending on whether the test is a fit of product and concept, product improvement, cost reduction/profit improvement, or acceptance of new and established products versus competition, questions will vary to reflect these differences.

Fit of Product and Concept

Since the objective is to determine what expectations were created and if they were met or exceeded, the respondents are shown the concept and asked questions about it. In addition, they use the product and respond to a questionnaire designed to evaluate the product based on actual experience with it. Comparisons between how the product was expected to perform and how it actually performed constitute the evaluation for fit. Products are served using monadic or sequential monadic test plans. Side-by-side paired comparisons and discrimination tests are not applicable. Comparisons being made by respondents are from concept to product and vice versa, not between products.

Product Improvement

Since the objective is to determine which, if any, product consumers prefer over another, a repeat pairs testing is often used in these situations. Other techniques that could be used are sequential monadic, side-by-side comparison, and BIB design. Monadic testing could be used in some situations but would require larger sample sizes. Triangle discrimination is not applicable since it is a measure of difference, not preference. Once the consumers are qualified, they are seated at an interviewing station and are served products in proper order and/or pairings. They fill out a self-administered or interviewer-administered questionnaire about the product. In some cases the survey is administered with the use of a personal computer.

Cost Reduction/Profit Improvement

Since the objective is to determine if consumers can, in fact, discriminate between products, repeat pairs testing or triangle discrimination tests are specifically designed for this situation. Other techniques that could be used are sequential monadic, side-by-side comparison, BIB, and monadic testing. (Monadic testing would require very large sample sizes.) After qualification, the consumers are seated in an interviewing station and are served products in the proper order and/or pairings. The survey is administered as mentioned for product improvements.

Acceptance of New and Established Products versus Competition

Since the objective is to determine how products compare to one another and identify areas of concern or benefit, product testing is usually done on a paired comparison basis, using either sequential monadic or side-by-side tests. Monadic tests are acceptable if a benchmark for comparison is provided. Discrimination testing techniques are not appropriate.

In-Home Usage

In-home usage product evaluations are generally used if preparation of the product, use in a "real world" situation, or use by multiple family members, are important factors. Consumers generally are recruited in the same way as previously discussed in the central location test section. Consumers then are given one or two products to use in their homes over a specified period of time. After usage, consumers are usually contacted by telephone to evaluate the products. In some cases the recontact is made by mail or in person. Attention to the specific research objectives of the type of product being tested must be given to fit the technique to the research need as discussed in the central location section.

Sampling Considerations

In general, the sample for these product tests should be drawn from a minimum of three cities or regions. When usage of or interest in a product is known or expected to vary greatly by geographic region, additional sample elements should be added to fill out the geographic areas. Respondents are to be recruited from the general population (i.e., through shopping mall or grocery store intercept, over the telephone, door-to-door, or mail). Since the primary purpose is to get a representative sample of category users, using customer lists/organization lists are acceptable with the proper controls and restrictions.

Most of these tests use a minimum sample size of 120 per product while some major companies want between 150 to 180 respondents per product/product pair. Specific decision rules and sample sizes can be calculated to accommodate various levels of risk as defined by levels of confidence and statistical power (see Appendix D). If respondents are prerecruited and/or there is a home-use test, respondents must be overscheduled by at least 20 percent to ensure that the right final sample size will be acquired.

OTHER CONSIDERATIONS

Usage Period Criteria

One of the primary considerations for the appropriate usage period is its *length*. The major issues to be considered in determining length are:

- *Freshness dates.* If a product has limited shelf life, usage periods may have to be chosen to reflect this.
- *Seasonality of product.* If the product is used at certain times of the year, such as eggnog, or only on certain days of the week, the usage period must allow for the unique product-usage patterns.
- *Flexibility of product.* Multiple-use products, such as ketchup, generally require longer trial periods to allow for the product to be used in several ways. Single-use items, such as coffeepot filters, need only be used once or twice since all uses are alike.
- *Usage occasions.* Multiple occasions should be taken into consideration. Although the product is used for the same basic pur-

pose (e.g., dishwashing detergent), it may perform differently under various usage occasions (lunch dishes versus dinner pots and pans). Usage periods must be sufficient to allow for multiple uses on different occasions. Single-occasion products may only require one usage cycle.

- *Amount of product to be placed.* Consideration must be given to how much of the product is available to be placed, the amount that is normally purchased, and the size of the household.
- *Normal usage rate.* Consider the normal rate at which products are used, including the frequency of use.
- *Timing.* Care should be taken to avoid a time period that includes unusual calendar events such as national or religious holidays where usage may be atypical.

In home-use testing, the usage period may either be *limited* or *extended*. Limited use (1 to 7 days) is most appropriate if:

- The product has limited shelf life.
- Usage is seasonal.
- The product is used primarily for one purpose.
- The product is readily available.
- Usage is fairly frequent and rate of use is high.
- Timing is tight and fielding needs to be completed before a holiday or to meet a deadline.
- The package contains enough product for only one use.

The basic advantages of a limited usage period are:

- Data collected may be of higher quality, since memory is not relied on so heavily.
- More control over the test situation with a shorter test period, uncontrolled variables are less likely to intervene and skew results.
- The study is completed in less time.
- More "real world" for some products or categories.

The disadvantages are:

- Evaluations are based on limited product experiences, in some cases only one usage situation.

- Some aspects are not evaluated, such as freshness over time, storage, etc.
- May unfairly highlight product differences which, over time or in the "real world," would not be noticed.

The extended-usage period approach is most applicable in the following situations:

- Products are shelf-stable.
- Seasonality of usage is *not* a concern.
- The product has multiple uses.
- The product has a basic function, but may perform differently under various conditions or circumstances.
- Sufficient products are available.
- Normal usage rate and/or frequency of use are low.
- Usage will not overlap any holiday or unique market periods.
- The package contains enough products for an extended-usage period.

The primary advantages of the extended-usage approach are:

- Evaluations are based on more extensive product experience, including various usage situations and over time.
- Additional product characteristics such as freshness, storage, etc., can be evaluated.
- More "real world" for some products. Less danger of biasing responses by requiring usage of test products at higher frequency rate than usual.

Disadvantages of the extended-usage period are:

- Relies more heavily on memory, especially if callback interview is completed at the end of the usage period.
- May minimize product differences since so much time passes from use to use.
- Uncontrolled variables are more likely to bias results. If an extended-usage period is allowed, the consumer may be sensitized to the category, be more receptive to information, or be exposed to information or change his or her opinion between the time he

or she begins using the first and second products. This means the fieldwork takes longer to complete, delaying results.

Brand Identification

Another issue in designing product use tests is whether to actually name the product or not. Product tests may be conducted with (branded) or without (blind) brand identification. In either case, product labeling requirements must be met in terms of ingredient lists, etc.

The *branded* approach to product testing is most appropriate for product tests when:

- The brand name of the product is well-known.
- The objective of the research is to measure consumer's perceptions of products, including competitive products.
- The product is unique or distinctive.

Advantages of the branded approach are:

- Is more "real world" because most products (excluding generics) carry a brand name and are evaluated in combination with a brand name.
- Allows the manufacturer to take advantage of the power of a good brand name.

A disadvantage is that the brand could contaminate product evaluations if effect of brand name is unknown or uncontrolled.

A *blind* approach to product testing is best applied when:

- Brand name is unknown, as with a new product that could be under an umbrella or carry its own brand name.
- Any time the chance that the brand name may alter product perceptions and the research objective is to measure real product differences causes concern.
- The primary objective is to measure product differences such as cost reductions, reformulations.

When testing blind, products are identified by product name or code letters only, not brand. Specific advantages of blind or unbranded testing are:

- Elimination of brand reduces the number of variables that could have unknown effects.
- Blind tests allow comparison of actual product differences, not perceptions of them.

Disadvantages include

- Is less "real world" since, in the marketplace, brand and product do interact.
- Brand sometimes has a powerful effect. Testing without brand, when the brand has a very strong reputation, subjects the product to a more stringent test than will occur in the marketplace. The danger of killing a new product could succeed if identified by the popular brand name. On the other hand, the New Coke case study vividly illustrates what can happen when extensive blind taste tests on a marketing icon are done and radical marketing decisions are made on the results without factoring in the brand influences.

Usage Situations

The two primary usage situations that are appropriate for product testing are *in-home testing* and *central location testing*. The in-home method is commonly used. With this type of product testing, the consumer is given the product to use in his or her home over a specified period of time. If more than one product is placed, they are placed simultaneously and each is clearly marked "use first" and "use second." Generally a letter is included with the test product. The letter thanks the consumer for participation and lays out the test rules. It should include

- Assurance of product quality.
- Explanation to use the product as respondent normally would.
- Statement that the respondent must prepare and eat some of the product personally.

- Statement about the timing of usage period (i.e., use over the next six or seven days).
- Approximate date of the callback if telephone or in person, or, requested mailback date for mail panels.
- Name and phone number of a contact person at the field agency, in case there are any questions.

The respondent prepares the product or products over the specified time period, evaluates the product(s), and reports the information when recontacted by phone, in person, or by mail.

The in-home approach to product testing is most effective when:

- Preparation of the product is an important element. This includes situations when the product is difficult to prepare, can be fixed several different ways, is used as an ingredient in other food items, or performs differently under different conditions or usage situations.
- Labeling requirements do not disclose any information about the product that may bias responses.
- Instructions are being tested for clarity or understanding.
- Product is used by other family members and their opinions will affect the purchase decision.
- Product has multiple uses that could not be replicated in a central location.
- A more thorough evaluation of the product under varying conditions is required.
- Product shelf life or storage are issues. If the product changes over time and usage, or requires storage, in-home testing provides a better testing situation.

The advantages of in-home testing are:

- Is more "real world" because the consumer evaluates the product as it will actually perform in the household.
- Other family members get to use/taste the product and can express their opinions.
- Comprehensive evaluations can be obtained about various aspects of the product, including packaging, shelf life, storage, etc.

The disadvantages are:

- Less control over the preparing/testing situation.
- Not as immediate; more time is required to obtain results.
- Overplacement is required since not all respondents who take home a product can be reached to complete evaluations. As a result, nonresponse bias could occur.
- Complete labeling is required, so consumers will know differences in ingredients.
- Evaluations depend on respondent's memory.

The central location method of product testing is also commonly used. With this type of test, consumers test the product at a central location, not in their homes. This can be done either on a prerecruited basis, or in a store or a mall intercept. All testing is conducted on the location and evaluation results are obtained immediately.

Food product is usually prepared by field services or company technicians or home economists and served to the respondents, one at a time, for their evaluations. In some instances, the consumer may open and prepare the product personally, in order to gain additional product exposure.

The occasions when a central location test is most appropriate are:

- Product evaluation is the key objective and only a few measurements are taken.
- Preparation is relatively easy and does not vary much from usage to usage. An example would be frozen entrees. Conversely, if preparation is complex, company personnel or a home economist should be involved.
- Product is consumed or used by itself, not as an ingredient in preparing other products.
- Labeling requirement would disclose information about the product that may bias responses.
- Shelf life or storage is not an issue; in other words, the product is shelf stable and one package contains product for only one usage.
- The consumer's evaluations are the key issue, and opinions of other family members are not required.
- Many products are to be tested.

- Incidence of qualification is low and screening is done by telephone.

Advantages of central location testing are:

- Good control over the test since all products are prepared and tested under the same, controlled situations.
- Evaluations are obtained immediately at the time of usage.
- Consumer's knowledge of the product is limited to what they are told, so ingredient changes can be disguised.
- Consumer's knowledge of the product can be controlled through progressive disclosure of product features.
- Less costly than door-to-door placement.
- Exhibits, videotapes, or displays can be used.
- Placement interview can be longer and include more information.
- Sample can be more representative than one drawn door-to-door.

The primary disadvantages of the central location method are:

- Less "real world" than in-home testing since someone else prepares and serves the product, making it more "researchy."
- Evaluations are limited to a specific situation, so are less comprehensive and not technically projectable to other situations.
- Other members of the family do not get an opportunity to evaluate the product.

Number of Callbacks

Another consideration for designing an in-home product test concerns the appropriate number of callbacks. In most sequential monadic product tests, *one* callback is conducted after both products have been used. No questions are asked about any product until all products have been used.

In some cases, however, a callback may be made after each product has been used. Consumers are asked to evaluate the first product before the second one is used. If the callback is personal, this allows the interviewer to remove the first product.

One Callback

A one-callback design will be used in almost all sequential monadic product testing situations. The advantages of one callback are:

- No danger of contamination of data due to "education" of the respondent. The concern here is that the questions asked on the first callback may teach the respondent how to use and evaluate the second product.
- May be more "real world" since consumers rely on their memories of product performance in making actual purchase decisions.
- Less expensive than conducting two callbacks. The amount of savings varies by method of interviewing. Largest savings will be realized with personal interviewing, and the smallest with mail recontacts.

The disadvantages include

- Potential loss or contamination of data due to confusion over which product performed in what way.
- Relies heavily on respondent's memory since evaluations are often made of usage experiences many days in the past.
- Product differences may be minimized since respondents may not be able to read small differences.
- If test product is used many times over the test period, the respondent is asked to summarize reactions and there may be some hazing or carryover.
- Questionnaire must be shorter. Since one callback is being conducted, not as much detailed information can be obtained about each product.
- No monadic ratings can be obtained or analyzed separately.
- First product may be removed and second product delivered if callbacks/recontacts are personal. This would minimize risk of confusion or product usage out of order. Obviously, this cannot be done with one callback.

Two Callbacks

A callback after each product test is rarely used. One possible application would be when wear out is a potential concern, but is not known to exist. By conducting a callback after the first product is used, the monadic evaluations are preserved and comparisons can be made by position.

Advantages of multiple callbacks include

- Evaluations are obtained immediately after each product is used.
- Memory failure is less of a problem.
- Monadic ratings are obtained on each product with 50 percent of the sample (assuming balanced rotation).
- More detailed information can be gathered about each product.
- Use of a test plan and looking at monadic ratings can control for position bias.

Disadvantages of multiple callbacks include

- "Education" of the respondent by participating in the first callback may contaminate data collected at the second callback.
- Effect of position bias may be higher.
- Less "real world," more "researchy."
- More costly than conducting one callback.

Placement Issues

Product tests involve placement/usage and evaluation. At central location tests, all of these are conducted at the same time and place, but for in-home tests they are separate. The basic methods of gathering data in product tests are:

1. Mail
2. Personal
   a. Door-to-door
   b. Intercepts
   c. Prerecruited central locations
3. By telephone
4. Weighted purchase intent

The following section will give an overview of the usage applications of each as well as their advantages and disadvantages. Each method will be evaluated in terms of its use for placement and callbacks.

Mail Techniques

Mail placements are frequently used for placing products. A delivery service can also be used. This may be done through a mail panel organization, unannounced (through a mass mailout, product drop, or using lists), and on a prescreened basis to specific consumers who have agreed to participate. Mail placements are best utilized when:

- The product is shelf stable, does not require special handling or storage, and is small enough and/or light enough to be deliverable.
- When budgets are limited, this may be a cost-effective way to test certain products.
- A national sample or one including hard-to-reach respondents is required.
- No exhibits or a limited number of exhibits are necessary.
- Tight timing is *not* necessary.

Unannounced mailouts are used when category usage is not an issue, or incidence is very high. In these cases screening for usage is not necessary. *Prescreened mailouts* are used when usage screening is important, incidence of usage is lower, or when the product is more expensive.

The advantages of mail or delivery service placement are:

- Less expensive. Mail is usually an inexpensive way of distributing product.
- Larger samples. Large samples can be drawn covering wide areas and including hard-to-reach respondents.

Disadvantages are:

- Loss of control over who receives and uses the product.
- Product may be lost or damaged in shipment.

- Not suitable for many products, such as frozen food or large products.
- A great deal of product must be distributed to get a sufficient number of evaluations.

Mail callbacks/evaluations may also be used in product testing. After product placement, mail may be used to gather consumer opinions of the products tested. A questionnaire is included with the product, or is mailed out as a follow up.

Mail is most efficiently used to obtain evaluations when:

- Questions asked are relatively straightforward, easy to understand, and follow.
- Timing is *not* critical.
- Budgets are limited.

The specific advantages include

- Less expensive way to obtain responses.
- Large samples can be utilized with relative efficiencies.
- Sample can include geographically dispersed and hard-to-reach people.
- No interviewer bias exists since no interviewer is employed.
- Some simple exhibits can be used.

Disadvantages include

- Poor control over who completes the questionnaire, and under what conditions.
- Questionnaire must be pretty basic and includes no clarification of confusing questions or open-ended questions.
- The fielding portion of the study takes weeks longer.
- Pretesting takes as long as a complete study.
- Nonresponse bias could be a problem. Low return rates are common except with a mail panel organization. Return rates as low as 10 to 20 percent can be expected for a mass mailing, but mail panels yield up to a 75 percent return.
- Low return rate requires that more products be distributed to obtain adequate number of evaluations.

- Sample is not truly representative.
- Mail panel respondents may be biased because of previous exposure to other products and caution should be taken when using them.

Personal Techniques

Personal interviewing is appropriate for almost every type of research study. If costs were not a major concern, personal interviewing could be used for both product placements and callbacks. Personal interviewing may be done door-to-door, as intercepts, or at central locations on a prerecruited basis.

Door-to-door placements are particularly appropriate when:

- The product requires special handling, is perishable or non-mailable.
- Exhibits are used.
- Incidence of qualification is fairly large (50 percent or more).
- Attitudinal information is required before the usage period.
- Observations are required of actual consumer behavior, such as handling or opening the package.
- Timing is important and the extra couple of weeks for mail panel interviewing is unacceptable.
- Sample requirements are stringent. If the sample must be a random one, including numerous sampling points, and interviews cannot be done by telephone, door-to-door interviewing is the alternative.
- Target group of consumers in identified and cannot be reached using other personal methods such as Hispanic housewives.

The advantages of door-to-door placement are:

- Flexibility. Almost anything can be done, with greater latitude in questionnaire length and format.
- Questionnaire can include more detailed questions. Responses can be probed and open-ended questions clarified.
- Exhibits can be used with ease.
- Observations can be made of actual behavior, instead of respondent's report of behavior such as the difficulty of opening the package.

- Sample can be more representative. In theory, a random sample of dwelling units can be drawn, but is not very practical.
- Convenience. Since the respondents are in their home, they can usually participate with little inconvenience.
- Perishable products need not leave refrigeration, since coolers can be used by interviewers.
- Timing. A study can be executed in a shorter period of time using simultaneous placement in several markets.

Disadvantages of door-to-door placement are:

- Cost. The major drawback of door-to-door interviewing is high cost. Costs often reach several times as much per interview as phone or mall research and much more than mail research.
- Sample. In practice, obtaining a truly representative sample door-to-door is difficult and it cannot be nationally representative.
- Execution of door-to-door studies often creates problems because of sampling points in unsafe neighborhoods, necessity to interview nights and weekends because of the high percentage of working women, and necessity of making numerous callback attempts due to respondents being unavailable.
- Supervision. It is difficult to directly supervise door-to-door since interviewers are largely on their own in sample neighborhoods.
- Product may be difficult to carry and store.

Door-to-Door Callbacks. If products are placed by door-to-door interviewing, callbacks are usually conducted in the same way, since there are cost efficiencies involved because sample households are already identified. If paired comparisons are being used and only one product was left at placement, then the callback doubles as placement of the second product and removal of the first. This technique is seldom used. Other occasions when door-to-door placements might be advisable include when exhibits are used, when observations of consumer behavior are required, or when the rate of use is being measured.

The advantages of this approach to callbacks include

- Flexibility, greater latitude in questionnaire length and format is provided, questionnaire can include more detailed questions.
- The respondents' questions about the test and the questionnaire can be immediately cleared up and open-ended questions clarified.

- Exhibits can be easily used.
- Observations can be made of actual behavior instead of respondents simply reporting their behavior.
- Rates of usage can be measured by observing the amount of the product used.
- The danger of misusing products is minimized.
- Respondent is expecting the interviewer, since an appointment is made.
- Is convenient for the respondent.

Disadvantages include

- Executional problems that occur when respondents are not home for their appointments and multiple attempts are necessary to complete the interview.
- Evening and weekend interviewing is costly and may be unsafe.
- Difficulty providing supervision.
- The product may be difficult to carry and/or store.
- The method is generally more expensive to execute than alternatives.

Intercepts

Placements. Intercepts for placements are very common and flexible. The intercept approach can be used for about any type of qualification criteria for low incidence to universal. The method is particularly suitable when the placement interview is fairly short (less than fifteen minutes). Intercepts are also very appropriate when large sample sizes are required and a good geographical representation is needed. Also, when the product in question is nonperishable or can be out of refrigeration for short times. Sometimes a research situation calls for a personal callback, but incidence of qualification is too low to permit door-to-door interviewing, but is high enough to make a mall intercept feasible. Other circumstances that may help dictate an intercept placement are when exhibits or displays are required, attitudinal information is needed before the usage period, observations are required of actual consumer behavior, and fast turnaround is essential.

The specific advantages of intercept placements are numerous and cost is a major factor. Intercepts are usually much less expensive than door-to-door or prerecruited central location placements. As a guideline, mall intercepts are usually more cost efficient than prerecruited central location sampling for incidence levels as low as 5 to 10 percent. Another advantage is control. The intercept format allows for direct supervision of the interviewing process. Malls contain a variety of stores that draw from many different groups of consumers so the sample venue generally provides a good cross section of respondents. In addition, a large number of consumers can be screened for participation in a survey in a short period of time. Another advantage is that there is a large network of field service organizations throughout the country that provide trained interviewing staff, PC (personal computer) interviewing capabilities, food preparation kitchens, and professional supervision.

The primary disadvantages of the method are:

- Sampling generally is not as representative as a properly executed door-to-door study and definitely is not as representative as a telephone study.
- Interview length is somewhat limited in an intercept situation. In malls, the interview should not exceed twenty minutes and should be not much longer than eight minutes in a grocery store.
- The product may not be compatible to this type of interviewing/placement.
- Some malls are overused and many consumers refuse to be interviewed.

Callbacks. As a general rule intercepts are not used as callbacks. However, in some circumstances they may be appropriate. If only one callback is required, the shopping mall is frequently visited by area residents, or the respondents are given an incentive to return on a specific day.

The limited advantages of an intercept callback are:

- It may be less expensive than door-to-door callbacks.
- Exhibits or displays may be used.
- Supervision is easily provided.
- Quotas can be easily watched and controlled.
- Reminder calls can be used to measure response rate.

On the other hand, the disadvantages of intercept callbacks include

- High dropout rate (many will not return requiring a large over-placement, often 30 percent or more).
- Difficulty in controlling usage period.
- Nonresponse bias.
- High refusal rate.
- Its perception and reality of being inconvenient to many consumers.

Prerecruited Central Locations

Placement and Evaluation. The prerecruited central location approach is suitable when the product preparation is complicated or requires a lot of time. If multiple products are being tested and the test plan is rather complicated, a prerecruit to a central location is a good idea. Other circumstances that make this method appropriate include: the objective is to test for discrimination; incidence of qualification is fairly low; timing is important and fieldwork must be completed in a short period of time; special equipment or lighting is needed; interview is lengthy (more than twenty minutes); the product is shelf stable; labeling information would bias the respondent; the product is used by itself rather than as an ingredient; and preparation is not an issue.

The advantages of such an approach are:

- Fieldwork can be completed quickly.
- Exhibits or displays can be used.
- Questionnaires can be longer with more detailed evaluations.
- Sample controls for usage can be included.
- A controlled testing environment is provided.
- The consumers' knowledge of the product is limited to what they are told.
- And multiple alternatives can be tested quickly.

The disadvantages of prerecruited placement include

- It requires payment of an incentive.
- Is less "real world" than in-home usage.
- Evaluations are limited to specific situations.
- Respondents are the only product evaluators.
- The cost is higher than intercepts and much higher than mail studies.

If consumers are coming to a central location to pick up the product for a placement only, it is much more cost efficient to have them use the product(s) and evaluate them at the same time. Having consumers come in just to pick up the product(s) and take it home for use is probably more expensive than conducting a prerecruited central location product test. However, at very low incidence rates, this method may be less expensive than placing products through a mall intercept.

Callbacks. Prerecruited callbacks are used only on very rare occasions. However, sometimes placement may be made for in-home usage and consumers may be asked to return to a central location to report product evaluations. Situations that dictate this response are when large displays, videocassettes, or other exhibits need to be used at the time of the callback evaluation, and when consumers are required to use the product to make something and bring in the results for evaluation.

Advantages of this method are:

- It allows for home use.
- Exhibits can be used.
- Interviews can be lengthy.
- Actual product results can be seen and evaluated.
- If participants are geographically dispersed, it could be a cost-effective way to obtain evaluations.

Disadvantages include

- It is more costly than central location tests with evaluations done immediately.
- Incentives must be given for people to come in.
- Is impractical since more efficient ways are available to complete entire interviews at one time.

Telephone Recruiting

Placements

Telephone recruiting for placements is very appropriate when incidence of qualification is low, sample needs to be drawn from numerous geographically diverse locations, product testing will be conducted at a central location or products can be mailed or delivered by field service agencies, lists of names of potential respondents are provided, and when no exhibits are used in the placement interview.

The basic advantages of this approach are:

- Is an inexpensive way to locate and recruit respondents when incidence is low.
- Control and supervision of screening can be provided.
- Sampling is very flexible (samples of neighborhoods, Standard Metropolitan Statistical Areas [SMSAs].
- Sales districts or national random digits can be used).
- Hard-to-reach respondents can be included.
- Is not dependent on weather.
- Timing is quick.

Disadvantages of telephone recruiting for placements are:

- Is less personal than face-to-face.
- Respondents may not be familiar with market research or may be skeptical and refuse to participate.
- Interviews must be fairly short.
- No exhibits can be used.
- Certain questions such as those using lengthy scales cannot be administered over the phone.

Callbacks

The telephone is used to complete callback evaluation interviews when the sample is geographically dispersed, no exhibits are necessary, questionnaires are short, and timing is critical. This inexpensive way to obtain consumer opinions has the same advantages and disadvantages that telephone contact for placement has.

Weighted Purchase Intent

The weighted purchase intention scale has been used for several decades as a way to estimate penetration for a concept in the early idea phase of product development and on the simulated test-market basis. The penetration estimate is based on the combination of a weighted sum of the five-point purchase intention scale combined with a frequency of purchase estimate and other promotion and distribution assumptions. Several models such as BASES, ASSESSOR, and others are available from specific market research firms.

SUMMARY

Product testing can be some of the most important market research conducted by a company in the highly competitive environment facing firms at the end of the decade. Sequentially, such testing follows the stages of product development including concept testing, development testing, fit of product/concept, and testing of the product with consumers. Techniques used in testing the product with consumers include monadic tests, paired comparisons, BIB design, repeated or double pairs and triangle tests, each with their own strengths and weaknesses. Such tests can be performed in two basic settings: central location and in-home tests. Numerous decisions that must be made regarding the execution of product tests in these locations were discussed.

NOTE

1. McGuire, E. Patrick. 1973. *Evaluating New Product Proposals*. New York: Conference Board.

Appendix A

Sample Research Proposals

SAMPLE 1

*Market-Penetration Study
for Planetary-Gear-Set-Driven Products*

*Proposal Submitted to Sherwood Winch Company
St. Louis, Missouri**

January 2006

Background

Sherwood Winch Company is conducting the strategic planning necessary to evaluate opportunities within markets that have or will be developing a demand for planetary-gear-set-driven product lines. The specific purpose of this study is to identify the markets or market segments that currently are unserved or are marginally served *and* which provide the existing or potential demand for a new supplier of a specific planetary-gear-set-driven product line.

Strong growth in energy and mineral markets underpinned the success of the largest construction contractors in 2005. Construction firms in the United States alone reported the dollar sales for contracts signed in 2005 were 25 percent over the performance for 2004. The strongest growth was realized in the oil, gas, and energy-related fields, with mining, marine, public works, and defense projects showing excellent growth potential for the near term. Because of intense competition from the continual introduction of new, more efficient lines of equipment from suppliers serving these markets, it is imperative to have the most accurate and timely feedback of the tempo, trends, and requirements of this dynamic marketplace. Greater demands being placed on the contractors, along with increased reliance on technology advances, make it necessary for the successful suppliers of the

---

*Names, dates, and locations have been changed in this sample proposal.

future to be the initiator and formulator of the needs of the marketplace, based on a clear understanding of emerging needs and trends.

Sherwood Winch Company, for some time, has been aware of the potential for gear sets that provide a greater efficiency and permit continuous duty usage. Central to the purpose of this study will be obtaining firsthand knowledge from key user firms of the design characteristics required for known market usages of planetary-gear sets.

The *goal of Sherwood Winch Company,* therefore, is to *set the pace* with planetary-gear-driven products that industry now requires, but with which it is not presently adequately supplied. Because of the importance of market data to strategic planning, it is necessary to prepare a reliable forecast of this fast evolving technology-oriented industry. The proposed study will concentrate on providing a comprehensive background of customer and competitor dynamics from which to evaluate future market penetration strategies for Sherwood Winch Company.

Scope and Methodology

To achieve the optimal results from the planetary-gear-products market penetration program, a two-phase study is recommended. Each phase would incorporate a different approach and methodology. This twofold approach is designed to maximize the quality and depth of the results while minimizing the variable cost to Sherwood Winch Company.

Phase I results will be based on interviews with a select and carefully designed sample of decision makers from OEM's (original equipment manufacturers) and end users. After identifying firms and decision makers whose viewpoints will provide a variety of perspectives on the planetary-gear products business the first phase will feature open-ended discussions with these decision makers. These discussions will build on and be tailored toward the individual expertise of the person interviewed as well as his or her firm's perspective and sector of industry. This *first phase* then will serve to *identify the market alternatives* that might or could be expected for planetary-gear products usage and to determine agreement for the market trends expected by this select sample of decision makers. Phase I, therefore, will be *qualitative in thrust* and based on 40 personal interviews.

Phase II will be based on the foundation built in Phase I. Phase II, however, will sample a wide variety of OEM's and end users *and* potential end users to further explore market opportunities and *quantify* existing market dynamics for planetary product requirements. But more important, it would provide a complement to and expansion of the perspective gained from Phase I in determining the trends to be expected in the future. By utilizing the appropriate statistical techniques, factors will be identified that underlie the pulse and direction of the marketplace as it now is, *and* which form the basis of the marketplace trends and marketing appeals that can be expected to emerge in the future. Phase II will be based on a carefully drawn sample of 300 interviews that will focus on each subsector of industry being examined. Phase II will result in the detailed analysis that will satisfy the study objectives of this market-penetration program.

Planetary Products Market-Penetration Program
Study Objective

The objectives of the market research to be done for the planetary-gear products market-penetration program are suggested as follows:

I. Determine market size by number of units of planetary-gear-driven products for 1998-2005:
   A. Market segments:
      1. Excavators:
         a. planetary swing (upper) drives
         b. crawler-track drives
      2. Log loaders and other logging equipment:
         a. planetary crawler-track drives
         b. swing (upper) drives
         c. planetary winches
         d. planetary-gear speed reducers for winch drives in lieu of complete winches
      3. Mobile cranes:
         a. planetary-gear winches
         b. swing (upper) drives
         c. crawler-track drives
         d. speed reducers for winch drives in lieu of complete winches
      4. Truck cranes:
         a. planetary-gear winches
         b. planetary-gear (upper) swing drives
         c. speed reducers for winch drives in lieu of complete winches
      5. Pedestal cranes:
         a. planetary-gear winches
         b. swing (upper) drives
         c. speed reducers for winch drives in lieu of complete winches
      6. Compactors:
         a. planetary crawler-track drives
         b. swing (upper) drives
         c. planetary winches

7. Blast hole drills:
   a. planetary crawler-track drives
   b. swing (upper) drives
   c. planetary winches
8. Paving machines:
   a. planetary crawler-track drives
   b. speed reducers
9. Offshore (jack-up) drilling platforms:
   a. planetary speed reducers
   b. independent winches
10. Fishing boats:
    a. planetary winches
    b. speed reducers
11. Workboats:
    a. planetary winches
    b. speed reducers

B. Planetary product specifications (product sizes):
   1. Excavator swing (upper) drives and other speed reducers used in high-shock applications: 3,500 ft. lbs. to 16,000 ft. lbs.:
      a. indicate top four to five categories
   2. Crane (upper) swing drives: 6,000 ft. lbs. to 24,000 ft. lbs. (non–high-shock applications):
      a. top four to five categories
   3. Track drives ("propel boxes"): 7,000 ft. lbs. to 32,000 ft. lbs.:
      a. top four to five categories
   4. Speed reducers: 6,000 ft. lbs. to 24,000 ft. lbs. (non–high-shock applications):
      a. top four to five categories
   5. Determine design (safety) factor for each application

II. Determine major customers for each product category: ·
   A. Planetary-gear winches
   B. Planetary-gear speed reducers for winch drives and drives for offshore (jack-up) platforms
   C. Planetary-gear (upper) swing drives on cranes
   D. Planetary-gear crawler-track drives

III. Identify major competitors and relative market share (to include self-manufacturers):
   A. For product categories:
      1. Planetary-gear winches
      2. Planetary-gear speed reducers for winch drives and drives for offshore (jack-up) platforms

        3. Planetary-gear (upper) swing drives on cranes
        4. Planetary-gear crawler-track drives
    B. Determine strengths and weaknesses:
        1. Design
        2. Manufacturing
        3. Marketing
        4. Price
        5. Service
        6. Others

IV. Analysis of customer attitudes toward current suppliers and the possibility of a new source supply:
    A. Determine approaches used by current suppliers:
        1. Advertising
        2. Literature
        3. Personal sales calls
    B. Identify services offered by current suppliers
    C. Determine customer satisfaction with current sales approaches and services offered
    D. Measure market receptivity to a new supplier of planetary products:
        1. As a limited specialized product supplier
        2. As a broadscale product line supplier

V. Profitability analysis of major competitors:
    A. Product categories:
        1. Planetary-gear winches
        2. Planetary-gear speed reducers for winch drives
        3. Planetary-gear (upper) swing drives on cranes
        4. Planetary-gear crawler-track drives
    B. Measure cost and profitability data for two to three major suppliers in each product category:
        1. Major equipment lines
        2. Parts and service

VI. Determine importance of various customer purchase criteria for planetary-gear products:
    A. Product specifications:
        1. Life expectancy
        2. Physical size
        3. Duty-cycle requirements
        4. Torque ratings required
        5. Weight requirements
        6. Design (safety) factors required

B. Means of distribution:
   1. Direct
   2. Distributor
VII. Determine customer attitudes toward importance of product prefer-
     ences, features, and appeals:
   A. By type of product:
      1. Price
      2. Lead time/availability
      3. Prior relationship with manufacturer
      4. Proximity to distribution point
      5. Warranty
      6. After-sales service
      7. Spare parts availability
      8. Design factors specified
VIII. Identify interaction of influence among decision makers involved in
      the selection of suppliers:
   A. Engineering
   B. Manufacturing
   C. Purchasing
   D. Operations
   E. Other
 IX. Recommended market penetration strategy for identified planetary-
     gear products:
   A. By identified market segments:
      1. Market targeting
      2. Market positioning

What Is Expected of the Research Organization?

In addition to satisfying the specific study objectives, Sherwood Winch
management expects the research project team to objectively evaluate the
purchasing criteria used by those who buy and specify in decisions to select
planetary-gear products within the markets being studied. In a sense, the research team is expected to provide Sherwood Winch with an independent
evaluation of how business is obtained in this industry, pricing structures,
what customers think of the state of the art for planetary-gear products, and
what steps Sherwood Winch might take to identify specific "niche markets"
and move quickly into a competitive position within this growth-oriented
industry.

Study Design Approach

In order to provide a multifaceted "self-correcting" approach to this project, we propose to have two consultant teams working the problem simultaneously. The first team will build the data from the bottom up, based upon field interviews and widespread personal contacts. The second team will work from the top down, developing an industry model and profitability analysis of major planetary-gear suppliers that simulates industry activity and accounts for major input from secondary sources of information. The second team will also engage in a limited number of "special personal interviews" with knowledgeable industry contacts to verify competitive data on a macro basis.

Corroborative Data

In addition to using the results of interviews for information on which to build our fact base, it is also proposed that an examination and analysis of other sources of data be made to give insight and broaden the scope of the study. For example, because of our experience in construction and petroleum industry markets, *nonproprietary* information that we have already developed and which is contained within our files, will be used to strengthen the evaluation of these markets. Likewise, published reports and secondary sources of data will be used as background for the financial analysis of major suppliers of planetary-gear-set products.

The Report

Phase I will be presented in the form of a *preliminary bound* report. Phase II will also be compiled into a bound report. The Phase II report will consist of tables, a written analysis, an executive summary, and conclusions and recommendations. Phase II will be the *comprehensive analysis,* which will satisfy the study objectives. A detailed index of tables and a table of contents will make the final volume a valuable reference tool.

Phase I is expected to take six to seven weeks to complete. Phase II will require an additional seven to nine weeks. We are currently in a position to begin work by early June.

Presentation

A personal presentation and discussion of each phase of the study will be made within ten days from time of notice of completion of each respective phase of the study.

Cost

Phase I of this study will require a budget of $24,400 for professional services. Direct expenses for this phase of the study, such as travel expenses, long-distance telephone charges, and associated costs (i.e., computer costs, graphics, special reports, or directories required) will be invoiced in addition to the professional services charges. These are billed at our actual cost and are not expected to exceed $6,250.

Phase II of the study, to be initiated upon completion of Phase I, will require $29,300 for the professional services budget. Direct expenses, once again, will be an additional bill at our actual cost. Direct expenses for travel and communications for Phase II are not expected to exceed $8,450. Should savings in travel and communications expenses be found, our billing will reflect the smaller amount.

An invoice of 25 percent of the total professional services fees and direct expenses will be submitted ten days after work has begun on Phase I. In addition, invoices for professional services fees and direct expenses to date will be sent monthly with the final invoice sent upon completion of Phase II of the report.

Policy of the Research Team

Our background and experience qualify us to undertake the task as outlined. To protect your interests, we agree that any proprietary information Sherwood Winch may furnish us or that is developed during the course of this study will be safeguarded in accordance with our established professional standards.

We look forward with great interest to working with Sherwood Winch on this timely project. Our very best effort will be given to satisfying the study objectives contained herein. A signed copy of one of the enclosed proposals will constitute our authority to begin work.

The Research Team

Melissa R. Hewlett
President

Accepted by Sherwood Winch Company
By: _____
Title: _____
Date: _____
Purchase Order Number: _____

SAMPLE 2

Proposed Employee Communication
Evaluation and Strategy

Proposal Submitted to Steveco Company of America
Belzu, California*

July 2006

Background

The management of the Steveco Company of America, Belzu, California, is currently evaluating their formal methods of internal communication. The goal is to more effectively communicate programs, policies, and general information to their employees. In order to achieve this goal and be assured of a communication strategy that is both realistic and practical, management must have an accurate understanding of the attitudes and expectations of its employees. Without such information, the level of understanding and effectiveness achieved by traditional means of internal communication is left largely to chance.

It has been said that, regardless of the message or the channel of the message, communication rests most explicitly in the ears of the hearer. Peter Drucker states that downward communication, that is, communication from management to the workforce, can work only after it has been informed and shaped by upward communication. In essence, downward communication is a response to the values, beliefs, and aspirations of those who are receiving the message. An understanding of these values, beliefs, and aspirations is necessary for downward communication to work effectively and for shared understandings of reality and mutual goals to exist.

The major challenge facing any organization, therefore, is to create a work environment in which its people can contribute to the mutually understood goals of the corporation. Of necessity, this means the workforce needs information—it needs feedback, as well as the personal flexibility and psychological support to interact, understand, and accomplish corporate goals as management defines them. This burden must be borne, not simply at the management level, but all the way down to the supervisory or foreperson level, who must maintain relationships with their people that permit open and honest two-way communication on every issue of importance to the audience.

---

*Names, dates, and locations have been changed in this sample proposal.

The understanding of these general principles is necessary to the approach and formulation of an effective communication strategy at Belzu. General observations drawn from our Belzu plant tour and associated conversations were:

1. There are three distinct groups of employees at Belzu:

Group	Current Orientation	Affiliation
Headquarters Mgt.	Steveco	Stevens
Operations Mgt.	Job Function	Technicians
Hourly Employees	Self	Unions

2. The rotating shift of the hourly employees (an operational necessity), currently contributes to "organizational apathy." But it need not.
3. The employees have been losing their sense of belonging, corporate identity, and loyalty to a large, uncommunicative company that sacrifices their jobs to economics (fuel prices). Individuals feel they have no control over their destiny (job security) … regardless of whether or not they do a good job. Those who once prided themselves as being Steveco's finest, have difficulty assimilating the loss of this distinction, not because of their work, but due to rising fuel costs. The unfortunate result is a weakening morale which, over time, leads to organizational apathy, poor job attitudes, carelessness, and … accidents.

Although no single individual expressed the problem in these terms, we believe that this underlies the *root cause* of Steveco's Belzu communication/accident problem.

To this end, an effective attitude survey program that provides for feedback and problem resolution is necessary in preparing a reliable and effective communication strategy. The basic purpose of the proposed study will be:

1. To study and evaluate internal communications and their effectiveness.
2. To identify and focus upon those methods that will increase and maintain the effectiveness of the safety program.

The implied needs, deduced from conversations with plant managers, are:

1. To recommend solutions to the personal and psychological distance between headquarters management, operational management, and the hourly employees.
2. To recommend a means of reducing the accident rate at the plant.
3. To revitalize an "esprit de corps," a sense of identity, pride, and purpose in being an employee of Steveco.

The specific objectives of this study then will be:

1. To make an evaluation of the effectiveness of Steveco's various channels of communication.
2. To determine employee attitudes toward management and supervisory level communication.
3. To measure employee perceptions of how well-informed they are.
4. To determine employee awareness of management's goals and policies.
5. To measure awareness of specific aspects of the safety program.
6. To determine employee attitudes toward the importance of being a Steveco employee and contributing to the overall objectives set forth by management.
7. To identify factors related to motivational enhancement and job satisfaction.
8. To evaluate the importance employees place on traditional communication tasks.
9. To identify existing informal patterns of communication.
10. To determine the communication strategies necessary to most effectively achieve management goals and enhance motivational enrichment.

The ultimate goals of this study then will be to provide effective and practical solutions to the communication and safety needs of Steveco, Belzu. Specifically, these goals will recommend an effective communication program that will have as its purpose the anticipation of problems *and* opportunities and the ability to effectively communicate company goals and policies in terms that will be understood by the employees. In addition, they will identify the root causes of the current level of accidents and to recommend changes to *reduce accidents*.

It is proposed that Steveco and our research team work cooperatively in the study in order to maximize the results and minimize the time and variable cost to Steveco.

Detailed Study Objectives

The objectives of the communication research study are to be as follows:

I. Preliminary Analysis (Phase I)
   A. Evaluate the effectiveness of Steveco's various channels of communication:

    1. According to division.
      a. Chemical
      b. Refinery
      c. Smelting
      d. Other
    2. According to job function.
      a. Management
      b. Superintendent
      c. Foreperson
      d. Worker
      e. Other
    3. According to the mode of communication.
      a. Oral
      b. Written
        (1) Newsletter
        (2) Bulletin board
        (3) Other

B. Determine employee attitudes toward management and supervisor-level communications:
    1. Determination of message importance.
    2. Reliability of communication channel.
    3. Importance of repetition to understanding and retention.

C. Measure employee perceptions of how well informed they are:
    1. For general company policy.
    2. For specific programs.
    3. For individual work groups.
    4. For adjoining work groups.
    5. For future welfare or benefits.

II. Detailed Analysis (Phase II)

A. Determine employee awareness of management's goals and policies:
    1. General policies.
    2. Management's concerns toward the workforce.
    3. Purpose of individual work units.
    4. Purpose of individual divisions.
    5. Function of Steveco, Belzu, as a part of Steveco corporate.

B. Measure awareness of level of specific aspects of the safety program:
    1. Reason for importance.
    2. Peer acceptance of program.
    3. Effectiveness of various promotional communication tools.
    4. Individual areas of caution.

C. Determine employee attitudes toward importance of being a Steveco employee and contributing to overall objectives set forth by management:
   1. By division.
   2. By job function.
   3. By years employed by Steveco.
   4. By age.
   5. By race.
D. Identify factors related to motivational enhancement and job satisfaction:
   1. Security.
   2. Importance of job/craft.
   3. Relationships.
   4. Purpose.
   5. Environment.
   6. Importance of total picture/corporate goals.
E. Evaluate importance employees place on traditional communication tasks:
   1. To build morale and foster employee communication tasks.
   2. To keep employees informed and to avoid misinformation and rumors.
   3. To motivate employees toward greater productivity.
   4. To create an employee constituency that will support the company with legislators and on other.
   5. To reduce employee turnover.
   6. To help avoid strikes and other labor unrest.
   7. To encourage employees to invest in the company.
F. Identify existing informal patterns and lines of communication:
   1. According to division.
   2. According to job functions.
G. Develop a demographic and psychographic profile of employees:
   1. Demographic.
      a. Age
      b. Sex
      c. Marital status
      d. Number of children
      e. Number of years with Steveco
      f. Job functions
      g. Distance traveled to work
   2. Psychographic factors.
      a. Individual pursuits/interests
      b. Family interests

    c. Leader/follower
    d. Activist/inactive
    e. Pessimist/optimist
    f. Achievers/maintainers
    g. Traditional/trend-conscious
H. Determine communication strategy necessary to most effectively achieve management goals and enhance motivational enrichment:
    1. To improve communications.
    2. To improve morale.
    3. To build a sense of pride in being a Steveco employee.
    4. To reduce accidents.
    5. To maintain and improve productivity.

Planning the Study

The study shall consist of a two-phase effort. Phase I will be a preliminary investigation obtained by focus group interviews and a sampling of personal interviews. Phase II will consist of a major survey effort both in the plant and by telephone at home that will provide the detailed, quantitative analysis from which an effective, practical communication strategy will be developed.

The preliminary phase will begin with four focus group sessions that will explore employee and supervisor attitudes and perceptions toward plant communication in general and the safety program in specific. A focus group involves an open discussion with 8 to 12 peers led by a trained group moderator (from our staff) who is adept at probing and guiding the discussion. The groups are exploratory in their purpose and are designed to elicit insights and concepts from which to design a much more strategic and meaningful survey questionnaire.

The focus group sessions will be closely followed by approximately forty personal interviews. The personal interviews will provide input to refine the design of the survey analysis. They will also provide timely preliminary conclusions and recommendations. Phase I is expected to take approximately four to six weeks to complete.

Phase II of the study will be based on a sample of interviews with Steveco. The sample will be drawn in such a way that it will be representative of the entire workforce. A specific series of interview questions designed around the study objectives will be formulated. This structured questionnaire will have been pretested in the personal interviews to ensure that each survey interview obtains the optimum in information and each question is worded so that it is clearly understood. Each interview will be designed to take approximately twenty minutes to conduct. A total of 400 interviews will be made.

Tabulations and statistical analysis will be made at the completion of the interviewing to yield the optimum by way of interpretation of the significance of differences and relationships among the attitudes and other factors examined in the study. Phase II is expected to take an additional eight weeks to complete.

Corroborative Data

In addition to using the results of interviews for information on which to build our fact base, an examination and analysis of other sources of data will be made to give insight and broaden the scope of the study. This will include secondary information and available reports by experts in this field. In addition, nonproprietary information that we have already developed, which is contained within our files, will be used to strengthen the evaluation.

Presentation

A personal presentation and discussion of each phase of the study will be made within ten days from time of notice to completion of each respective phase of the study.

Cost

Phase I of this study will require a budget of $24,800 for professional services. Direct expenses for this phase of the study, such as travel expenses, long-distance telephone charges, and associated costs (i.e., special equipment required) will be invoiced in addition to the professional service charges. These are billed at our actual cost and are not expected to exceed $6,500.

Phase II of the study, to be initiated upon completion of Phase I, will require $35,400 for the professional services budget. Direct expenses once again will be billed additionally at our actual cost. Direct expenses for travel and communications for Phase II are not expected to exceed $8,450. Should savings in travel and communications expenses be found, our billing will reflect the smaller amount. Invoices will be submitted monthly, beginning ten days after work has begun, reflecting the professional service fees and direct expenses for that time period.

Survey Alternative

Should a lower budget alternative be desired, the methodology will be based on 300 survey interviews. The study objectives for this alternative would be as outlined in the preliminary analysis of the detailed study objectives. This study would also be presented in the form of a bound report with the personal presentation. The cost for this study would be $18,150 for professional service fees with direct expenses billed additionally. The time parameters would involve approximately eight weeks.

Policy of the Research Team

Our background and experience help to qualify us to undertake the task as outlined. To protect your interests, we agree that any proprietary information Steveco may furnish us with or that is developed during the course of this study will be safeguarded in accordance with our established professional standards.

We look forward with great interest to working with Steveco on this timely project. If this proposal is acceptable, please sign and return one of the attached copies indicating your approval to proceed. A signed copy of one of the enclosed proposals will constitute our authority to begin work.

The Research Team

Lawrence L. Albritton
President

Accepted by Steveco Company of America
By: _____
Title: _____
Date: _____
Purchase Order Number: _____
Study Option: _____

Appendix B

Sources of Secondary Data

CONSUMER DATA SOURCES

Census of the Population (Government Printing Office). Taken every ten years, this source reports the population by geographic region, with detailed breakdowns according to demographic characteristics, such as sex, marital status, age, education, race, income, etc.

Consumer Market and Magazine Report. Published annually by Daniel Starch, this source describes the household population of the United States with respect to a number of demographic variables and consumption statistics. The profiles are based on a large probability sample and they give good consumer behavioral and socioeconomic characteristics.

County and City Data Book. Bureau of the Census (Government Printing Office). Published every five years, this publication gives statistics on population, income, education, employment, housing, retail, and wholesale sales for various cities, Standard Metropolitan Statistical Areas (SMSAs), and counties.

Editor and Publisher Market Guide. Published annually by Editor and Publisher Co., it contains information on 265 metro areas including population, number of households, industries, retail sales, and climate.

Guide to Consumer Markets. Published annually by Conference Board, this source provides data on the behavior of consumers, under the headings of: population, employment, income, expenditures, production and distribution, and prices.

Historical Statistics of the United States from Colonial Times to 1970. This volume was prepared as a supplement to the *Statistical Abstract.* This source provides data on social, economic, and political aspects of life in the

United States. It contains consistent definitions and thus eliminates incompatibilities of data in the Statistical Abstracts caused by dynamic changes over time.

Marketing Information Guide. Published monthly by the Department of Commerce, this source lists recently published studies and statistics that serve as a useful source of current information to marketing researchers.

Rand McNally Commercial Atlas and Marketing Guide (Chicago: Rand McNally Company). Published annually, this source contains marketing data and maps for some 100,000 cities and towns in the United States. It includes such things as population, auto registrations, basic trading areas, manufacturing, transportation, population, and related data.

Sales Management Survey of Buying Power. Published annually by *Sales and Marketing Management* magazine, this source provides information such as population, income, retail sales, etc., again broken down by state, county, and SMSA, for the United States and Canada.

COMPANY DATA SOURCES

Almanac of Business and Industrial Financial Ratios. Published annually by Prentice-Hall, this source lists a number of businesses, sales, and certain operating ratios for several industries. The computations are from tax returns supplied by the IRS, and the data allow comparison of a company's financial ratios with competitors of similar size.

Directory of Corporate Affiliations. Published annually by National Register Publishing Company, Inc., this source lists approximately 3,000 parent companies and their 16,000 divisions, subsidiaries, and affiliates.

Directory of Intercorporate Ownership. Published by Simon & Schuster, Volume 1 contains parent companies, with divisions, subsidiaries, overseas subsidiaries, and American companies owned by foreign firms. Volume 2 provides an alphabetical listing of all the entries in Volume 1.

Fortune Directory. Published annually by *Fortune* magazine, this source presents information on sales, assets, profits, invested capital, and employees for the 500 largest U.S. industrial corporations.

Fortune Double 500 Directory. Published annually in the May-August issues of *Fortune* magazine, this source offers information on assets, sales, and profits of 1,000 of the largest U.S. firms, fifty largest banks, life insurance companies, and retailing, transportation, utility, and financial companies. In addition, this source ranks foreign firms and banks.

Hoover's Handbook of American Business. Published by Hoover's Business Press, this two-volume work provides profiles of 750 large companies in the United States.

Mergent's Manuals. Published annually, this source provides income statements and balance sheets for companies and government units.

Middle Market Directory. Published annually by Dun & Bradstreet, this source lists companies with assets in the range of $500,000 to $999,999. The directory offers information on some 30,000 companies' officers, products, sales, and number of employees.

Million Dollar Directory. Published annually by Dun & Bradstreet, this source offers the same information as the Middle Market Directory, only for companies with sales over $9 million or 180 employees.

Moody's Industrial Manual. Published annually, this source provides information on selected companies' products and description, history, mergers and acquisition record, principal plants and properties, principal offices, as well as seven years of financial statements and statistical records.

Moody's Manual of Investments. This source documents historical and operational data on selected firms and five years of their balance sheets, income accounts, and dividend records.

Moody's Manuals. This source list includes manuals entitled Banks and Finance, Municipals and Governments, Public Utilities, Transportation. These manuals contain balance sheet and income statements for various companies and government units.

Reference Book of Corporate Managements. Published annually by Dun & Bradstreet, this source gives a list of 2,400 companies and their 30,000 officers and directors.

Sheldon's Retail Directory of the United States and Canada. Published annually by Phelon, Sheldon & Marsar, Inc., this source supplies the largest chain, department, and specialty stores, by state and city, and by Canadian province and city. This source also includes merchandise managers and buyers.

Standard and Poor's Register of Corporations, Directors, and Executives. Published annually by Standard and Poor, this source provides officers, sales, products, and number of employees for some 75,000 U.S. and Canadian corporations.

State Manufacturing Directories. Published for each state, these sources give company addresses, products, officers, etc., by geographic location.

Thomas Register of American Manufacturers. Published annually by the Thomas Publishing Company, this source gives specific manufacturers of individual products, as well as the company's address, branch offices, and subsidiaries.

Wall Street Journal Index. Published monthly, this source lists corporate news, alphabetically, by firm name, as it has occurred in *The Wall Street Journal.*

MARKET DATA SOURCES

American Statistics Index: A Comprehensive Guide and Index to the Statistical Publications of the U.S. Government. Published monthly by the Congressional Information Service, this source indexes statistical publications of federal agencies, and it is a useful starting point for obtaining market data.

Ayer Directory of Publications. Published annually by Ayer Press, this source is a comprehensive listing of newspapers, magazines, and trade publications of the United States, by states, Canada, Bermuda, Republics of Panama and the Philippines, and the Bahamas.

Bureau of the Census Catalog (Government Printing Office). Published quarterly, this source is a comprehensive guide to Census Bureau publications. Publications include agriculture, foreign trade, governments, population, and the economic census.

Business Conditions Digest. Bureau of Economic Analysis, Department of Commerce (Government Printing Office). Published monthly, this source gives indications of business activity in table and chart form.

Business Cycle Developments. Bureau of the Census (Government Printing Office). Published monthly, this source provides some seventy business activity indicators, that give keys to general economic conditions.

Business Periodicals Index. This source lists articles by subject heading from 150 or more business periodicals. It also suggests alternate key words that can be used to determine a standard of relevance in environmental analysis.

Business Statistics. Department of Commerce. Published biennially, this source is a supplement to "The Survey of Current Business." It provides information from some 2,500 statistical series, starting in 1939.

Census of Business (Government Printing Office). Published every five years, this source supplies statistics on the retail, wholesale, and service trades. The census of service trade compiles information on receipts, legal form of organization, employment, and number of units by geographic area.

Census of Manufacturer (Government Printing Office). Published every five years, this source presents manufacturers by type of industry. It contains detailed industry and geographic statistics, such as the number of establishments, quantity of output, value added in manufacture, employment, wages, inventories, sales by customer class, and fuel, water, and energy consumption.

Census of Retail Trade (Government Printing Office). Taken every five years in the years ending in 2 and 7, this source provides information on 100 retail classifications. Statistics are compiled on number of establishments, total sales, sales by product line, size of firms, employment and payroll for states, SMSAs, counties and cities of 2,500 or more.

Census of Selected Service Industries (Government Printing Office). Taken every five years, in years ending in 2 and 7, this source compiles statistics on 150 or more service classifications. Information on the number of establishments, receipts, payrolls, etc., is provided for various service organizations.

Census of Transportation (Government Printing Office). Taken every five years, in years ending in 2 and 7, this source presents three specific surveys: Truck Inventory and Use Survey, National Travel Survey, and Commodity Transportation Survey.

Census of Wholesale Trade (Government Printing Office). Taken every five years, in years ending in 2 and 7, this source provides statistics of 150 wholesale classifications. Information includes numbers of establishments, sales, personnel, payroll, etc.

Commodity Yearbook. Published annually by the Commodity Research Bureau, this source supplies data on prices, production, exports, stocks, etc., for 100 commodities.

County Business Patterns. Departments of Commerce and Health, Education and Welfare. Published annually, this source gives statistics on the number of businesses by type and their employment and payroll broken down by county.

Directories of Federal Statistics for Local Areas, and for States: Guides to Sources. Bureau of the Census (Government Printing Office). These two directories list sources of federal statistics for local areas, and for states, respectively. Data includes such topics as population, health, education, income, finance, etc.

Directory of Federal Statistics for Local Areas: A Guide to Sources (Government Printing Office). This source looks at topics such as population, finance, income, education, etc., in a local perspective.

Economic Almanac. Published every two years by the National Industrial Conference Board, this source gives data on population, prices, communications, transportation, electric and gas consumption, construction, mining and manufacturing output, in the United States, Canada, and other selected world areas.

Economic Indicators. Council of Economic Advisors, Department of Commerce (Government Printing Office). Published monthly, this source gives current, key indicators of general business conditions, such as GNP (gross national product), personal consumption expenditures, etc.

F and S Index. This detailed index on business-related subjects offers information about companies, industries, and products from numerous business-oriented newspapers, trade journals, financial publications, and special reports.

Federal Reserve Bulletin (Washington, DC: Federal Reserve System Board of Governors). Published monthly, this publication offers financial data on interest rates, credit, savings, banking activity; an index of industrial production; and finance and international trade statistics.

Handbook of Economic Statistics. Economics Statistics Bureau. Published annually, this source, presents current and historical statistics of U.S. industry, commerce, agriculture, and labor.

Market Analysis. A Handbook of Current Data Sources. Written by Nathalie Frank and published by Scarecrow Press of Metuchen, NJ, this book offers sources of secondary information broken down on the basis of indexes, abstracts, directories, etc.

Market Guide (New York: *Editor and Publisher* magazine). Published annually, this source presents data on population, principal industries, transportation facilities, households, banks, and retail outlets for some 1,500 U.S. and Canadian newspaper markets.

Measuring Markets: A Guide to the Use of Federal and State Statistical Data (Government Printing Office). This publication lists federal and state publications covering population, income, employment, taxes, and sales. It is a useful starting point for the marketing researcher who is interested in locating secondary data.

Merchandising. Published annually in the March issue of this magazine is the "Statistical and Marketing Report," which presents charts and tables of sales, shipments, product saturation and replacement, trade in, and import/export figures for home electronics, major appliances, and housewares. Also appearing annually in the May issue is the "Statistical and Marketing Forecast." This gives manufacturer's sales projections for the coming year and is useful in forecasting certain market factors.

Monthly Labor Review. Published monthly by the U.S. Bureau of Labor Statistics, this source compiles trends and information on employment, wages, weekly working hours, collective agreements, industrial accidents, etc.

Predicasts (Cleveland, OH: Predicasts, Inc.). This abstract gives forecasts and market data, condensed to one line, from business and financial publications, trade journals and newspapers. It includes information on products, industries and the economy, and it presents a consensus forecast for each data series.

Public Affairs Information Services Bulletin (PAIS). Similar to, but different from, the *Business Periodicals Index,* this source includes more foreign publications, and it includes many books, government publications, and many nonperiodical publications.

Reader's Guide to Periodical Literature. This index presents articles from magazines of a general nature, such as *U.S. News and World Report, Time, Newsweek, Saturday Review*, etc. It also suggests alternate key words that provide initial insight into the nature of the environment.

Standard and Poor's Industry Survey. Published annually, this source offers current surveys of industries and a monthly Trends and Projections section, useful in forecasting market factors.

Standard and Poor's Trade and Securities Statistics. Published monthly by Standard and Poor Corporation, this source contains statistics on banking, production, labor, commodity prices, income, trade, securities, etc.

Statistical Abstract of the United States. Bureau of the Census (Government Printing Office). Published annually, this source serves as a good initial reference for other secondary data sources. It includes data tables covering social, economic, industrial, political and demographic subjects.

Statistics of Income. Internal Revenue Service. Published annually, this source gives balance sheet and income statement statistics, prepared from federal income tax returns of corporations, and broken down by major industry, asset size, etc.

Survey of Current Business. Bureau of Economic Analysis, Department of Commerce (Government Printing Office). Published monthly, this source presents indicators of general business, personal consumption expenditures, industry statistics, domestic trade, earnings and employment by industry, real estate activity, etc.

U.S. Industrial Outlook (Government Printing Office). Published annually, this source provides a detailed analysis of approximately 200 manufacturing and nonmanufacturing industries. It contains information on recent developments, current trends, and a ten-year outlook for the industries. This source is useful in forecasting the specific marketing factors of a market analysis.

COST DATA SOURCES

Business Publication Rates and Data. Published by Standard Rate & Data Service, Inc. This index lists various trade publication sources.

Economic Census (Government Printing Office). A comprehensive and periodic canvass of U.S. industrial and business activities, taken by the Census Bureau every five years. In addition to providing the framework for forecasting and planning, these censuses provide weights and benchmarks for indexes of industrial production, productivity, and price. Management uses these in economic or sales forecasting, and analyzing sales performance, allocating advertising budgets, locating plants, warehouses and stores, and so on.

Encyclopedia of Associations. Published by Gale Research Co. May acquaint a researcher with various associations for cost data pertaining to desired industry.

Gale Directory of Databases. Published by Gale Research Co. twice a year, this directory lists more than 12,000 databases, 3,000 database producers, and 2,000 online services and vendors.

Moody's Investors Services, Inc. Published by Standard and Poor Corporation, this is a financial reporting source that includes many large firms.

Standard Corporation Records. Published by Standard and Poor Corporation, this is a publication of financial reporting data of the larger firms.

COMPUTERIZED DATABASES

Most certainly the quickest way to search thousands of periodicals for information of interest to marketers is via one of the many computerized databases available. Using either CD-ROM or online technologies available at many public or college libraries, these databases are generally very user-friendly and either inexpensive or free to use. Some of the ones most useful to the market researcher are described in the following.

DIALOG. Maintains more than 600 databases including ABI/INFORM, which abstracts more than 1,000 business journals, and PROMT (Predicasts Overview of Marketer and Technologies) with summaries and full text from 1,000 publications.

FINDEX. Indexes and abstracts more than 50,000 research reports by U.S. and international research firms.

GENERAL ADVICE

The number and complexity of information sources may discourage the novice secondary-source researcher from pursuing this line of research. Our advice to the uninitiated researcher is to take the problem to the business reference librarian at the nearest university library. He or she can save considerable wasted time and effort by directing the researcher to those sources most likely to provide the solution to information problems. We also recommend the following short list of sources for those researchers who want to pursue their searches alone, but who need a few broad-based sources to get started.

- *Business Information, How to Find It, How to Use It*—Michael R. Gavin, author. The second edition was published in 1992 by Oryx Press. More recent editions may be available.
- *Directories in Print—Gale Research Co.* Indexes over 10,000 published directories.
- *Directory of On-Line Databases*—Euadra Associates, Santa Monica, CA. Updated periodically.
- *Encyclopedia of Associations*—Gale Research lists over 20,000 trade associations by subject area, including addresses and phone numbers. Many trade associations are very helpful in meeting information needs.
- *Encyclopedia of Business Information Sources*—Also by Gale Research, this encyclopedia is updated frequently.

Appendix C

Sample Questionnaires

MAIL QUESTIONNAIRE

November 21, 2006

Dr. Reed Graham
Medical Plaza
2140 S. 78th E. Ave.
Tulsa, OK 74129

Dear Dr. Graham:

Marketing Research Associates is conducting a study in the Tulsa area concerning HOME NURSING CARE.

You have been chosen as one in a group of doctors selected to represent the physician sentiment in this area. Response to this questionnaire is completely voluntary, yet we hope you choose to record your feelings on the short form enclosed.

This information will be used to help our client develop more effective nursing services.

Your response will be held in the strictest confidence. We are interested only in the collective responses of the physicians in this group. To help us achieve this goal, please do not put your name on the survey form or on the enclosed, self-addressed return envelope.

We hope that you choose to help our client help you by taking a few moments to answer the enclosed questions.

Thank-you.

Sincerely,
Robert E. Stevens, President
Marketing Research Associates

Home Nursing Care

Thank-you for your cooperation. You can be sure that your responses will remain confidential. We are only interested in the total response trends of your selected group. Do not place your name on this form.

Please answer each question by placing an "X" in the appropriate space.

1. What is your specialty?
   A. _____ Internal Medicine   D. _____ Ophthalmology
   B. _____ Family Practice   E. _____ Urology
   C. _____ Surgery   F. _____ Cardiovascular
           and/or Thoracic Surgery
2. How many years have you been in practice?
   A. _____ 0–10 years   C. _____ 21–30 years
   B. _____ 11–20 years   D. _____ over 30 years
3. What percentage of your patients do you estimate to be over 65 years of age?
   A. _____ 0–20%   D. _____ 61–80%
   B. _____ 21–40%   E. _____ over 80%
   C. _____ 41–60%
4. Where do most of your patients live?
   A. _____ North Tulsa   D. _____ West Tulsa
   B. _____ East Tulsa   E. _____ Don't know
   C. _____ South Tulsa
5. Rate each factor according to the importance you place on it when selecting a nursing service for patient referral.
   Use the following scale and circle the number that corresponds best with your opinion.

very unimportant	important	moderately unimportant	undecided/ don't know	moderately important	important	very important
1	2	3	4	5	6	7

A. Skill and training of nurses   1   2   3   4   5   6   7

B. Nurses following physicians' directions   1   2   3   4   5   6   7

C. Feedback to physician of patient's condition   1   2   3   4   5   6   7

D. Fees charged per visit   1   2   3   4   5   6   7

E. Third-party reimbursement
   of nursing fees   1   2   3   4   5   6   7

F. Availability during "off-hours"
   (weekends, holidays, etc.)   1   .2   3   4   5   6   7

6. Rate each of the following local nursing services in terms of how you believe it satisfies each factor.

Use the following scale and circle the number that corresponds best with your opinion.

very unimportant	important	moderately unimportant	undecided/ don't know	moderately important	important	very important
1	2	3	4	5	6	7

A. *Kimberly Nurses:*

1. Skill and training of nurses   1   2   3   4   5   6   7

2. Nurses following physicians'
   directions   1   2   3   4   5   6   7

3. Feedback to physician
   of patient's condition   1   2   3   4   5   6   7

4. Fees charged per visit   1   2   3   4   5   6   7

5. Third-party reimbursement
   of nursing fees   1   2   3   4   5   6   7

6. Availability during "off-hours"
   (weekends, holidays, etc.)   1   2   3   4   5   6   7

B. *Medical Personnel Pool:*

1. Skill and training of nurses   1   2   3   4   5   6   7

2. Nurses following physicians'
   directions   1   2   3   ·4   5   6   7

   3. Feedback to physician
      of patient's condition   1   2   3   4   5   6   7

   4. Fees charged per visit   1   2   3   4   5   6   7

   5. Third-party reimbursement
      of nursing fees   1   2   3   4   5   6   7

   6. Availability during "off-hours"
      (weekends, holidays, etc.)   1   2   3   4   5   6   7

C. *Tulsa County Public Health Nursing Service:*

   1. Skill and training of nurses   1   2   3   4   5   6   7

   2. Nurses following physicians'
      directions   1   2   3   4   5   6   7

   3. Feedback to physician
      of patient's condition   1   2   3   4   5   6   7

   4. Fees charged per visit   1   2   3   4   5   6   7

   5. Third-party reimbursement
      of nursing fees   1   2   3   4   5   6   7

   6. Availability during "off-hours"
      (weekends, holidays, etc.)   1   2   3   4   5   6   7

D. *Homemakers Upjohn:*

   1. Skill and training of nurses   1   2   3   4   5   6   7

   2. Nurses following physicians'
      directions   1   2   3   4   5   6   7

   3. Feedback to physician
      of patient's condition   1   2   3   4   5   6   7

   4. Fees charged per visit   1   2   3   4   5   6   7

5. Third-party reimbursement
   of nursing fees   1   2   3   4   5   6   7

6. Availability during "off-hours"
   (weekends, holidays, etc.)   1   2   3   4   5   6   7

E. *Pro-Med:*

1. Skill and training of nurses   1   2   3   4   5   6   7

2. Nurses following physicians'
   directions   1   2   3   4   5   6   7

3. Feedback to physician
   of patient's condition   1   2   3   4   5   6   7

4. Fees charged per visit   1   2   3   4   5   6   7

5. Third-party reimbursement
   of nursing fees   1   2   3   4   5   6   7

6. Availability during "off-hours"
   (weekends, holidays, etc.)   1   2   3   4   5   6   7

F. *Quality Care:*

1. Skill and training of nurses   1   2   3   4   5   6   7

2. Nurses following physicians'
   directions   1   2   3   4   5   6   7

3. Feedback to physician
   of patient's condition   1   2   3   4   5   6   7

4. Fees charged per visit   1   2   3   4   5   6   7

5. Third-party reimbursement
   of nursing fees   1   2   3   4   5   6   7

6. Availability during "off-hours"
   (weekends, holidays, etc.)   1   2   3   4   5   6   7

7. Which nursing service would you probably use if you were going to refer a patient to a home nursing service? (Please rank in order of preference from 1 through 7.)

A. _____ Pro-Med

B. _____ Homemakers Upjohn

C. _____ Tulsa County Public Health Nursing Service

D. _____ Quality Care

E. _____ Medical Personnel Pool

F. _____ Kimberly Nurses

G. _____ Other (please specify:_____)

8. How frequently do patients request to be referred to a specific nursing service?

A. _____ never

B. _____ 1-20% of the time

C. _____ 21-40% of the time

D. _____ 41-60% of the time

E. _____ 61-80% of the time

F. _____ over 80% of the time

Thank-you for your responses and assistance in making this study possible. Any additional comments you wish to make would be appreciated. Please feel free to use the following space to record them.

PERSONAL INTERVIEWING GUIDE

Motel Study

Date _____

INTERVIEWING GUIDE   Inn _____

Interviewer _____ Interview # _____

1. What is the purpose of your present trip?
2. How do you usually go about arranging for a room?
   (Probe for factors influencing development and use of strategy.)
3. Have you used the reservation services of other motel or hotel chains?
   How do you think the reservation services of this motel compare to the
   others you are familiar with?
4. Are there specific things you like or dislike about making reservations?
   What about this motel's reservation services?
5. Is there anything missing in present reservation services that you feel
   would be an improvement?
6. (If not volunteered in previous question) How would you react to the idea
   of all reservations being made only by telephone?
   a. One-number system
   b. Physical evidence and personal contact

MOTEL STUDY DEMOGRAPHICS

1. In which one of the following age categories do you belong?

   Under 25 ____   45 to 54 ____

   26 to 34 ____   55 to 65 ____

   35 to 44 ____   Over 65 ____

2. Sex: Male ____   Female ____

3. What is your occupation?
   1. Professional-technical ____
   2. Top manager or owner ____
   3. Middle-manager ____
   4. Sales ____
   5. Craftsperson ____
   6. Operatives ____
   7. Service ____
   8. Clerical ____
   9. Laborer ____
   10. Armed Forces ____

    11. Miscellaneous ____
    12. Not in labor force ____

4. What type of company do you work for?
    1. Manufacturing ____
    2. Wholesaling or retailing ____
    3. Service ____
    4. Education ____
    5. Professional ____
    6. Government ____
    7. Other ____
    8. Retired ____

5. What is the highest level of education you have reached?
    1. Some grade school ____
    2. Completed eighth grade ____
    3. Some high school ____
    4. Graduate-high school ____
    5. Some college ____
    6. Graduate-four years college ____
    7. Graduate work ____

6. Which of the following categories most nearly approximates your annual family income?
    1. 0 to $4,999
    2. $5,000 to $7,999
    3. $8,000 to $10,999
    4. $11,000 to $13,999
    5. $14,000 to $16,999
    6. $17,000 and over

7. Approximately how many nights do you spend in motels or hotels each year? ____

TELEPHONE QUESTIONNAIRE

Retail Banking Survey

[1-3]

Hello, am I speaking with the man/lady of the house? (IF NO, ASK TO SPEAK TO THAT PERSON.)

Hello, I am _____ . We are conducting a marketing research project with area residents. This study deals with financial institutions and we need your help in this project. Your answers will be confidential and used only in combination with the responses of other people.

1a. Do you or a member of your household work for a bank, savings and loan, credit union, advertising, public relations, or market research firm?

_____ YES (Terminate)
_____ NO

1b. Do you have a checking or savings account with a local financial institution?

_____ YES
_____ NO (Terminate)

[4] 2. How long have you lived in this area?

_____ 0-2 years[1]
_____ 3-5 years[2]
_____ 6-12 years[3]
_____ 13-20 years[4]
_____ Over 20 years[5]
_____ Refused[6]

[5] 3. What is the name of your primary financial institution?

_____ Central Bank[1]
_____ First American Bank[2]
_____ Hibernia National Bank[3]
_____ Pelican Homestead[4]

_____ People's Homestead[5]
_____ Premier Bank[6]
_____ Other[7]

4. What services are you currently utilizing at your primary financial institution? (READ)

[6]   _____ Automatic Teller Machines
[7]   _____ Personal Loans
[8]   _____ Automobile Loans
[9]   _____ Home (Mortgage) Loans
[10]   _____ Telephone Bill Paying Service
[11]   _____ VISA/MasterCard Services
[12]   _____ Safe Deposit Box
[13]   _____ Checking Account
[14]   _____ Savings Account
[15]   _____ Trust Account
[16]   _____ Money Market Deposit Account
[17]   _____ CDs and Investment Instrument
[18]   _____ Individual Retirement Accounts (IRAs)
[19]   _____ Overdraft Protection
[20]   _____ Educational Loans
[21]   _____ Other

[22] 5. How long have you done business with your primary financial institution?

_____ Less than 1 year[1]
_____ 1-2 years[2]
_____ 3-5 years[3]
_____ 6-12 years[4]
_____ Over 12 years[5]

[23] 6. Do you also have accounts at other institutions?

_____ YES[1]
_____ NO[2] (Skip to question 9)

7. What services do you currently utilize at this institution?

[24]   _____ Automatic Teller Machines
[25]   _____ Personal Loans
[26]   _____ Automobile Loans

[27] ____ Home (Mortgage) Loans
[28] ____ Telephone Bill Paying Service
[29] ____ VISA/MasterCard Services
[30] ____ Safe Deposit Box
[31] ____ Checking Account
[32] ____ Savings Account
[33] ____ Trust Account
[34] ____ Money Market Deposit Account
[35] ____ CDs and Investment Instrument
[36] ____ Individual Retirement Accounts (IRAs)
[37] ____ Overdraft Protection
[38] ____ Educational Loans
[39] ____ Other

[40] 8. (If secondary financial institutions) How long have you done business with your secondary financial institution?

     ____ Less than 1 year[1]
     ____ 1-2 years[2]
     ____ 2-5 years[3]
     ____ 6-12 years[4]
     ____ Over 12 years[5]

[41] 9. Have you changed your primary financial institution while living in this area?

     ____ YES[1]
     ____ NO[2] (Skip to question 13)

[42]10. How long ago did you make that change?

     ____ Less than 1 year[1]
     ____ 1-2 years[2]
     ____ 3-5 years[3]
     ____ 6-12 years[4]
     ____ Over 12 years[5]

[43]11. What did you change from?

     ____ Bank to a savings and loan[1]
     ____ Bank to a credit union[2]
     ____ Savings and loan to a bank[3]
     ____ Savings and loan to a credit union[4]

____ Credit union to a bank[5]
____ Credit union to a savings and loan[6]
____ Other[7]

[44]12. What was the main reason you changed financial institutions?

____ Poor service at old[1]
____ Better location of new[2]
____ Unsure of stability of old/felt safer at new institution[3]
____ Interest rates higher at new[4]
____ Other, specify[5]_____

[45]13. On a scale of 1 to 5, where "1" is strongly dissatisfied and "5" is very satisfied, how would you rate your satisfaction with your primary financial institution?

Strongly dissatisfied   1   2   3   4   5   Very satisfied

[46]   If dissatisfied (1 or 2), ask: Why are you dissatisfied?

____ Poor service at old[1]
____ Better location of new[2]
____ Unsure of stability of old/felt safer at new institution[3]
____ Interest rates higher at new[4]
____ Other, specify[5]_____

14. Now I would like you to think for a moment about financial institutions in this area. As I mention several factors about financial institutions, please tell me which one comes to mind first for each factor. It does not matter if you have ever done business with them or not. This is simply your initial impression or opinion.

		Central Bank	First Amer.	Hibernia Nat.	Pelican Home.	People's Home.	Premier Bank	Other
[47]	a. Best managed	1	2	3	4	5	6	7
[48]	b. Friendliest, most personalized service	1	2	3	4	5	6	7
[49]	c. Most customer-oriented	1	2	3	4	5	6	7
[50]	d. Most progressive and up-to-date	1	2	3	4	5	6	7

			1	2	3	4	5	6	7
[51]	e.	Best for investment-oriented customers	1	2	3	4	5	6	7
[52]	f.	The most innovative in the marketplace	1	2	3	4	5	6	7
[53]	g.	The financial institution most involved in community leadership and activities	1	2	3	4	5	6	7

			Central Bank	First Amer.	Hiber Nat.	Pelican Home.	People's Home.	Premier Bank	Other
[54]	h.	Strongest financial base	1	2	3	4	5	6	7
[55]	i.	Best reputation for being successful, reliable, and honest	1	2	3	4	5	6	7
[56]	j.	The one you would recommend	1	2	3	4	5	6	7
[57]	k.	The one you would never recommend	1	2	3	4	5	6	7
[58]	l.	Has the best advertising	1	2	3	4	5	6	7
[59]	m.	The leader among local financial institutions	1	2	3	4	5	6	7
[60]	n.	Has the best service	1	2	3	4	5	6	7
[61]	o.	Makes fewest errors on accounts	1	2	3	4	5	6	7
[62]	p.	Friendliest, most knowledgeable employees	1	2	3	4	5	6	7
[63]	q.	Is the best place for people like you	1	2	3	4	5	6	7

15. Do you remember recently seeing or hearing advertising for local financial institutions? If yes, which ones?

[64]   ____ Yes, Premier
[65]   ____ Yes, Hibernia
[66]   ____ Yes, Pelican
[67]   ____ Yes, Other
[68]   ____ No (Skip to question 17)

16. On what media did you hear the advertising? (Mark all that apply)

[69]   ____ Heard TV advertising
[70]   ____ Heard radio advertising
[71]   ____ Saw a newspaper ad/article
[72]   ____ Saw new sign going up
[73]   ____ Billboards
[74]   ____ Someone told me about it
[75]   ____ Other_____

[76]17. Now just a few questions about you. Are you:

____ Single with no children[1]
____ Married with no children[2]
____ Married with children at home[3]
____ Single with children at home[4]
____ Married with no children at home[5]
____ Single with no children at home[6]
____ Refused[7]

[77]18. Which age category do you fit into? (READ)

____ 18-24[1]   ____ 56-64[5]

____ 25-34[2]   ____ 65 and older[6]

____35-44[3]   ____ refused[7]

____45-54[4]

[78]19. What is the category that includes your total family income? (READ)

____ Under $15,000[1]   ____ $65,000 to $79,999[6]

____ $15,000 to $24,999[2]   ____ $80,000 to $94,999[7]

_____ $25,000 to $34,999[3]   _____ $95,000 to $109,999[8]

_____ $35,000 to $49,999[4]   _____ Over $110,000[9]

_____ $50,000 to $64,999[5]   _____ Don't know/refused[10]

[79]20. Are you: (READ)

     _____ A high school graduate[1]

     _____ A high school graduate with some college[2]

     _____ A college graduate[3]

     _____ A college graduate with some graduate school[4]

     _____ A graduate degree holder[5]

     _____ Refused[6]

[80]21. Sex: (Do not ask unless necessary)

     _____ Male[1]

     _____ Female[2]

[81]22. Which of the following most closely approximates your average monthly balance in your checking account(s)? (READ)

     _____ Under $250[1]

     _____ $251 to $500[2]

     _____ $501 to $1,000[3]

     _____ $1,001 to $2,000[4]

     _____ Over $2,000[5]

     _____ Refused[6]

[82]23. What is the approximate amount you have invested in CDs, money market deposit accounts, Individual Retirement Accounts (IRAs), or other types of high-yield investments with financial institutions? (READ)

     _____ None[1]

     _____ Under $10,000[2]

_____ $10,001 to $25,000[3]

_____ $25,001 to $75,000[4]

_____ Over $75,000[5]

_____ Refused[6]

[83]24. Finally, what would be a typical monthly balance for your savings accounts? (READ)

_____ None[1]

_____ Under $2,500[2]

_____ $2,501 to $5,000[3]

_____ $5,001 to $7,500[4]

_____ $7,501 to $10,000[5]

_____ Over $10,000[6]

_____ Refused[7]

Thank-you very much for your time and cooperation.

Appendix D

Statistical Sampling Concepts

THE STATISTICAL SIDE OF SAMPLING

The sample size for a probability sample depends on the standard error of the mean, the precision desired from the estimate, and the desired degree of confidence associated with the estimate. The standard error of the mean measures sampling errors that arise from estimating a population from a sample instead of including all of the essential information in the population. The size of the standard error is the function of the standard deviation of the population values and the size of the sample.

$$\sigma_{\bar{x}} = \frac{\sigma}{\sqrt{\eta}}$$

where $\sigma_{\bar{x}}$ = standard error; σ = standard deviation; and η = sample size.

The precision is the size of the plus-or-minus interval around the population parameter under consideration, and the degree of confidence is the percentage level of certainty (probability) that the true mean is within the plus-or-minus interval around the mean. Precision and confidence are interrelated and, within a given size sample, increasing one may be done only at the expense of the other. In other words, the degree of confidence or the degree of precision may be increased, but not both.

The main factors that have a direct influence on the size of the sample are:

1. *The desired degree of confidence associated with the estimate.* In other words, how confident does the researcher want to be in the results of the survey? If the researcher wants 100 percent confidence, he or she must take a census. The more confident a researcher wants to be, the larger the sample should be. This confidence is usually expressed in terms of 90, 95, or 99 percent.
2. *The size of the error the researcher is willing to accept.* This width of the interval relates to the precision desired from the estimate. The greater the precision, or rather the smaller the plus-or-minus fluctua-

tion around the sample mean or proportion, the larger the sample requirement.

The basic formula for calculating sample size for variables (e.g., age, income, weight, height, etc.) is derived from the formula for standard error:

$$\sigma_{\bar{x}} = \frac{\sigma}{\sqrt{\eta}}$$

$$\eta = \frac{\sigma^2}{\sigma_{\bar{x}}^2}$$

The unknowns in the formula above are $\sigma_{\bar{x}}$ (standard error), σ (standard deviation), and η (sample size). In order to calculate the sample size, the researcher must:

1. Select the appropriate level of confidence.
2. Determine the width of the plus-or-minus interval that is acceptable and calculate standard error.
3. Estimate the variability (standard deviation) of the population based on a pilot study or previous experience of the researcher with the population.
4. Calculate sample size (solve for n).

For example, a researcher might choose the 95.5 percent confidence level as appropriate. Using the assumptions of the central limit theorem (that means of samples drawn will be normally distributed around the population means, etc.), the researcher will select a standard normal deviate from the following choices:

Level of Confidence	Z Value
68.3%	1.00
75.0	1.15
80.0	1.28
85.0	1.44
90.0	1.64
95.0	1.96
95.5	2.00
99.0	2.58
99.7	3.00

This allows the researcher to calculate the standard error ($\sigma_{\bar{x}}$). If, for example, the precision width of the interval is selected at 40, the sampling error on either side of the mean must be 20. At the 95.5 percent level of confidence, $Z = 2$ and the confidence interval equals $\pm Z\sigma_{\bar{x}}$.

Then the standard error is equal to 10.

$$CL = \bar{\chi} \pm Z\sigma_{\bar{x}}$$
$$CI = \pm Z\sigma_{\bar{x}}$$

where $Z = 2$ at 95.5 percent level; $2_x\sigma_{\bar{x}} = 20$; $\sigma_{\bar{x}} = 10$; CL = confidence limits; and CI = confidence interval.

Having calculated the standard error based on an appropriate level of confidence and desired interval width, we have two unknowns in the sample size formula left, namely sample size (η) and standard deviation (σ). The standard deviation of the sample must now be estimated. This can be done by either taking a small pilot sample and computing the standard deviation or it can be estimated on the knowledge and experience the researcher has of the population. If you estimate the standard deviation as 200, the sample size can be calculated.

$$\sigma_{\bar{x}} = \frac{\sigma}{\sqrt{\eta}}$$
$$\eta = \frac{\sigma^2}{\sigma_{\bar{x}}^2}$$
$$\eta = \frac{(200)^2}{(10)^2}$$
$$\eta = \frac{40,000}{100}$$
$$\eta = 400$$

The sample size required to give a standard error of 10 at a 95.5 percent level of confidence is computed to be 400. This assumes that assumptions concerning the variability of the population were correct.

Another way of viewing the calculation of sample size required for a given precision of a mean score is to use the following formula:

$$\eta = \frac{Z^2\sigma^2}{h^2}$$

where Z = value from normal distribution table for desired confidence level; σ = standard deviation; η = sample size; and h = desired precision $\pm$. Using the same information as used in the previous example, the same result is obtained:

$$\eta = \frac{(2)^2 (200)^2}{(20)^2}$$

$$\eta = \frac{(4)(40,000)}{(400)}$$

$$\eta = \frac{160,000}{400}$$

$$\eta = 400$$

Tables in most statistical books are provided to allow you, at several given confidence levels, to select the exact sample size given an estimated standard deviation and a desired width of interval.

Determining sample size for a question involving proportions (e.g., those who eat out/do not eat out, successes/failures, have access to Internet/do not have access, etc.) or attributes is very similar to the procedure followed for variables. The researcher must:

1. Select the appropriate level of confidence.
2. Determine the width of the plus-or-minus interval that is acceptable and calculated the standard error of the proportion $\sigma_{\bar{p}}$.
3. Estimate the population proportion based on a pilot study or previous experience of the researcher with the population.
4. Calculate the sample size (solve for η).

The basic formula for calculating sample size for proportions or attributes is derived from the formula for standard error of the proportion:

$$\sigma\bar{p} = \sqrt{\frac{pq}{\eta}}$$

where $\sigma\bar{p}$ = standard error of proportion; p = percent of successes; and q = percent of nonsuccess (l-p).

Assume that management has specified that there be a 95.5 percent confidence level and that the error in estimating the population not be greater than $\pm$ 5 percent (p $\pm$ 0.05). In other words, the width of the interval is 10 percent. A pilot study has shown that 40 percent of the population eats out over four times a week.

$$CI = \pm Z \sigma \bar{\rho}$$

$$2\sigma\bar{\rho} = \frac{\pm CI}{2}$$

$$\sigma\bar{\rho} = \frac{0.05}{2}$$

$$\sigma\bar{\rho} = 0.025$$

Substituting in:

$$\sigma\bar{\rho} = \sqrt{\frac{pq}{\eta}}$$

$$\eta = \frac{p \cdot q}{\sigma\bar{\rho}^2}$$

$$\eta = \frac{(.40)(.60)}{(.025)^2}$$

$$\eta = \frac{.24}{.000625}$$

Another way to view calculating the sample size required for a given precision of a proportion score is to use the following formula:

$$\eta = \frac{Z^2(p \cdot q)}{h^2}$$

where Z = value from normal distribution table for desired confidence level; ρ = btained proportion; $q = 1 - \rho$; and h = desired precision ±.

Using the same information as used in the previous example, the same result is obtained:

$$\eta = \frac{(2)^2(.40 \times .60)}{(.05)^2}$$

$$\eta = \frac{(.4)(.24)}{.0025}$$

$$\sigma_{\bar{x}} = \frac{\sigma}{\sqrt{\eta}}$$

$$\eta = 384$$

The sample size required to give a 95.5 percent level of confidence that the sample proportion is within ± 5 percent of the population proportion is 384.

Tables in statistics books provide a simple method for selecting sample size at several alternative confidence levels given an estimated value of the proportion (p) and a desired confidence interval.

Since sample size is predicated on a specific attribute, variable, proportion, or parameter, a study with multiple objectives will require different sample sizes for the various objectives. Rarely is a study designed to determine a single variable or proportion. Consequently, to get the desired precision at the desired level of confidence for all variables, the larger sample size must be selected. In some cases, however, one single variable might require a sample size significantly larger than any other variable. In this case, concentrate on the most critical variables and choose a sample size large enough to estimate them with the required precision and confidence level desired by the researchers/clients.

Sample Size/Sample Error

Overview

The ultimate objective in selecting a sample size is to obtain a sample size that is large enough to allow measurement of real differences and which, due to sampling error, will not lead to incorrect decisions.

This section is designed to review research, Type I and II errors, and explain how sample errors relate to decision criteria.

Type I and II Two Errors

Most marketing research studies are trying to prove or disprove a hypothesis. A hypothesis is a statement that we would like to prove as either true or false in the real world.

A hypothesis can also be developed on the basis of existing data. For example, a study may show that 60 percent of the men and 40 percent of the women prefer Product A. A hypothesis that may result from this data is that more men than women prefer Product A. The method used to prove this assertion involves statistical testing.

In statistics it is commonly assumed that two populations (samples) are equal until proven otherwise. This is called the null hypothesis. The alternate hypothesis is that the two populations are not equal. This is accepted at a particular level of significance if the data indicate that differences between the groups exist. Our decision choices can be shown as:

The Real World

Research Conclusion	The same number of men and women prefer Product A	More men than women prefer Product A
The same number of men as women prefer Product A	Correct Decision	Type II Error
More men than women prefer Product A	Type I Error	Correct Decision

A Type I error is identifying a difference that does not exist, or stated another way, finding a difference when there is not one. A Type II error is not identifying a difference that actually does exist. In other words, a Type II error is not finding a difference when there is one. Saying things are different when they are really the same (Type I) is generally of greater concern. Type II error is related to sample size. The larger the sample, the more likely to find real differences and make fewer Type II errors.

Sampling Errors

In making a decision, the measures obtained must be viewed in terms of sampling errors and related back to decision criteria. Numbers obtained cannot be viewed as absolute, or an incorrect decision may be drawn.

For example, a decision criteria may be written to call for preference of A over B. If 52 percent of your sample of 100 preferred A, your decision criteria technically would be met. However, the error around the 52 percent is ± 9.8 percent. This means your actual preference could vary from 42.2 percent to 61.8 percent. This range would lead to different conclusions. Thus, you should conduct tests of significance on actual data to determine if there is actually a "statistically" significant difference between values.

Appendix E

Sample Final Report

PILOT STUDY
OF FINANCIAL INSTITUTION

Prepared for:
Bill Berry, President
Financial Institution
January 2006

Table of Contents

Introduction

The following study was conducted to assist Financial Institution with the planning necessary to determine future courses of action in response to changing market conditions. This involves developing a database from which conclusions can be drawn about positioning strategy, market-share goals, and promotional strategy. The purpose of this study was to analyze the retail banking market in the City area. The study analyzed market share by primary financial institution, services utilized by primary and secondary institution, images of financial institutions, and advertising awareness.

Research Objectives

The specific research objectives of this study were as follows:

1. What is the market share for primary institutions for the major financial institutions in the area?
2. How do customers utilize the utilization of various services at both primary and secondary institutions?
3. What is the level of satisfaction with primary institutions and the reasons for any dissatisfaction?
4. What are the changes in primary institutions by respondents and the reasons for any changes?
5. What is respondents' image of various financial institutions on a series of image characteristics?
6. What is the level of advertising awareness and media exposure of respondents?
7. What is respondents' socioeconomic characteristics such as age, sex, income, education, etc.?

Research Methodology

To accomplish these objectives, telephone interviews were conducted with 299 area residents who used the services of local financial institutions. Respondents were randomly selected from the City area telephone book to assure a representative sample was used as the basis of data analysis.

The respondents were surveyed using a structured questionnaire designed to respond to the project's specific research objectives. The questionnaire was thoroughly pretested before being administered to improve the quality of the measuring instrument. The resulting data were edited, entered into computer files, and processed by a statistical analysis program to provide a comprehensive set of tables and cross-tabulations for the study. The tables included number of respondents and percentages by response to each question, and chi-square analysis of the cross-tabulations of the data by primary financial institution to identify differences in response patterns to the questions contained in the questionnaire.

Executive Summary

- A survey of 299 City area respondents was completed during the months of November and December 2005. The survey involved the use of a structured questionnaire administered by telephone to randomly selected area residents who had an account with a local financial institution. The questionnaire was pretested to assure the completeness and accuracy of responses. A typical respondent could be described as follows: married; male; between the ages of 35-44; lived in the area for 6-12 years; median income of $35,000 to $49,999; attended or graduated college.
- Each respondent was asked to identify his or her primary financial institution. City Bank was by far the most frequently mentioned financial institution (47 percent) followed by The First National Bank (14 percent) and Public Bank (11 percent).
- The services utilized most frequently at the primary financial institution were checking accounts, savings accounts, ATMs, and investment instruments. Fifty-one percent of the respondents had done business at their primary institution for six or more years and 52 percent were highly satisfied with their primary financial institution.
- Thirty-eight percent of the respondents reported having an account at a secondary institution. The most frequently utilized services were savings (18 percent), checking (14 percent), and investment instruments (13 percent). The majority of the respondents have done business with their secondary financial institutions for over six years. The high proportion of respondents with secondary institutions may indicate a preference for multiple financial relationships or a lack of cross-selling by primary institutions.
- Sixty-two (20.7 percent) of the respondents stated they had changed their primary financial institution since living in the area and of this group 62.9 percent had done so in the last five years. This indicates the volatility of the market with major changes (Public and The First National) during that time period. Based on this study and supplemental sources on deposits, it appears that City Bank and The First National

Bank have both gained market share at the expense of Public Bank. Most respondents who reported switching financial institutions changed from one bank to another.

- The main reason respondents gave for switching primary financial institutions was poor service. This theme was echoed in responses to another question on dissatisfaction with their current primary institution. Poor service was named by 55 percent of the respondents who expressed dissatisfaction with their current primary financial institution. Keeping current customers satisfied with the service received appears to be a safeguard against dissatisfaction and ultimate switching from one financial institution to another.

- Respondents were also asked to respond to seventeen image characteristics to measure the image of several different institutions. City Bank was the most frequently mentioned institution on every item except "The one you would never recommend." City Bank was followed most closely by The First National Bank, and Public Bank was a distant third.

- Respondents appear to see City Bank, The First National Bank, and to some extent Public Bank as well-managed, progressive, innovative, customer-oriented institutions with a strong financial base, local, and involved in community activities. They were viewed as providing the best service, leaders among local financial institutions with friendly, knowledgeable employees—the one they would recommend to others and best for people similar to themselves.

- Respondents were also asked questions to determine advertising awareness and media exposure for financial institution advertising. When the three financial institutions with the most active promotional campaigns (The First National Bank, Public Bank, and Premier Homestead) were compared, 29 percent remembered seeing or hearing an ad for The First National Bank, 22 percent remembered Public Bank, and 17 percent remembered Premier Homestead. Media exposure for these campaigns were: (1) saw/heard TV ad—43 percent; (2) heard radio ad—27 percent; and (3) saw newspaper ad—16 percent. All other media accounted for only 14 percent.

Findings

This section presents the findings of the study. The first part shows the characteristics of the respondents who participated in the project, followed by a question-by-question analysis of the results of the study.

Sample Characteristics

TABLE E.1. Length of Time Respondents Have Lived in This Area

Length of Time	Frequency	Percent
0-2 Years	40	13
3-5 Years	67	23
6-12 Years	52	17
13-20 Years	41	14
Over 20 Years	92	31
Don't Know/Refused	7	2
Total	299	100

TABLE E.2. Marital Status of Respondents

Marital Status	Frequency	Percent
Single with No Children	74	26
Married with No Children	50	17
Married with Children at Home	86	30
Single with Children at Home	12	4
Married with No Children at Home	53	18
Single with No Children at Home	11	4
Refused	4	1
Total	290	100

TABLE E.3. Age Category of Respondents

Age Category	Frequency	Percent
18-24	44	15
25-34	84	29
35-44	55	19
45-54	44	15
55-64	28	10
65 and older	20	7
Refused	13	5
Total	288	100

TABLE E.4. Total Family Income of Respondents

Total Family Income	Frequency	Percent
Under $15,000	22	7
$15,000 to $24,999	44	15
$25,000 to $34,999	48	16

TABLE E.4 *(continued)*

$35,000 to $49,999	49	17
$50,000 to $64,999	33	11
$65,000 to $79,999	7	2
$80,000 to $94,999	—	—
$95,000 to $109,000	—	—
Over $110,000	8	3
Don't Know/Refused	88	29
Total	299	100

TABLE E.5. Education Level of Respondents

Education Level	Frequency	Percent
High School Graduate	52	17
High School Graduate with Some College	88	30
College Graduate	102	34
College Graduate with Some Graduate School	15	5
Graduate Degree	18	6
Don't Know/Refused	24	8
Total	299	100

TABLE E.6. Sex of Respondents

Sex	Frequency	Percent
Male	150	52
Female	140	48
Total	290	100

TABLE E.7. Average Monthly Balance in Checking Account of Respondents

Monthly Balance	Frequency	Percent
Under $250	24	8
$250 to $500	43	14
$501 to $1,000	63	21
$1,001 to $2,000	27	9
Over $2,000	51	17
Don't Know/Refused	91	31
Total	299	100

TABLE E.8. Amount Respondents Have Invested in CDs, Money Market Deposit Accounts, Individual Retirement Accounts (IRAs), or Other High-Yield Investments

Amount Invested	Frequency	Percent
None	82	28
Under $10,000	41	14
$10,001 to $25,000	38	13
$25,001 to $75,000	27	9
Over $75,000	7	2
Don't Know/Refused	103	34
Total	298	100

TABLE E.9. Typical Monthly Balance for Nonchecking Savings Account of Respondents

Monthly Balance	Frequency	Percent
None	32	11
Under $2,500	38	13
$2,501 to $5,000	37	12
$5,001 to $7,500	32	11
$7,501 to $10,000	19	6
Over $10,000	37	12
Don't Know/Refused	104	35
Total	299	100

Primary Institution/Services Utilized by Respondents

Each respondent was asked to identify his or her primary financial institution. The results revealed the following statistics.

TABLE E.10. Respondents' Primary Financial Institution

Financial Institution	Frequency	Percent
City Bank	136	47
First Bank	25	9
The First National Bank	39	14
Premier Homestead	13	4
City Homestead	19	7
Public Bank	33	11
Other	24	8
Total	289	100

Of the 289 customers interviewed, 136 or 47 percent stated that City Bank was their primary financial institution. The First National Bank was the primary financial institution for 39 or 14 percent of the respondents. Of those surveyed, Public Bank was preferred by 11 percent or 33 of the respondents as their primary financial institution.

The following table shows the services utilized by respondents at their primary financial institution.

TABLE E.11. Services Utilized by Respondents at Primary Financial Institution

Service	Frequency	Percent
Automatic Teller Machine	162	54
Personal Loan	48	16
Automobile Loan	47	16
Home (Mortgage) Loans	28	9
Telephone Bill Paying Service	7	2
VISA/MasterCard Service	85	28
Safe Deposit Box	58	19
Checking Account	286	96
Savings Account	229	77
Trust Account	11	4
Money Market Deposit Account	23	8
CDs and Investment Instrument	116	39
Individual Retirement Accounts (IRAs)	54	18
Overdraft Protection	69	23
Educational Loan	17	6
Other	14	5

Of those surveyed, 286 or 96 percent have a checking account with their primary financial institution. A savings account was the second largest service utilized by 229 respondents or 77 percent. The automatic teller machine was used by 162 respondents or 54 percent. CDs and other investment instruments were used by 116 or 39 percent of those surveyed at their primary financial institution. Only 7 or 2 percent of those surveyed used the telephone bill paying service at their primary financial institution. Another infrequently used service by respondents is the trust account, used by 11 or 4 percent.

TABLE E.12. Length of Time Respondents Have Done Business with Their Primary Financial Institution

Length of Time	Frequency	Percent
Less Than 1 Year	34	12
1-2 Years	30	10
3-5 Years	79	27
6-12 Years	82	28
Over 12 Years	67	23
Total	292	100

Of those surveyed, 28 percent or 82 respondents have done business with their primary financial institution for 6-12 years. Seventy-nine respondents or 27 percent have done business with their primary financial institution for 3-5 years. Of those surveyed, 51 percent have done business with their primary financial institution for 6 or more years.

Services Utilized at Secondary Financial Institution

Of those respondents interviewed, 112 or 38 percent have accounts at a secondary financial institution. The following table outlines the services used by the respondents at their secondary financial institution.

TABLE E.13. Services Utilized by Respondents at Secondary Financial Institution

Service	Frequency	Percent
Automatic Teller Machine	8	3
Personal Loan	11	4
Automobile Loan	17	6
Home (Mortgage) Loan	25	8
Telephone Bill Paying Service	1	—
VISA/MasterCard Service	15	5
Safe Deposit Box	5	2
Checking Account	42	14
Savings Account	53	18
Trust Account	3	1
Money Market Deposit Account	3	1
CDs and Investment Instruments	38	13
Individual Retirement Accounts (IRAs)	17	6
Overdraft Protection	1	—
Educational Loans	6	2
Other	2	1

Those respondents who have a secondary financial institution use a savings account as the primary service (53 respondents or 18 percent). A checking account as a service at a secondary financial institution was used by 42 of the respondents or 14 percent. Of those surveyed, 38 or 13 percent utilized CDs and investment instruments at their secondary financial institution. The services utilized least by respondents at their secondary financial institution were telephone bill paying service, overdraft protection, and trust accounts.

TABLE E.14. Length of Time Respondents Have Done Business with Their Secondary Financial Institution

Length of Time	Frequency	Percent
Less Than 1 Year	5	4
1-2 Years	14	12
2-5 Years	28	25
6-12 Years	32	28
Over 12 Years	36	31
Total	115	100

Of those surveyed who have a secondary financial institution, the majority (59 percent) have done business with their secondary institution for over 6 years. This indicates that either respondents prefer to have more than one financial institution or that primary institutions are not doing a good job of cross-selling their services.

Changes in Primary Financial Institutions

Respondents were asked if they had changed primary financial institutions while living in this area. Of those surveyed, 62 or 21 percent had changed primary financial institutions. The following table shows how long ago the change was made.

TABLE E.15. How Long Ago Respondents Changed Primary Financial Institutions While Living in This Area

How Long Ago Change Was Made	Frequency	Percent
Less Than 1 Year	13	21
1-2 Years	8	13
3-5 Years	18	29
6-12 Years	10	16

Over 12 Years	13	21
Total	62	100

Of those surveyed who changed primary financial institutions while living in this area, 18 or 29 percent, made that change 3-5 years ago. This indicates a great deal of volatility in the customer base of financial institutions in the area. In the last 5 years 63 percent have changed their primary financial institution.

The following table states what type of change was made when respondents changed primary financial institutions.

TABLE E.16. Type of Financial Institution Change Made by Respondents

Category	Frequency	Percent
A Bank to a Savings and Loan	3	5
A Bank to a Credit Union	2	3
A Savings and Loan to a Bank	5	8
A Savings and Loan to a Credit Union	—	—
A Credit Union to a Bank	—	—
A Credit Union to a Savings and Loan	—	—
A Bank to another Bank	50	84
Total	60	100

Of those surveyed who changed primary financial institutions while living in this area, 84 percent or 50 respondents changed from one bank to another bank. The other types of changes made were from a savings and loan to a bank with 5 respondents or 8 percent making this type of a change, 5 percent of the respondents changed from a bank to a savings and loan, and 3 percent changed from a bank to a credit union.

The following table will outline the main reason respondents changed primary financial institutions while living in this area.

TABLE E.17. Main Reason Respondents Changed Primary Financial Institutions

Reason for Change	Frequency	Percent
Poor Service at Old	22	34
Better Location of New	14	22
Unsure of Stability/Felt Safer at New	9	14
Interest Rates Higher at New	5	8
Other	14	22
Total	64	100

According to those surveyed, the most frequent reason to change primary financial institutions was *poor* service. Twenty-two percent of respondents also stated that a better location was the reason they changed. Of those surveyed who have changed primary financial institutions, 14 percent changed because they were unsure of the stability of their current bank and felt safer at another institution, 8 percent changed to get a higher interest rate, and 22 percent stated some other reason for their decisions to change primary financial institutions.

The following table will look at respondents' level of satisfaction with their current primary financial institution. Respondents were asked to rank their financial institution on a scale of 1 to 5, where 1 is strongly dissatisfied and 5 is very satisfied.

TABLE E.18. Respondents' Satisfaction with Their Primary Financial Institution

Category		Frequency	Percent
Strongly Dissatisfied	-1	2	1
	-2	9	3
	-3	31	11
	-4	97	33
Very Satisfied	-5	152	52
Total		291	100

The overall level of satisfaction with the primary financial institutions of respondents was fairly high. Of those surveyed, 52 percent or 152 respondents were very satisfied with their primary financial institution. A satisfaction rating of "4" was given to primary financial institutions by 97 respondents or 33 percent. Of those surveyed, 31 or 11 percent gave their primary financial institution a satisfaction level of "3." Only 2 respondents or 1 percent were strongly dissatisfied with their primary financial institution with a rating of "1," and 9 respondents or 3 percent gave a rating of "2."

Respondents that rated their overall level of satisfaction with their primary financial institution as "Strongly Dissatisfied -1 or -2," were asked to specify why they were dissatisfied. The findings are in Table E.19. This table reinforces the earlier findings that poor service, or at least what customers perceive as poor service, causes dissatisfaction and eventual departure from a particular financial institution.

TABLE E.19. Respondents' Reason for Dissatisfaction with Primary Financial Institution

Category	Frequency	Percent
Poor Service	6	55
Bad Location	—	—
Unsure of Stability	5	` 45
Interest Rates Are Low	—	—
Other	—	—
Total	11	100

Of those surveyed, only 11 expressed dissatisfaction with their primary financial institution. The main reason cited for dissatisfaction was "Poor Service," indicated by 55 percent of the respondents. Respondents' second major reason for dissatisfaction was "Unsure of Stability," indicated by 5 respondents or 45 percent.

Images of Financial Institutions

Respondents were asked to express their initial impression or opinion about financial institutions in the area. Those surveyed were asked to mention what financial institution came to mind when the interviewer mentioned each factor about financial institutions. The results are listed in Table E.20.

TABLE E.20. Respondents' Perceptions of Local Financial Institutions

Factor	City Bank	First Bank	First Nat.	Premier Home	City Home	Public Bank	Other
Best managed	51%	6%	20%	4%	2%	12%	5%
Friendliest, most personalized service	47	8	16	6	5	12	6
Most customer-oriented	46	10	19	5	3	12	5
Most progressive and up-to-date	39	5	33	5	2	13	3
Best for investment-oriented customers	38	8	30	6	4	10	4
Most innovative in the market	43	5	32	4	1	12	3
The financial institution most involved in community leadership and activities	66	6	14	2	2	6	4

Strongest financial base	37	7	31	5	2	14	4
Best reputation for being successful, reliable, and honest	53	8	16	4	2	12	5
The one you would recommend	45	9	21	4	2	13	6
The one you would never recommend	10	21	6	9	30	12	12
Has the best advertising	59	5	17	4	2	12	1
The leader among local financial institutions	49	7	26	3	1	10	4
Has the best service	43	9	21	5	3	12	7
Makes fewest errors on accounts	43	10	18	5	6	11	7
Friendliest, most knowledgeable employees	44	10	17	7	5	11	6
Is the best place for people similar to you	46	9	21	5	2	11	6

Of those responding, the table shows the percentage of respondents that chose each of the banks for the various factors. In all of the categories City Bank was the number one choice, except on the question that asked respondents to name the "One financial institution they would never recommend." The respondents perceptions on City Bank were highest when asked to name the financial institution "Most involved in community leadership and activities," with 66 percent of those surveyed choosing City Bank. When respondents were asked to name the financial institution with the "Best reputation for being successful, reliable, and honest," "Best managed," and "The leader among local financial institutions," City Bank was clearly the favorite choice. City Bank was the dominant choice in several other categories as well. When respondents were asked which financial institution has the friendliest, most personalized service; the most customer-oriented; most innovative; has the best service; and makes fewest errors on accounts, City Bank had the highest percentages in each of these categories.

In several of the categories City Bank and The First National Bank were the two obvious favorites. When respondents were asked to name the financial institution that is the "Most progressive and up-to-date," 39 percent chose City Bank and 33 percent chose The First National Bank. When asked to name the financial institution with the "Strongest financial base," 37 percent chose City Bank and 31 percent chose The First National Bank.

Advertising Awareness

Respondents were asked if they remembered recently seeing or hearing advertising for any of the local financial institutions.

The following table states which financial institutions were remembered by respondents for advertisements.

TABLE E.21. Respondents' Recollection of Recent Advertisements by Local Financial Institutions

Financial Institution	Frequency	Percent
Public Bank	47	22
The First National Bank	61	29
Premier Homestead	37	17
All Others	67	32
Total	212	100

Sixty-one respondents (29 percent) remembered recently seeing or hearing advertisements for The First National Bank. Of those surveyed, 67 or 32 percent remembered advertising for "Other," which would include any of the financial institutions in the area except the ones mentioned above (Public, The First National, and Premier Homestead).

The following table outlines the media source remembered by respondents as advertising for a local financial institution.

TABLE E.22. Media Source Remembered by Respondents in Advertisements for a Local Financial Institution

Media Source	Frequency	Percent
Heard TV Advertising	98	43
Heard Radio Advertising	62	27
Saw a Newspaper Ad/Article	36	16
Saw a New Sign Going Up	8	3
Billboards	21	9
Someone Told Me About It	3	1
Other	2	1
Total	230	100

Ninety-eight respondents (43 percent) cited TV as the media source remembered for advertisements for a local financial institution. Radio was the second largest media source remembered, cited by 62 respondents or 27 percent. Advertising through the paper was remembered by 16 percent of the respondents.

Conclusions and Recommendations

The Sample

The sample consisted of interviews with residents in the City area who had an account with a local financial institution. Of the 299 area residents who were surveyed, 52 percent were male and 48 percent were female. A typical respondent is described as a married male between the ages of 35-44, who has lived in this area for 6-12 years, with a median income of $35,000 to $49,999, and has attended or graduated from college.

Primary Financial Institution

Of the 299 residents who were surveyed, 47 percent named City Bank as their primary financial institution, followed by The First National Bank, named by 14 percent of the respondents.

TABLE E.23. Primary Financial Institution

Financial Institution	Frequency	Percent
City Bank	136	47
First Bank	25	9
The First National Bank	39	14
Premier Homestead	13	4
City Homestead	19	7
Public Bank	33	11
Other	24	8
Total	289	100

Services Utilized at Primary Financial Institution

Once the primary financial institution of respondents was established, respondents were asked which services they utilized at their primary financial institution. The following chart lists those services used most by residents who were surveyed.

TABLE E.24. Services Utilized at Primary Institution

Service	Frequency	Percent
Checking Account	286	96
Savings Account	229	77

Automatic Teller Machine	162	54
CDs and Investment Instruments	116	39
VISA/MasterCard Service	85	28

Of those surveyed, 96 percent utilize a checking account at their primary financial institution, and 77 percent utilize a savings account. Fifty-one percent of the respondents have done business with their primary financial institution for 6 or more years.

Services Utilized at Secondary Financial Institution

Of those surveyed, 38 percent have accounts at a secondary financial institution. The following chart shows the services used most frequently by those with secondary financial institutions.

TABLE E.25. Services Utilized at Secondary Institution

Service	Frequency	Percent
Savings Account	53	18
Checking Account	42	14
CDs and Investment Instruments	38	13
Home (Mortgage) Loan	25	8

Of those respondents with secondary financial institutions, 59 percent have done business with their financial institution for 6 or more years.

Changes in Primary Financial Institutions

Of those surveyed, 21 percent had changed primary financial institutions while living in this area. Respondents were asked what type of change they made, and 84 percent changed from one bank to another. The main reason respondents changed primary financial institutions while living in this area was due to poor service.

This finding coincides with respondents' level of satisfaction or dissatisfaction with their primary financial institution. Fifty-two percent of those surveyed were very satisfied with their primary financial institution, and 4 percent of those surveyed were strongly dissatisfied. Those respondents who stated they were dissatisfied were then asked why they were dissatisfied. Fifty-five percent of those stated their main reason for dissatisfaction was poor service.

Images of Financial Institutions

Respondents were asked to express their initial impression about financial institutions in the area to determine the image of several local financial institutions. The overall favorite in all of the categories (except for "The financial institution you would never recommend"), was City Bank. Some of the characteristics respondents were asked about were: Which local financial institution is well-managed, progressive, innovative, customer-oriented, with a strong financial base, and involved in the community? The local institution mentioned first by the majority of the respondents was City Bank. The First National Bank was the respondents' second most frequently mentioned, and Public Bank came in a distant third.

Advertising Most Remembered and Media Source

To determine advertising awareness and media exposure for local financial institutions, respondents were asked to identify financial institutions for which they recalled seeing or hearing advertising. When The First National Bank, Public Bank, and Premier Homestead (the three local financial institutions with the most active promotional campaigns) were compared, 29 percent remembered seeing or hearing an ad for The First National Bank, 22 percent remembered Public Bank, and 17 percent remembered Premier Homestead. Those who did recall seeing or hearing ads for financial institutions were also asked to identify the media sources where they saw or heard the ads. The media source most frequently remembered was TV (43 percent), radio ads (27 percent), and newspaper ads (16 percent).

Recommendations

Recommended action or decisions by management would be listed at this point. None were part of this example study. As noted in the research objectives, the study provided answers to a number of questions about market conditions and management used the results in a number of ways. Researchers were not requested to make recommendations in any particular area.

RETAIL BANKING SURVEY

[1-3]

Hello, am I speaking with the man/lady of the house? (IF NO, ASK TO SPEAK TO THAT PERSON.)

Hello, I am _____ . We are conducting a marketing research project with area residents. This study deals with financial institutions and we need your help in this project. Your answers will be confidential and used only in combination with the responses of other people.

    1a. Do you or a member of your household work for a bank, savings and loan, credit union, advertising, public relations, or market research firm?

        ____ YES (Terminate)
        ____ NO

    1b. Do you have a checking or savings account with a local financial institution?

        ____ YES
        ____ NO (Terminate)

[4] 2. How long have you lived in this area?

        ____ 0-2 years[1]
        ____ 3-5 years[2]
        ____ 6-12 years[3]
        ____ 13-20 years[4]
        ____ Over 20 years[5]
        ____ Refused[6]

[5] 3. What is the name of your primary financial institution?

        ____ Central Bank[1]
        ____ First American Bank[2]
        ____ Hibernia National Bank[3]
        ____ Pelican Homestead[4]
        ____ People's Homestead[5]

_____ Premier Bank[6]
_____ Other[7]

4. What services are you currently utilizing at your primary financial institution? (READ)

[6]   _____ Automatic Teller Machines
[7]   _____ Personal Loans
[8]   _____ Automobile Loans
[9]   _____ Home (Mortgage) Loans
[10]   _____ Telephone Bill Paying Service
[11]   _____ VISA/MasterCard Services
[12]   _____ Safe Deposit Box
[13]   _____ Checking Account
[14]   _____ Savings Account
[15]   _____ Trust Account
[16]   _____ Money Market Deposit Account
[17]   _____ CDs and Investment Instrument
[18]   _____ Individual Retirement Accounts (IRAs)
[19]   _____ Overdraft Protection
[20]   _____ Educational Loans
[21]   _____ Other

[22] 5. How long have you done business with your primary financial institution?

_____ Less than 1 year[1]
_____ 1-2 years[2]
_____ 3-5 years[3]
_____ 6-12 years[4]
_____ Over 12 years[5]

[23] 6. Do you also have accounts at other institutions?

_____ YES[1]
_____ NO[2] (Skip to question 9)

7. What services do you currently utilize at this institution?

[24]   _____ Automatic Teller Machines
[25]   _____ Personal Loans
[26]   _____ Automobile Loans
[27]   _____ Home (Mortgage) Loans
[28]   _____ Telephone Bill Paying Service

[29]   ____ VISA/MasterCard Services
[30]   ____ Safe Deposit Box
[31]   ____ Checking Account
[32]   ____ Savings Account
[33]   ____ Trust Account
[34]   ____ Money Market Deposit Account
[35]   ____ CDs and Investment Instrument
[36]   ____ Individual Retirement Accounts (IRAs)
[37]   ____ Overdraft Protection
[38]   ____ Educational Loans
[39]   ____ Other

[40] 8. (If secondary financial institutions) How long have you done business with your secondary financial institution?

    ____ Less than 1 year[1]
    ____ 1-2 years[2]
    ____ 2-5 years[3]
    ____ 6-12 years[4]
    ____ Over 12 years[5]

[41] 9. Have you changed your primary financial institution while living in this area?

    ____ YES[1]
    ____ NO[2] (Skip to question 13)

[42]10. How long ago did you make that change?

    ____ Less than 1 year[1]
    ____ 1-2 years[2]
    ____ 3-5 years[3]
    ____ 6-12 years[4]
    ____ Over 12 years[5]

[43]11. What did you change from?

    ____ Bank to a savings and loan[1]
    ____ Bank to a credit union[2]
    ____ Savings and loan to a bank[3]
    ____ Savings and loan to a credit union[4]
    ____ Credit union to a bank[5]
    ____ Credit union to a savings and loan[6]
    ____ Other[7]

[44]12. What was the main reason you changed financial institutions?

    ____ Poor service at old[1]
    ____ Better location of new[2]
    ____ Unsure of stability of old/felt safer at new institution[3]
    ____ Interest rates higher at new[4]
    ____ Other, specify[5]_____

[45]13. On a scale of 1 to 5, where "1" is strongly dissatisfied and "5" is very satisfied, how would you rate your satisfaction with your primary financial institution?

Strongly dissatisfied 1 2 3 4 5 Very satisfied

[46]   If dissatisfied (1 or 2), ask: Why are you dissatisfied?

    ____ Poor service at old[1]
    ____ Better location of new[2]
    ____ Unsure of stability of old/felt safer at new institution[3]
    ____ Interest rates higher at new[4]
    ____ Other, specify[5]_____

14. Now I would like you to think for a moment about financial institutions in this area. As I mention several factors about financial institutions, please tell me which one comes to mind first for each factor. It does not matter if you have ever done business with them or not. This is simply your initial impression or opinion.

		Central Bank	First Amer.	Hiber-nia Nat.	Pelican Home.	People's Home.	Premier Bank	Other
[47]	a. Best managed	1	2	3	4	5	6	7
[48]	b. Friendliest, most personalized service	1	2	3	4	5	6	7
[49]	c. Most customer-oriented	1	2	3	4	5	6	7
[50]	d. Most progressive and up-to-date	1	2	3	4	5	6	7
[51]	e. Best for investment-oriented customers	1	2	3	4	5	6	7

			Central Bank	First Amer.	Hiber Nat.	Pelican Home.	People's Home.	Premier Bank	Other
[52]	f.	The most innovative in the market-place	1	2	3	4	5	6	7
[53]	g.	The financial institution most involved in community leadership and activities	1	2	3	4	5	6	7
[54]	h.	Strongest financial base	1	2	3	4	5	6	7
[55]	i.	Best reputation for being successful, reliable, and honest	1	2	3	4	5	6	7
[56]	j.	The one you would recommend	1	2	3	4	5	6	7
[57]	k.	The one you would never recommend	1	2	3	4	5	6	7
[58]	l.	Has the best advertising	1	2	3	4	5	6	7
[59]	m.	The leader among local financial institutions	1	2	3	4	5	6	7
[60]	n.	Has the best service	1	2	3	4	5	6	7
[61]	o.	Makes fewest errors on accounts	1	2	3	4	5	6	7
[62]	p.	Friendliest, most knowledge-able employees	1	2	3	4	5	6	7
[63]	q.	Is the best place for people like you	1	2	3	4	5	6	7

15. Do you remember recently seeing or hearing advertising for local financial institutions? If yes, which ones?

[64]   ____ Yes, Premier
[65]   ____ Yes, Hibernia
[66]   ____ Yes, Pelican
[67]   ____ Yes, Other
[68]   ____ No (Skip to question 17)

16. On what media did you hear the advertising?
(Mark all that apply)

[69]   ____ Heard TV advertising
[70]   ____ Heard radio advertising
[71]   ____ Saw a newspaper ad/article
[72]   ____ Saw new sign going up
[73]   ____ Billboards
[74]   ____ Someone told me about it
[75]   ____ Other_____

[76]17. Now just a few questions about you. Are you:

____ Single with no children[1]
____ Married with no children[2]
____ Married with children at home[3]
____ Single with children at home[4]
____ Married with no children at home[5]
____ Single with no children at home[6]
____ Refused[7]

[77]18. Which age category do you fit into? (READ)

____ 18-24[1]   ____ 56-64[5]

____ 25-34[2]   ____ 65 and older[6]

____ 35-44[3]   ____ refused[7]

____ 45-54[4]

[78]19. What is the category that includes your total family income? (READ)

_____ Under 15,000[1]   _____ $65,000 to $79,999[6]

_____ $15,000 to $24,999[2]   _____ $80,000 to $94,999[7]

_____ $25,000 to $34,999[3]   _____ $95,000 to $109,999[8]

_____ $35,000 to $49,999[4]   _____ Over $110,000[9]

_____ $50,000 to $64,999[5]   _____ Don't know/refused[10]

[79]20. Are you: (READ)

_____ A high school graduate[1]

_____ A high school graduate with some college[2]

_____ A college graduate[3]

_____ A college graduate with some graduate school[4]

_____ A graduate degree holder[5]

_____ Refused[6]

[80]21. Sex: (Do not ask unless necessary)

_____ Male[1]

_____ Female[2]

[81]22. Which of the following most closely approximates your average monthly balance in your checking account(s)? (READ)

_____ Under $250[1]

_____ $251 to $500[2]

_____ $501 to $1,000[3]

_____ $1,001 to $2,000[4]

_____ Over $2,000[5]

_____ Refused[6]

[82]23. What is the approximate amount you have invested in CDs, money market deposit accounts, Individual Retirement Accounts (IRAs), or other types of high-yield investments with financial institutions? (READ)

     ____ None[1]

     ____ Under $10,000[2]

     ____ $10,001 to $25,000[3]

     ____ $25,001 to $75,000[4]

     ____ Over $75,000[5]

     ____ Refused[6]

[83]24. Finally, what would be a typical monthly balance for your savings accounts? (READ)

     ____ None[1]

     ____ Under $2,500[2]

     ____ $2,501 to $5,000[3]

     ____ $5,001 to $7,500[4]

     ____ $7,501 to $10,000[5]

     ____ Over $10,000[6]

     ____ Refused[7]

Thank-you very much for your time and cooperation.

Index

A.C. Nielsen Company, 40, 63, 64, 92, 96
Acceptance testing, 305
Accuracy, 66, 73, 75, 85, 98, 111, 117, 145, 149, 171, 182, 183, 190, 250, 274, 280, 393
Activities, interests, and opinions (AIO), 101
Actual interview, 158, 168
Administration methods, 140
Advantage(s), 5, 22, 40, 114, 119, 122, 125, 136, 186, 202, 228, 231, 252, 280, 282, 287, 289, 291, 305, 309, 323, 335
Agency for International Development (AID), 276
AIO (activities, interests, and opinions), 101
Allocation of resources, 202
Alternatives, identifying, 3
Analysis, discriminant, 243
Analysis of selected cases, 32
Analysis stage, 141, 145, 191, 226
Analyst, skepticism of, 218, 229
Analyzing data, 16, 217, 225, 227
Approach, 3, 7, 8, 12, 13, 15, 16, 17, 20, 26, 28, 32, 34, 35, 58, 103, 106, 113, 125, 145, 158, 160, 161, 188, 194, 195, 225, 227, 232, 236, 243, 268, 278, 279, 281, 291, 292, 299, 300, 304, 308, 310, 311, 312, 314, 315, 322, 323, 325, 333, 334, 336, 338, 342, 347, 350
Arbitron Radio Market Reports, 96
Artificial setting, 125
Asking questions, 30, 103, 104, 135, 146
ASSESSOR, 339

Association, 32, 61, 92, 137, 202, 218, 238, 240, 241, 246, 269, 291
bivariate, 237, 239, 242
multivariate, 36, 198, 221, 237, 242, 243, 272
Attitude-type questions, 206
Attitudinal data, 3
Audits and Surveys (research firm), 64
Availability, 281, 309, 310, 346
Awareness, 9, 14, 17, 18, 39, 79, 102, 145, 351, 352, 392, 394, 408

Background information, 142, 168, 269, 270, 276
BASES, 67, 339
Behaviors, 30, 32, 66, 75, 101, 102, 109, 118, 142, 150, 177, 213
BehaviorScan, 39, 40, 96
Benchtop analysis, 302
BIB (balanced incomplete block) test, 311, 312, 318, 319, 339
Blind approach, 323
Brainstorming, 300
Brand identification, 323
Briefings, 168, 177
British Overseas Trade Board, 269
Budget, 23, 27, 63, 68, 126, 190, 192, 268, 270, 278, 289, 290, 294, 348, 355, 356
Burgoyne (research firm), 64
Burke (research firm), 65, 67
Buyers, 54, 227, 360

Order a copy of this book with this form or online at:
http://www.haworthpress.com/store/product.asp?sku=5156

THE MARKETING RESEARCH GUIDE
Second Edition

_____in hardbound at $69.95 (ISBN-13: 978-0-7890-2416-9; ISBN-10: 0-7890-2416-0)

_____in softbound at $49.95 (ISBN-13: 978-0-7890-2417-6; ISBN-10: 0-7890-2417-9)

Or order online and use special offer code HEC25 in the shopping cart.

COST OF BOOKS_____

☐ **BILL ME LATER:** (Bill-me option is good on US/Canada/Mexico orders only; not good to jobbers, wholesalers, or subscription agencies.)

☐ Check here if billing address is different from shipping address and attach purchase order and billing address information.

POSTAGE & HANDLING_____
(US: $4.00 for first book & $1.50 for each additional book)
(Outside US: $5.00 for first book & $2.00 for each additional book)

Signature_____

SUBTOTAL_____

☐ **PAYMENT ENCLOSED: $**_____

IN CANADA: ADD 7% GST_____

☐ **PLEASE CHARGE TO MY CREDIT CARD.**

STATE TAX_____
(NJ, NY, OH, MN, CA, IL, IN, PA, & SD residents, add appropriate local sales tax)

☐ Visa ☐ MasterCard ☐ AmEx ☐ Discover
☐ Diner's Club ☐ Eurocard ☐ JCB

Account # _____

FINAL TOTAL_____
(If paying in Canadian funds, convert using the current exchange rate, UNESCO coupons welcome)

Exp. Date_____

Signature_____

Prices in US dollars and subject to change without notice.

NAME_____

INSTITUTION_____

ADDRESS_____

CITY_____

STATE/ZIP_____

COUNTRY_____ COUNTY (NY residents only)_____

TEL_____ FAX_____

E-MAIL_____

May we use your e-mail address for confirmations and other types of information? ☐ Yes ☐ No
We appreciate receiving your e-mail address and fax number. Haworth would like to e-mail or fax special discount offers to you, as a preferred customer. **We will never share, rent, or exchange your e-mail address or fax number.** We regard such actions as an invasion of your privacy.

Order From Your Local Bookstore or Directly From
The Haworth Press, Inc.
10 Alice Street, Binghamton, New York 13904-1580 • USA
TELEPHONE: 1-800-HAWORTH (1-800-429-6784) / Outside US/Canada: (607) 722-5857
FAX: 1-800-895-0582 / Outside US/Canada: (607) 771-0012
E-mail to: orders@haworthpress.com

For orders outside US and Canada, you may wish to order through your local sales representative, distributor, or bookseller.
For information, see http://haworthpress.com/distributors

(Discounts are available for individual orders in US and Canada only, not booksellers/distributors.)

PLEASE PHOTOCOPY THIS FORM FOR YOUR PERSONAL USE.
http://www.HaworthPress.com

BOF04